Literacy for All Young Learners

Literacy for All Young Learners

Mary Renck Jalongo, PhD

Gryphon House
www.gryphonhouse.com

Copyright

Published by Gryphon House, Inc.

P. O. Box 10, Lewisville, NC 27023

800-638-0928; 877-638-7576 (fax)

Visit us on the web at www.gryphonhouse.com.

Library of Congress Cataloging-in-Publication Data

Jalongo, Mary Renck.

 Literacy for all young learners / by Mary Renck Jalongo.

    pages cm

Includes bibliographical references and index.

ISBN 978-0-87659-568-8

1. English language--Study and teaching--Foreign speakers--Activity programs. I. Title.

PE1128.A2J343 2015

428.0071--dc23

2015003788

Bulk Purchase

Gryphon House books are available for special premiums and sales promotions as well as for fund-raising use. Special editions or book excerpts also can be created to specifications. For details, call 800-638-0928.

Disclaimer

Gryphon House, Inc. cannot be held responsible for damage, mishap, or injury incurred during the use of or because of activities in this book. Appropriate and reasonable caution and adult supervision of children involved in activities and corresponding to the age and capability of each child involved are recommended at all times. Do not leave children unattended at any time. Observe safety and caution at all times.

Table of Contents

Preface

My first experience with a young English language learner occurred when I was a kindergartner. An Italian boy with olive skin and glossy black curls arrived at our school wearing red leather fisherman sandals. At recess, three boys began to make fun of him, saying, "He's wearing girls' shoes! Girls' shoes! Girls' shoes!" The boys continued to pursue him until the newcomer stood behind the school building, back against the wall, with tears streaming down his flushed face. I told the boys to stop but they ignored me. Finally, I resorted to throwing sand and they ran off, threatening to tell the principal. What happened was much worse: They told Miss Klingensmith. She was the person I pretended to be when I played school; she was the one who would inspire me to pursue a career in early childhood education. Above anyone else at that school, I did not want to disappoint Miss Klingensmith. She listened as I explained what had happened, and to her everlasting credit, my only punishment was to promise never to throw sand again.

Over the years, I have amassed many more experiences with young children who did not speak English and were newcomers to a school: as a Future Teachers of America volunteer; as a new teacher; as a volunteer for the Teacher Corps—a sort of stateside version of the Peace Corps; in a community preschool that included the children of migrant farm workers; and as a doctoral student in a university-based preschool that included the children of international students, many of whom did not speak English. As a college professor, I have had the opportunity to work with college students with dual majors in education and Spanish. They completed their student teaching in an elementary school where English was the language of instruction in the morning and Spanish was the language of instruction in the afternoon. During the summer, I supervised their internship in a public school in Mexico. Thus, young children whose first language is not English—and their teachers—have been a significant part of my professional career. This book has given me the opportunity to synthesize what I've learned from personal experience and from research.

Acknowledgments

Books are the culmination of many years of professional work, extensive reading, problem solving, reflective practice, and writing for other purposes. I would like to thank everyone who has contributed to this process throughout my career: young children and their families, my college students and professional colleagues, and my teachers and mentors.

Two people who made a large contribution to this book are doctoral candidates and graduate assistants at Indiana University of Pennsylvania, Elizabeth Octave and Nicole Olbrish. They prepared the Common Core State Standards grid that is included in each activity, reviewed websites and apps, suggested additional children's books, and made suggestions about the letters to families. Marianela D. Davis translated the letters to families into Spanish. Their work is very much appreciated and has enhanced the quality of this book.

—M. R. J.

Literacy for All Young Learners

Who is the young English language learner? The designation *English language learner* (ELL) is commonly used to refer to children who do not have English as a first language and are working to acquire proficiency in English. What are the realities for the young child who arrives at a school or center with little or no proficiency in English? The first, frequently overwhelming, experience is that the language of communication and instruction will be one that the child does not understand. Unless large numbers of children speak the same first language—such as Spanish-speaking children in Miami or Albuquerque—chances are that the child will be immersed in English from the very first day. While peers or an occasional community volunteer may speak the child's first language, there may not be anyone to interpret or translate. As a result, it will be up to the "regular" teacher—preschool or primary—to offer a curriculum that meets the developmental needs of all learners.

Introduction

Most of the time, the amount and kind of support offered to ELLs are entirely up to the teacher. If teachers make effective use of evidence-based strategies, English language learners will become valued members of the classroom community, will acquire a positive first impression of education, and will make the most of educational opportunities. If, on the other hand, teachers decide that a child with limited English proficiency is an inconvenience and take a sink-or-swim approach, then the child will feel like an outsider, question his competence, and have diminished opportunities to learn.

Misconceptions about Second-Language Learning

Supporting the young ELL relies on a combination of accurate information, pedagogical skills, and a commitment to supporting every child's learning. Often, misconceptions about young English language learners get in the way of making early childhood classrooms effective learning environments for them.

English language learners are not just found in urban settings. ELLs can be found in all types of early childhood settings. The cultural and linguistic diversity of the children enrolled in early childhood programs has increased dramatically. According to the National Clearinghouse for English Language Acquisition, between 1997 and 2008 the number of English language learners enrolled in U.S. public schools increased by 51 percent. Today, one in nine students in the United States does not speak English as her first language; by 2025, the Pew Hispanic Center predicts that one in four students will be an English language learner.

Young children do not just pick up language; they need intensive and intentional instruction. Although young children's facility with languages can be impressive, language is first heard as a jumble of sounds. If you doubt this, just turn to a television or radio channel that broadcasts in a language you do not speak. At first, you cannot tell what pieces of that flow of speech represent a word, a phrase, or a sentence. Learners of a new language need *comprehensible input*, or an understanding of what they hear in a meaningful context. The more meaningful input a child is exposed to, the more progress the child can make in a second language.

The child's home language is not an impediment to acquiring English. The first language is a resource for learning the second language. Children are capable of developing emergent literacy skills in two languages simultaneously. And, being bilingual or multilingual offers significant advantages, including enhanced self-esteem, communication with family and friends, and the ability to apply knowledge of the first language to the second language. *Translanguaging*, or sometimes combining both languages into a single sentence, occurs naturally in young children. Consider what you do when someone speaks to you in an unfamiliar language and you want to communicate with that person. Your first instinct is to pay attention to nonverbal cues such as gestures, facial expressions, and pantomime. You also pay attention to the emotional tone of the message and intonation; for example, the rising pitch at the end of an utterance indicates a question. You latch onto any words that you recognize, such as a person's name, a word borrowed from English, repeated words, and cognates— words that sound similar, such as *accident* in English and *accidente* in Spanish. You consider the context and look for cues from the immediate environment. Just as your knowledge of a language scaffolds your efforts to make sense out of an unfamiliar language, the young child's knowledge of another language is a strength, not a liability.

Language learning is not limited to one area of the brain nor does it follow a steady, incremental path. Language learning involves many areas of the brain and tends to occur in spurts as new neural pathways are established. If your metaphor for language learning suggests evenly spaced steps, it is time to rethink. Research suggests that language development progresses unevenly, sometimes surging forward and at other times lingering at a plateau.

The seemingly simple act of looking at a picture book engages all areas of the brain, as the child uses motor skills to pick up a book and turn the pages, vision to look at the words and pictures, reasoning to interpret the meanings of the words, gestures or speech to respond to the pictures, and emotions to respond to the book's art and meaning.

Understanding Second-Language Learners

Stages in Learning English

Researcher Patton Tabors notes that young children must work through a series of revelations as they begin to learn a new language:

- Not everyone understands or speaks their language.
- The people who do not understand and speak their language speak a different language.
- If they want to communicate with these people, they need to learn this new and different language.

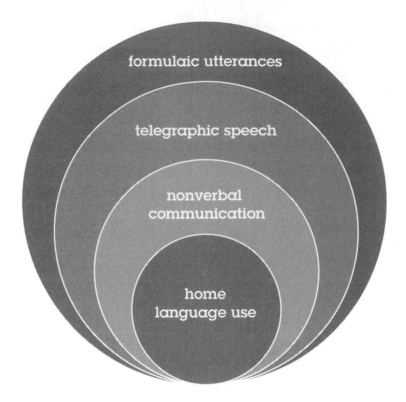

- **Home language use:** Although not all children do this, they may speak in their home language for a while before realizing they are not communicating. They may go through a period of speaking to others in their first language, even though everyone is responding in English. Even after they have begun speaking English, children may continue to use their first language with grandparents or other family members or may mix the two languages.

- **Reliance on nonverbal communication:** At this stage, children realize that they are not being understood and may use little or no language, relying instead on gestures and nonverbal utterances. For example, a child who needs assistance might whine or whimper. However, even if they are not producing English, this does not mean they are not receiving English. It is common to see these children standing on the sidelines as spectators, watching and listening to their peers. Other children may treat them like babies, speak to them as they would a much younger child, or simply ignore them. Some children go through a stage in which they attempt to sound like they are speaking English before they have acquired a vocabulary in English. This behavior parallels the stream of nonwords often produced by babies near the end of their first year—a flow of gibberish with the intonation of speech but with no (or few) recognizable words. Second language learners may repeat this stage much later. If adults cannot understand the child's first language, this important milestone may be overlooked because the adults assume the talk is in the first language. However, it is an important part of development because it shows that the child is trying on the sounds and intonation patterns of English.

- **Telegraphic speech:** Telegraphic speech, observed commonly in toddlers and young preschoolers, strips language down to the very essence (as adults once did when they sent telegrams and had to pay for each word). Second-language learners typically go through a similar phase. Telegraphic speech relies primarily on nouns, verbs, and words for social interaction. Articles, pronouns, word endings, and other grammatical pieces are left out. For example, a child may say "More juice" instead of "I want some more juice." At this point, children use the few words or phrases that they know.

- **Formulaic utterances:** If you have studied another language, you probably memorized common scripts along the lines of "Hello, my name is _____. What is your name? I am glad to meet you." Such scripts make communicating easier; young second-language learners use a version of this approach as well. Some of the more common expressions used by young children are "What's that?" "Lookit," or "How does it . . . ?"

Obstacles that Second Language Learners and Their Families Face

For many young children and their families, the transition to an English-language early childhood program represents challenges in a number of areas.

Online, we offer printable letters home in both English and Spanish, to help you connect with families. See www.gryphon-house.com.

- **Reduced circumstances:** A family's social status can be diminished as they attempt to reestablish their credentials in a new environment. Young ELLs' parents frequently are underemployed; for example, a medical doctor from Russia may not have a U.S. medical license and may be working two jobs to support her family. Reduced circumstances can affect children as well; for example, a gifted child may be treated by his preschool classmates as if he were a toddler because he does not speak English. Family socioeconomic status (SES) is a combination of family income, parents' education level, and job status. In the United States, higher income levels can mean access to more language-learning resources such as books, technology, cultural events, tutors, and enrichment programs. Thus, it is particularly important that teachers inform families about of all of the free and inexpensive resources available to them in the school and larger community.

- **Limited exposure to English:** Many families of English language learners are living in linguistically isolated households; no one in the household knows English well enough to accomplish routine tasks. This leads to a double bind in that they cannot acquire English unless they have social interaction with English-speaking individuals, yet these interactions do not occur until *after* they have acquired some English. The family will often continue to speak only the home language. As the children grow older, they often will serve as translators for their family members.

- **Changes in the physical environment and expectations for in-school routines:** Many young children who previously spent much of their time outdoors become nature deprived when they are kept indoors much of the time. Overcrowding, violence, and the absence of green spaces in the neighborhood can cause dramatic changes in the physical environment. A child may be accustomed to social expectations that differ significantly from those in her new country. When she behaves according to the old expectations, she may be embarrassed or even ridiculed by her new peers. Teachers can help by learning about the child's culture and working with the family to teach all of the children in the class about their new friend's background and country. They can also pay special attention to helping the young ELL learn the expectations of her new environment.

- **Rejection of the home language in an effort to fit in:** In the United States as well as some other countries, English not only dominates but also is associated with status, education, wealth, and power. One common yet disappointing outcome for many families is that children's proficiency in the ethnic language often declines. This can lead to disillusionment with the "American dream" as parents and families see their young children drifting away from their traditions, values, and language. In an English-dominant context, children often need more support to preserve and enhance their knowledge of their first language.

- **Lack of cultural information:** Educators can be uninformed or misinformed about the many different cultures, traditions, or religious observances among their students, and achieving understanding can be a challenge. For example, I know of some teachers who carefully planned a pizza party for the class families and were offended because the Muslim mothers would not eat. The teachers knew that Muslims do not eat pork, and they had been careful to order a vegetarian pizza. However, because the teachers used the same knife to cut both the sausage-and-pepperoni pizzas and the vegetarian pizza, religious observances prohibited the Muslim mothers from eating. Until the teachers understood this, they were inclined to think that they had "already done everything" to make the gathering a success.

Specific Activities Lead to Success in Literacy

In 2009, the National Early Literacy Panel (NELP) analyzed 299 predictive studies to arrive at a list of the early childhood activities that are associated with success in literacy. On that list were the activities that serve as the research base for this book, including:

- Oral language
- Concepts about print
- Name writing and other activities related to children's names
- Environmental print
- Alphabet knowledge
- Phonological processing
- Visual-perceptual skills
- Rapid Automatic Naming (instantly and correctly identifying letters, numbers, and words)
- Emergent (pretend) reading
- Emergent (pretend) writing
- Dialogic reading (interactive reading and discussion of books)
- Parent programs
- Vocabulary instruction
- Play-based literacy

Throughout this book, readers will find all of these principles and more put into practice. In my early days of teaching, I remember being boggled by the concept of individualizing when there were twenty-eight first graders in my classroom. I naïvely assumed that it meant planning a different activity for each child simultaneously. Later, I realized that the activities themselves were too prescriptive and limiting.

Optimize your ability to reach and teach a diverse group of children by planning open-ended activities that allow every child to participate at some level. For example, suppose that you are sharing a predictable big book with a group of preschoolers, one that is an action song with accompanying gestures. Some students will watch, listen, and rely mainly on the actions combined with oral language to understand the book. Others will study the illustrations to figure out what comes next in the song. Still others will rely on repetition, rhyme, and recall; they may begin by joining in on a few words or a refrain and eventually memorize the entire text. Just a few will actually decode the words and read them in the conventional sense. Thus, because the activity is not narrowly defined, everyone gets a chance to participate and experience success with literacy at some level.

Organization of This Book

This book is organized along a developmental continuum to make the activities more accessible to learners at different stages and to support teachers in differentiating instruction. It is based on Jerome Bruner's conceptualization of stages in learning.

- **Level I—Enactive: links oral language with physical activity**
  Using physical activity helps make oral language understandable. Use the enactive mode with young children who are new to English, particularly if their first language is not strong. Level I strategies are designated with the symbol to the right.

- **Level II—Iconic: links ideas with pictures**
  Initially, children need photographs or realistic drawings to make the connection with ideas, because it is difficult for them to fill in the blanks of more abstract symbols. As they progress through this stage, they learn to understand less realistic images that are still pictorial. Level II strategies are designated with the symbol to the right.

- **Level III—Symbolic: uses abstract symbols, such as letters, words, numerals, logos**
  It is not until children are interpreting symbols that they can become literate with print. Level III strategies are designated with the symbol to the right.

- **Extensions**
  Each of the sixty-five evidence- and standards-based activities in the book has an extension that is suitable for young children who are gifted and talented with language or for older students, such as second or third graders. The extensions are indicated by an icon that suggests a high level of proficiency with reading and writing.

Effectively Teaching ELLs

To effectively teach English language learners, consider the following approaches:

1. **Build on familiarity.** Imagine what it must be like to be a child from rural China and arrive at a well-equipped U.S. preschool. Surely, some of the materials found there must be mystifying. In my experience, breakthroughs in communication frequently happen when children interact with materials and do activities with which they are already familiar, such as water, sand, clay, and music and movement. For example, the three-year-old son of a Chinese graduate-student couple first attempted to speak English with peers while they played at the water table. The relaxed atmosphere, smaller group, and familiar materials

encouraged him to begin with an enthusiastic "Hi!" each time a child joined the group and "Bye-bye!" as the children exited. Next, he progressed to saying, "Look!" at whatever he was doing with the toys and water.

2. **Use a variety of approaches.** Multimodal approaches promote student engagement. If you combine gestures, objects, pictures, sounds, oral language, demonstrations of how things are done, and references to printed texts, you offer the largest number of children the greatest opportunity to learn. For example, introduce snack with pictures and the actual food containers; a demonstration of how to set the table; pantomimed actions of eating and drinking; and words that are commonly used in that context, such as *more* and *thank you*.

3. **Consider the children's emotions.** Young children often fear making a mistake and, at least initially, may remain silent as they listen and observe—even when they understand some of what is being said. Positive recognition from peers can fuel a child's motivation to speak out. The son of a graduate student from Saudi Arabia, for example, moved beyond one-word utterances for the first time when the class was singing. I had noticed him clapping and mouthing some of the words, and his mother shared that she had overheard him practicing at home. He surprised all of us one sunny afternoon when he enthusiastically joined in the song and the accompanying actions. The other children began to applaud spontaneously, and from that point forward, his English grew by leaps and bounds.

4. **Use repetition and intentional vocabulary instruction.** Researchers have found that, beginning at about age three, young children learn an estimated six to ten new words per day. However, they need about eight to ten meaningful repetitions of a word to make it part of their active vocabulary, so ordinary talk is often inadequate for developing vocabulary. When children are thrust into an environment where their language is not the language of instruction, it restarts this process. To bridge this vocabulary gap, young ELLs need teachers who provide context-rich encounters with a word, introduce key words in books before sharing them, use multimodal approaches, and supply child-friendly definitions of words.

5. **Get in touch with the beginner's mind.** As a beginning first- and second-grade teacher, I used to be puzzled when a not-yet-reader would volunteer to read aloud. Then, I realized that these children thought that knowing how to read would magically "just happen" to them someday. It is easy to see how this assumption could occur. Prior to attending school, we tell them that they will learn to read and that it will be fun, but we never say how long it might take or the huge investment of time, effort, and practice required. Adopting the child's point of view is essential to understanding how to support literacy all day and every day. It takes a beginner's mind.

Early childhood educators play an essential role in fostering and furthering language growth. The experiences that they provide are formative, irreplaceable, and set essential language-learning processes in motion. Giving young children a good start as learners is what early childhood education is all about.

What Is It?

Word Walls and E-Sorts to Build Vocabulary

Word walls are collections of developmentally appropriate words that are posted so that children can see them in print. Many classrooms have word walls with different purposes—for example, Words We Know: *yes, no, stop, I, Mom, love, cat, dog*; or Words for Pets: *dog, cat, hamster, fish*. Generally, a word wall is matched to instructional purposes; is cumulative so that, as new words are introduced, the familiar words remain; and serves as a support for students as they study, think about, read, and attempt to write words. An e-sort is an electronic, individualized word wall that the child can access digitally. Children can also use digital desktop publishing to create electronic word lists and share them with others. Older children can refer to word walls when they are writing in their journals as well.

Why Is It Important?

To become fluent readers and writers, children need to recognize many common words on sight. Not all words are spelled the way that they sound, and it is too time consuming to sound out every word. Hearing and understanding language or speaking words aloud and then seeing them in print support children's language growth.

How Does It Work?

Experts recommend building word walls with children over time, referring to them often as an instructional resource, and practicing reading the words in an interactive way with the children. To get more tips on using a word wall effectively, see Reading Rockets http://www.readingrockets.org/strategies/word_walls.

Connections with the Common Core Standards		
Age	**Category**	**Standard**
Kindergarten	Conventions of Standard English	L.K.1. Use frequently occurring nouns and verbs.
First Grade	Vocabulary Acquisition and Use	L.2.4. Determine or clarify the meaning of unknown and multiple-meaning words and phrases based on grade one reading and content, choosing flexibly from an array of strategies.
Second Grade	Phonics and Word Recognition	RF.2.3. Know and apply grade-level phonics and word-analysis skills in decoding words.
Third Grade	Phonics and Word Recognition	RF.3.3. Know and apply grade-level phonics and word-analysis skills in decoding words.

Leveled Adaptations

Level I: Relying on Actions and Oral Language

1. Create a word wall that has several of the most essential words for social interaction, such as *yes, no, please*, and *thank you*. Write these words in English as well as other languages spoken by the children.

2. Set up a game with a toy. The first child asks, "Would you like to play?" and the English language learner answers, "Yes, please." The first child hands over the toy, and the second child says, "Thank you." Use a pointer or small LED flashlight for children to highlight each word as it is said.

Level II: Relying on Visual Images

1. To make the connection between actions and oral language, take digital photographs of children doing helpful classroom tasks. Laminate the images and affix magnets or Velcro to the back of each.

2. Make a helper board listing the names of the children in the class and –ing verbs. You could add tasks such as watering the plants, feeding the fish, or setting the table.

3. Let the children place the photos to link the verbs for the tasks to children's names. Model the practice of referring to the board when determining who is responsible for a task.

4. For a bilingual word wall, share the bilingual book, *Bebé Goes Shopping* by Susan Middleton Elya. In this story, a child keeps grabbing strange items to put in the cart until he gets a box of animal crackers. Make silhouettes of the animals to represent the crackers that Bebé eats, such as a giraffe, a camel, and a bear. Make a matching set of the Spanish words: *jirafa, camello*, and *oso*. If there are children who speak other languages, these words can be posted as well.

Level III: Beginning to Use Symbols

1. Young children are learning names of all kinds of things, so create word walls of nouns. Next, develop a word wall of action words.

2. After you have developed these two word walls, try combining the words into simple sentences, such as: "Once there was a _____ , and he wanted to _____." Some of these sentences will be humorous. You can get more ideas for noun-verb combinations that begin with the same letter of the alphabet at http://www.toytheater.com/action-alphabet.php

3. As children gain experience with word walls, they can use them to produce their own original books. For example, a word wall with days of the week in multiple languages could be used with the children's book *Cookie's Week* by Cindy Ward. In this story, a kitten gets into all kinds of mischief, Monday through Saturday, and finally takes a rest on Sunday. Children can invent their own day-by-day account of a pet—real or hoped for—and what it might do.

Extensions

1. To challenge students with gifts and talents in working with words, consider having them learn about silent letters. Share the book *Silent Letters Loud and Clear* by Robin Pulver as a way to introduce this concept.

2. Have the children create their own e-sorts of words with silent letters using a program such as VoiceThread. Or, have them create word walls of specialized academic vocabulary related to a subject area, such as the names of dinosaurs.

Picture Book Recommendations

Daywalt, Drew. 2013. *The Day the Crayons Quit.* New York: Philomel. **(P, K, 1st, 2nd)**
This entertaining story stimulates children's imaginations by describing the antics of personified crayons. This book would lend itself to a word wall of the names of colors.

Dewdney, Anna. 2012. *Llama, Llama Hoppity-Hop.* New York: Penguin. **(T, P)**
In this rhyming board book, part of a series about Llama Llama, the activities are clapping, jumping, stretching, and moving. Make a picture word wall of the actions.

Elya, Susan. 2006. *Bebé Goes Shopping.* San Diego, CA: Harcourt Children's. **(P, K, 1st, 2nd, 3rd)**
Bebé is not at all helpful during a trip to the grocery store until Mama gives him a box of animal cookies to keep him occupied. Spanish words are interspersed throughout the book.

Fogliano, Julie. 2012. *And Then It's Spring.* New York: Roaring Book Press. **(P, K, 1st)**
After sharing this book, make a word wall of the seasons and descriptive words associated with each time of the year. Children can then refer to the word wall to construct books or create a picture of an activity that they enjoy during each season.

Fox, Mem. 2010. *Where Is the Green Sheep? Donde Esta la Oveja Verde?* Chicago, IL: Harcourt. **(T, P, K, 1st)**
Basic vocabulary is repeated and rhymed in this bilingual story about various kinds of sheep—and a particularly hard-to-find green one.

Janovitz, Marilyn. 2012. *Play Baby Play!* Naperville, IL: Source-books. **(T)**
Babies in a playgroup enjoy participating in all of the activities that include rolling around, ringing bells, and listening to stories.

Pulver, Robin. 2010. *Silent Letters Loud and Clear.* New York: Holiday House. **(1st, 2nd)**
The book follows a class who wants to ban silent letters because they make spelling too difficult. Including these silent-letter words in a word wall will help the readers to visualize their tricky spellings.

Sierra, Judy. 2012. *Suppose You Meet a Dinosaur: A First Book of Manners.* New York: Knopf. **(P, K, 1st)**
A little girl goes grocery shopping with her friendly dinosaur companion. In the process, they learn to use polite words, including *please, thank you*, and *excuse me*. Use this book to generate a word wall of polite words in multiple languages.

Teckentrup, Britta. 2012. *Animal Spots and Stripes.* San Francisco, CA: Chronicle. **(P, K)**
This is a brightly colored board book that teaches patterns. Use it to inspire a wall of words that describe patterns.

T = Toddlers (ages 1–2)
P = Preschool (ages 3–5)
K = Kindergarten (ages 5–6)
1st = First grade (ages 6–7)
2nd = Second grade (ages 7–8)
3rd = Third grade (ages 8–9)

Ward, Cindy. 1997. *Cookie's Week.* New York: Puffin. **(T, P, K, 1st)**

> A mischievous cat does something disruptive to the household every day—except Sunday, when she takes a rest. Use a word wall of days of the week before and after sharing the story. The children can create their own books with pages for each of the days.

Wild, Margaret. 2003. *Kiss Kiss!* New York: Simon and Schuster. **(T, P)**

> A baby hippo rushes outside to play and forgets to kiss his mom. All of the other jungle animals he meets along the way remind him of his omission. Have children retell the story with clip art images, stuffed toy animals, or puppets.

Online, we offer recommendations for apps that can help support children's literacy learning. Many apps are offered for free or at a low cost and are available on iTunes or Google Play. See www.gryphonhouse.com

What Is It?

Using Children's Names as a Starting Point for Alphabet Learning

Even before children pay much attention to other pieces of print, they often recognize and try to write their own names. The progression in children's name writing typically moves from random marks on paper to more controlled scribbles to shapes to letter-like shapes and then to actual letters. A child may represent her name with the first letter only and then gradually add more. The letters produced by young children usually appear to float on the page with no baseline, might be arranged in reverse order, or the child may simply run out of room on the page. Gradually, with additional practice, the child can write her first name in a recognizable way in letters of uniform size.

Why Is It Important?

Names have great personal significance for children and families. Some families prefer a unique name for their child while others follow tradition and name a child after another family member. Some cultures have naming rituals, such as a ceremony during which the child's name is selected. Therefore, it is particularly important for teachers to learn each child's name and to check with the family to be certain about the correct pronunciation.

How Does It Work?

By building on an interest in and familiarity with the letters in their own names, children can begin to understand the functions of print, increase their awareness of sound-symbol correspondence in words, identify letters, and print their names correctly. For advice on how to teach a child to write her name, step by step, see *Handwriting without Tears*, available at http://www.hwtears.com/files/Teaching_Children_Their_Name.pdf

Children are curious about one another's names, so this can be useful in teaching the alphabet and other print-recognition activities. If the class is large, begin with just some of their names. Do a simple sort, such as long names and short names.

	Connections with the Common Core Standards	
Age	**Category**	**Standard**
Kindergarten	Vocabulary Acquisition and Use	L.K.5. With guidance and support from adults, explore word relationships and nuances in word meanings.
First Grade	Craft and Structure	RI.1.4. Ask and answer questions to help determine or clarify the meaning of words and phrases in a text.
Second Grade	Phonics and Word Recognition	RF.2.3. Know and apply grade-level phonics and word analysis skills in decoding words.
Third Grade	Phonics and Word Recognition	RF.3.3. Know and apply grade-level phonics and word analysis skills in decoding words.

Leveled Adaptations

Level I: Relying on Actions and Oral Language

1. Take a digital photo of each child, and glue it onto paper with the child's first name neatly printed in upper- and lowercase manuscript letters. Laminate the cards so that they can be used all year.

2. Have the children sit in a circle. Give them turns being the mail carrier, supplying the child with a tote bag and hat. The mail carrier delivers the children's names and pictures by placing the laminated cards on the floor next to the correct persons.

3. As the mail carrier gives out the names, all of the children can say each child's name and clap the number of syllables that they hear, such as Sky-lar, two claps; Ro-lan-do, three claps; Gra-ci-el-la, four claps.

4. Send home examples of the child's name with the first letter capitalized and the rest in small letters, as it is written in school.

5. Do art activities that get the children more familiar with the letters in their names. For example, print each child's name on a piece of cardboard or construction paper with a broad-tip poster marker. Let the children glue confetti, stickers, or the little circles that result from using a hole punch onto their names to make the letters stand out.

6. Use masking tape or blue painter's tape to make the first letter of each child's name on heavy paper. Then, let her fingerpaint all around it so that the letter stands out after the tape is removed.

Level II: Relying on Visual Images

1. Make flash cards of each child's first name accompanied by a small digital photo. As you hold up each one, point out the clues that children can use to figure out a classmate's name; for example, *Juan* is a short name while *Mariposa* is a longer name.

2. Teach word configuration by making an outline of the shape of each child's name with construction paper. Have the children work in groups on name puzzles. In this activity,

they will match the construction-paper outline of the name to the correct print version by placing the configuration shape over the name. Start this game with a few examples that are very different, such as *Alyssa, Tim,* and *Giselle.* Group together names that are similar in shape, such as *John, Luke,* and *Lila.* Gradually add more names with fewer distinguishing characteristics, such as *Lisa* and *Paco.* To practice, hold up each name-outline card and ask, "Whose name is this? Is this student here today?" Some children will rely on the first letter to identify the name. Others will rely on configuration or visual memory, and still others will rely on letter sounds or sight-word recognition.

3. Make another type of word-configuration game by printing the children's names on letter strips that have a dotted line in the middle. Make a set of paper squares to use to cover small letters such as *a, e, c,* and *s.* Use rectangles set on the baseline to cover letters that are "sticks," such as *l, f, h,* and *k.* Use rectangles set at the dotted line to hang down for letters with "tails," such as *j, g,* and *p.* Cover the letters, and ask the children to guess the name that is covered.

Level III: Beginning to Use Symbols

1. Have the children do a letter search through old magazines to find all of the different type styles—lower- and uppercase, fonts, colors—in which the first letter of their name appears. Let them cut out the letters and make them into a collage.

2. Make a bulletin board or banners of children's names in large, clear print. Let the children decorate their names with their favorite things.

3. Researchers Carolyn Denton, Richard Parker, and Jan Jasbrouck suggest reading simple sentences into which children's names are inserted.

   ● Tell the children that they will read sentences that have words they know or can sound out; include the students' names in the sentences. For example, "(Child's name) loves to play," or "(Child's name) is a boy."

   ● Teach the words *a, and, the, he, she, we, it, was,* and *is.* If the children do not recognize a word, say the word (in a pleasant voice), and have them say it with you. Practice until they can identify the words quickly and accurately; point out their classmates' names in the sentence.

   ● Have the children practice reading the sentence several times until they can read it smoothly; create additional sentences with other students' names included.

Extensions

1. Read the book *A My Name Is Alice* by Jane Bayer to the children. In this book, the children have names that begin with every letter of the alphabet. Children can try making a similar book, using both the real names of their classmates and ones that they invent for any letter of the alphabet that has not been used.

2. Use music to extend the children's familiarity with classmates' names. For example, listen to "Mary Wore Her Red Dress"; then, sing it and substitute different children's names and articles of clothing into the song. Create a chart of each child's name and article of clothing. To hear the tune, visit http://www.youtube.com and type "Mary Wore Her Red Dress" in the search bar.

3. You might have children use the letters in their first, middle, and last names to design a monogram using different fonts, or have them invent a logo or label for themselves or their family.

Picture Book Recommendations

Bottner, Barbara. 2011. *An Annoying ABC.* New York: Knopf Books for Young Readers. **(P, K, 1st)**

This humorous story has a class full of children with names that begin with the letters *A* to *Z*. After listening to the story, post the letters in alphabetical order in the classroom, and then have each child use a sticky note to put his name next to the letter of the alphabet that it begins with.

Feldman, Jean, and Holly Karapetkova. 2009. *I Love Letters.* Silver Spring, MD: Gryphon House. **(P, K, 1st)**

This book features many different activities—such as the Name Game—designed to teach letters.

Hobbie, Holly. 2000. *Puddle's ABC.* New York: Little, Brown. **(T, P, K)**

One friend helps another learn how to write his name. Partner a child who can write his name with a child who is just learning to do this; have them practice in wet sand, on a magic slate, chalkboard, whiteboard, tablet computer, or an interactive whiteboard.

Mayer, Bill. 2008. *All Aboard: A Traveling Alphabet.* New York: Margaret McElderry. **(P, K, 1st)**

Things that go are the focus of this book that takes readers on a trip from *A* to *Z*.

Murphy, Stuart. 2011. *Write on, Carlos!* Watertown, MA: Charlesbridge. **(P, K, 1st)**

With help from his mom, Carlos learns how to locate each letter of his name in the alphabet and how to write the letters. Make an alphabet learning center where children can use magnetic alphabet letters, alphabet tiles, and alphabet blocks to spell out their names.

Wells, Rosemary. 2006. *Max's ABC.* New York: Viking. **(T, P, K)**

Pesky ants are the premise for this different take on an alphabet book. Combine it with the song "The Ants Go Marching." The song and lyrics in both English and Spanish are available on YouTube. Type "the ants go marching English Spanish" into the search bar.

Wells, Rosemary. 2008. *Yoko Writes Her Name.* New York: Hyperion. **(P, K)**

In this story, learning to write her name is a breakthrough for a kindergarten child from Japan. Provide children with a laminated card that shows the correct spelling of their names in upper- and lowercase letters so that they can trace and try to copy them.

Williams, Karen. 2010. *A Beach Tail.* Honesdale, PA: Boyds Mills. **(P, K, 1st)**

A boy draws a lion in the sand and makes the tail very long so that he can follow it back to where he began. Use it to introduce writing with a fingertip in a shallow pan of wet sand.

Williams, Karen, and Khadra Mohammed. 2009. *My Name Is Sangoel.* Grand Rapids, MI: Eerdmans. **(K, P, 1st)**

After sharing this book, create a class book with one page for each child that reads, "My name is _____." Have the children draw, pretend write, or copy their names. Take dictation from children who are not yet writing so that every child contributes a page to the book. This activity can be done on the computer as well.

Book Packs to Bring Picture Books into Homes

What Is It?

A book pack is an assortment of developmentally appropriate children's books suitable for reading aloud and related activities sent home with children in a durable, easily transportable container. It is circulated to children, parents, and families as a sort of miniature lending library that supports reading aloud at home.

Why Is It Important?

Many households lack reading materials suitable for young children. Researchers have found that children with books at home persist in their education, on average, three more years than those who do not own books. Having as few as twenty books in the home has a significant, positive benefit. Additionally, researchers have found that when families from low-income backgrounds are provided with appropriate children's books, easy-to-read suggestions for sharing books with toddlers, and encouragement for reading aloud at home, they are ten times more likely to read with children at least three days a week than families who do not have these supports. For some families, materials and activities sent home by teachers may be the only reading resources in the home that are well-matched to a child's level of understanding.

How Does It Work?

Begin by deciding what you will use as a container to transport the materials between school and home. You need something that is inexpensive and sturdy, closes tightly, is easy to clean and that a young child can carry. Some possibilities are heavy-duty ziplock plastic bags, backpacks, small plastic suitcases, large lunchboxes, or tote bags that have zippered tops.

Sort through your collection of books. Use paperback books; gently used ones are fine. Choose four to six books for each book pack, and make sure that the books are at different reading levels. You can categorize by theme, by a particular skill, or by story character.

Now that you have your book collection, create the following items:

- **A brief note to the parents and children introducing the book pack**
  This note should state the purpose of the book pack; explain what children will learn; be clear, easy to read, and error-free (and translated into another language as appropriate); build motivation to complete the activities, and describe the use and care of the materials.
- **Developmentally appropriate books**
  For example, you might include a wordless book so that a nonreader can use the illustrations to tell a story and include an easy reader with controlled vocabulary to support the emergent reader. Include dual-language books to support book sharing by families that do not have English as their first language. Carefully select additional books that go along with the theme; a school or public library may be able to assist with lists of recommended books. Free, printable minibooks are another inexpensive source of reading

material at different levels.. Lists of books arranged by topic and level are available at the DLTK site: http://www.dltk-teach.com/minibooks/index.htm or at the Scholastic site: http://www.scholastic.com/premium

- **An inventory card listing the book pack's contents**
  Use the inventory card to keep track of what each pack contains, and update it as the book pack is developed further. It also serves as a checklist so that families remember what books should be returned.

- **Interactive activities**
  Include simple games to play, pictures to color and label, letter trace-and-write sheets, and props that can be used to retell the story. If possible, add literacy materials such as a small whiteboard and washable marker or different types of writing paper and crayons and pencils.

- **A simple evaluation tool**
  Supply an evaluation slip that has sections for the parent and the child to rate how well they liked the book. Use a smiley face, neutral face, and frown for the child to mark. Ask the parents/families for suggestions to improve the book pack.

Connections with the Common Core Standards		
Age	**Category**	**Standard**
Kindergarten	Integration of Knowledge and Ideas	RL.K.7 With prompting and support, describe the relationship between illustrations and the story in which they appear.
First Grade	Integration of Knowledge and Ideas	RL.1.7 Use the illustrations and details in a text to describe its key ideas.
Second Grade	Integration of Knowledge and Ideas	RL.2.7 Use information gained from the illustrations and words in a print or digital text to demonstrate understanding of its characters, setting, or plot.
Third Grade	Integration of Knowledge and Ideas	RL.3.7 Explain how specific aspects of a text's illustrations contribute to what is conveyed by the words in a story.

Leveled Adaptations

Level I: Relying on Actions and Oral Language
Send home fingerplays and action rhymes that show the gestures to accompany the words, such as *Today Is Monday*, a song picture book by Eric Carle that has a different favorite food for every day of the week. To find the song on YouTube, type "today is Monday by loonytricky" in the search bar. Have each child list seven favorite foods and make their own song chart to take home.

Level II: Relying on Visual Images

Send home a thematic book pack, such as books in English and Spanish or a collection on camping (or pretending to camp).

Level III: Beginning to Use Symbols

Consider a book pack about a food that just about everyone eats, such as pizza.

Extensions

1. Plan a family night at which the parents and children help you assemble a variety of book packs. Begin by collecting many different paperback books. Put several of them that are related in some way together.

2. Identify and gather some suitable containers.

3. Prepare the supplies, such as the list of contents, the letter explaining the purpose, the interactive activities, a simple evaluation form, and any other reading and writing materials.

4. Sort the materials using a system such as self-adhesive colored dots to make it easy to match items to the correct container.

5. When the families arrive, they will put the packs together in assembly-line fashion.

6. After the packs are complete, let small groups use one of the book packs. Give them comment cards to get their questions, suggestions on how to improve them, or recommendations for other types of book packs that they would like to see.

Picture Book Recommendations

Spanish and English

Many children's favorites, such as *Chicka Chicka Boom Boom, The Very Hungry Caterpillar,* and *Ferdinand* are available in Spanish. More suggestions are at http://libraries.idaho.gov/files/Books-to-Go-spanish-10bags-master-list.pdf

Dominguez, Angela. 2013. *Maria Had a Little Llama/María Tenía una Llamita Pequeña*. New York: Holt. **(P, K)**

The nursery rhyme is illustrated and translated into Spanish.

Eastman, P.D. 1967. *Are You My Mother?* New York: Random House. **(T, P, K)**

Eastman, P.D. 2001. *¿Eres Mi Mamá?* New York: Random House. **(T, P, K)**

The classic book is available in both Spanish and English. Snort!

Howell, Theresa. 2003. *A Is for Airplane/A Es para Avion*. Lanham, MD: Cooper Square. **(P, K, 1st)**

The alphabet in both English and Spanish.

Mora, Pat. 2009. *Book Fiesta! Celebrate Children's Day/Book Day; Celebremos el Dia de los Ninos/el Dia de los Libros!* New York: HarperCollins. **(K, 1st, 2nd)**

Children can let their imaginations take flight with this delightful book.

Murphy, Mary. 2008. *I Like It When . . . /Me Gusta Cuando . . .* Boston, MA: HMH Books for Young Readers. **(T, P)**

In this charming board book, a little penguin lists his favorite things, including holding hands, dancing, and hugging.

T =	**Toddlers** (ages 1–2)
P =	**Preschool** (ages 3–5)
K =	**Kindergarten** (ages 5–6)
1st =	**First grade** (ages 6–7)
2nd =	**Second grade** (ages 7–8)
3rd =	**Third grade** (ages 8–9)

Camping Book Pack

Henkes, Kevin. 1997. *Bailey Goes Camping.* New York: Greenwillow. **(T, P, K)**

James, Helen. 2007. *S is for S'mores: A Camping Alphabet.* Ann Arbor, MI: Sleeping Bear. **(P, K, 1st, 2nd)**

Lessac, Frané. 2003. *Camp Granada: Sing-Along Camp Songs.* New York: Henry Holt. **(K, 1st, 2nd, 3rd)**

> A compilation of favorite camp songs suitable for sharing.

Mayer, Mercer. 2001. *Just Me and My Dad.* New York: Random House. **(T, P, K)**

Parrish, Peggy. 2003. *Amelia Bedelia Goes Camping.* New York: Greenwillow. **(P, K, 1st, 2nd)**

Rockwell, Anne. 1986. *The Night We Slept Outside.* New York: Aladdin. **(P, K, 1st)**

Ross, Maxim. n.d. *Let's Go Camping.* Amazon Digital Services. **(P, K, 1st, 2nd, 3rd)**

> This story describes the activities associated with camping and includes a picture glossary of camping.

Rylant, Cynthia. 1999. *Henry and Mudge and the Starry Night.* New York: Simon Spotlight. **(P, K, 1st, 2nd)**

Van Dusen, Chris. 2003. *A Camping Spree with Mr. Magee.* San Francisco, CA: Chronicle. **(K, 1st, 2nd)**

Book Pack on Pizza

Auch, Mary Jane. 2003. *The Princess and the Pizza.* New York: Holiday House. **(K, 1st, 2nd)**

Barbour, Karen. 1990. *Little Nino's Pizzeria.* Boston, MA: HMH Books for Young Readers. **(K, 1st, 2nd)**

Katz, Karen. 2004. *Grandpa and Me.* New York: Little Simon. **(T, P, K)**

Morton, Lone. 1998. *Get Dressed, Robbie/Vistete, Robertito.* Hauppauge, NY: Barron's. **(P, K, 1st)**

Steig, William. 2003. *Pete's a Pizza.* New York: HarperFestival. **(T, P, K)**

Walter, Virginia. 1998. *"Hi! Pizza Man!"* London, UK: Orchard. **(T, P, K)**

Wellington, Monica. 2006. *Pizza at Sally's.* New York: Dutton. **(P, K, 1st, 2nd, 3rd)**

> Describes the entire pizza-making process, starting with growing the tomatoes.

What Is It?

Literature Circles to Extend Story Comprehension

A literature circle is a small group of children who choose a book, make decisions concerning the reading and sharing of the text, and function as the facilitators of the discussion. In preschool or kindergarten, the basis for the literature discussion group often is a picture book that they have heard read aloud. For children in the primary grades, the reading material might be a poem, a picture book that children have selected to read, or a chapter book read aloud in class by the teacher or chosen by a small group of interested students.

For ELLs, choose a book that they have heard in both their home language and in English and have practiced several times using digital technology, working with an aide, or working with a peer or cross-age tutor. This will give them the background that they need to participate more fully in the discussion.

Why Is It Important?

Discussion is a major way for children to respond to what they read. Literature discussion in small groups encourages children to connect with literature, promotes higher-order thinking skills, improves listening and reading comprehension, and supports cooperative learning.

How Does It Work?

The teacher first models and directs the literature circles. Later, as children gain experience with discussions focused on a piece of literature, they can assume greater responsibility for managing literature circles. The teacher chooses several appropriate books and allows students to vote on one to discuss. Note that not only story books but also information books are suitable for sharing in this way. The book discussion process with young children typically includes the following phases:

- Previewing the story and making predictions based on the title, cover illustrations, and so forth
- Reading and wondering as the group reads the story and shares their thoughts about it
- Assembling children into smaller groups so that they can respond to the story briefly through talk, drawing, or short written responses
- Looking back to review what the whole group has learned from their experiences with the book
- For younger children or children with limited experiences in literature discussion, just five minutes may be sufficient at first. As children gain confidence and competence in interacting with books, allocate more time.

Connections with the Common Core State Standards

Age	Category	Standard
Kindergarten	Comprehension and Collaboration	SL.K.1. Participate in collaborative conversations with diverse partners about kindergarten topics and texts with peers and adults in small and larger groups.
First Grade	Comprehension and Collaboration	SL.1.1. Participate in collaborative conversations with diverse partners about first-grade topics and texts with peers and adults in small and larger groups.
Second Grade	Comprehension and Collaboration	SL.2.1. Participate in collaborative conversations with diverse partners about second-grade topics and texts with peers and adults in small and larger groups.
Third Grade	Comprehension and Collaboration	SL.3.1. Engage effectively in a range of collaborative discussions (one-on-one, in groups, and teacher-led) with diverse partners on third-grade topics and texts, building on others' ideas and expressing their own clearly.

Leveled Adaptations

Level I: Relying on Actions and Oral Language

1. Use the book *Goodnight, Goodnight, Construction Site* by Sherri Rinker with a group of three to five children.
2. Collect small toys to represent construction equipment that is mentioned in the book—crane truck, cement mixer, dump truck, bulldozer, and excavator. As each piece of equipment is mentioned and gets ready to retire for the evening, have children manipulate them in the ways described in the book in a small sand box. End each one by covering the item with a cloth to represent going to sleep.
3. During the literature circle, ask questions such as, "What do the trucks do during the day?" "What do the trucks do to get ready to go to sleep?" "What do you think will happen tomorrow morning?"
4. You might follow up with *Construction Countdown* by K. C. Olson, combining the book with plastic equipment to count.

Level II: Relying on Visual Images

1. Begin by reading aloud the book *Diggers Go* by Steve Light.
2. You can find free, realistic clip-art images of each of the types of equipment from this book in Microsoft Office clip art. Enlarge them, and label each one with the name of the equipment.
3. Read the story aloud and have the children imitate the sounds that the vehicles make.
4. Talk about the sounds that equipment makes using books such as *Demolition* by Sally Sutton and *Machines Go to Work in the City* by William Low. Then, make a class book of equipment and sounds.

Level III: Beginning to Use Symbols

1. The book *Goodnight, Goodnight, Construction Site* has twenty-four pairs of rhyming words. Make a word wall of the pairs of rhyming words for children to see, and ask them to clap when they hear the rhyme as the story is read aloud.

2. Use clip-art images of the types of equipment, and have children discuss what job each performs.

3. Find some information books on construction to add to their background knowledge, and then have them work in small groups to produce books that follow this pattern:

   I am a ____.

   Here's what I do ____.

   People need me because ____.

Extensions

1. Coach children with more advanced literacy skills in how to lead a small group of peers as they discuss books.

2. Provide them with a script of open-ended questions that can be used as the basis for discussion.

   What do you think? (each child has a turn after reading the book)

   What does ____ do?

   What else could ____ do?

   How do you think ____ feels when ____?

   Why does ____ feel that way? How can you tell?

   If you could talk to someone from this story, who would you choose? Why?

   What would you say to him or her?

   Is there anyone in this book who reminds you of yourself? Who? Why?

   Would you change anything about this story? What? How would you change it?

   If you were writing a sequel to this story, what would you have happen next?

   If you were writing a prequel, what would you have happen earlier?

   If you could talk to the author of this story, what would say or ask?

   What is the best part of the story? Why?

3. Monitor the groups, and provide the children with feedback.

Picture Book Recommendations

Garcia, Emma. 2007. *Tip Tip Dig Dig.* New York: Sterling. **(T)**

   Construction equipment, including a digger, mixer, crane, dump truck, bulldozer, and road roller, set to work in this simple book suitable for toddlers.

Light, Steve. 2013. *Diggers Go.* San Francisco, CA: Chronicle. **(T, P)**

   Part of a board-book series on vehicles, this one focuses on construction equipment and the sounds that each one makes. Use it to encourage play with toy vehicles.

Low, William. 2012. *Machines Go to Work in the City.* New York: Henry Holt. **(P, K, 1st, 2nd)**

   The illustrations and information in this book give it great appeal.

McMullan, Kate, and Jim McMullan. 2007. *I'm Dirty!* New York: HarperCollins **(T, P, K)**

   A backhoe gets progressively dirtier in this book, part of a series that includes *I'm Big!, I'm Mighty!, I Stink!, I'm Fast!,* and *I'm Bad!*

Meltzer, Lynn. 2011. *The Construction Crew.* New York: Henry Holt. **(T, P, K)**

Before building a new home, the construction crew demolishes an old building in this story told in rhyme.

Olson, K. C. 2004. *Construction Countdown.* New York: Henry Holt. **(P, K, 1st)**

This book uses different types of construction vehicles to count down from ten to one. All of the vehicles are working together, leading up to a surprise ending.

Rinker, Sherri. 2011. *Goodnight, Goodnight, Construction Site.* San Francisco, CA: Chronicle. **(T, P, K)**

Personified heavy equipment calls it a day in this gentle story that uses repetition and rhyme to create a quiet mood. Toddlers will enjoy spotting the equipment they may have seen elsewhere as well as joining in on the refrain.

Sutton, Sally. 2012. *Demolition.* Somerville, MA: Candlewick. **(P, K)**

Before construction begins, demolition might be necessary. This book introduces several demolition machines, accompanied by pictures and words that describe the sounds they make.

What Is It?

Environmental Print Activities to Teach Word Configuration

Environmental print refers to all of the print material—letters, numbers, logos, universal symbols—in the settings that young children experience. It includes labels and signs of all types, such as traffic signs; food packaging; junk mail; toy advertising; electronic and print billboards; images in magazines, newspapers, and newsletters; and so forth. Word configuration refers to the overall shape or outline of a word. Unlike the text of a book, environmental print emphasizes an individual word, letters, numerals, or a symbol such as the logo for a grocery-store chain. Children often recognize certain items, such as the packaging of their favorite breakfast cereal, long before they are independent readers. Environmental print activities capitalize on the words, letters, numbers, and symbols that children encounter in various contexts and use this familiarity to build literacy skills.

Why Is It Important?

Between one and two years of age, most children begin using nouns to label people, animals, places, and objects, and they tend to ask for the names of whatever they do not know. These first words usually have personal significance, such as names of family members, friends, pets, or foods. By the time that they reach preschool, many children also start to notice print in their environment and may begin to point it out or ask what a sign says. If a child writes *XOXO* to indicate hugs and kisses, draws a heart to represent the word *love*, or attempts to put a favorite food on a shopping list, the child understands that print conveys meaning.

How Does It Work?

Environmental print is a relevant and convenient way to draw young children's attention to print. Activities that focus on environmental print offer particular advantages for young ELLs. Many young children live in communities where they will see labels at the grocery store in English and in Spanish, for example. So, a routine trip to the store can be an opportunity to draw the child's attention to print in a meaningful context. Learning to use contextual cues—for example, knowing that the label they see in the produce department probably is the name of that food item—gives children a scaffold on which to build their guesses about a word's or symbol's meaning in their first language as well as in English.

Connections with the Common Core State Standards		
Age	Category	Standard
Kindergarten	Vocabulary Acquisition and Use	LK.5. Identify real-life connections between words and their use.
First Grade	Vocabulary Acquisition and Use	L.1.5. Identify real-life connections between words and their use.
Second Grade	Vocabulary Acquisition and Use	L.2.5. Identify real-life connections between words and their use.
Third Grade	Vocabulary Acquisition and Use	L.3.5. Identify real-life connections between words and their use.

Leveled Adaptations

Level I: Relying on Actions and Oral Language

1. On any given day, children arrive at school wearing, carrying, and using examples of environmental print, such as the images on their clothing or the names of colors on their crayons. Have the children take turns sharing something they know, such as what their T-shirt says.

2. Around the school building, children can see signs such as *stop, office*, or *exit* and universal logos for the boys' and girls' restrooms. Actual photographs of common signs are available on Microsoft Office clip art; select photographs rather than graphics when you search so that you have a realistic version of the sign. Show these photos to the children, and talk with them about what they mean.

3. Go on an environmental print hunt with the children, and collect examples of symbols around them that they can read. Emphasize the importance of knowing what these messages mean and how knowing it keeps them safe or solves a problem.

4. Because environmental print activities adapt readily to different levels of ability, you may want to have an environmental print learning center. This can be especially helpful for children who are learning English as a second language. For example, you can place some print materials, such as restaurant menus, in two languages in the center.

Level II: Relying on Visual Images

According to researcher Uta Frith, the first stage of word recognition is *logographic*: words are learned as whole units, more like a picture. Even some toddlers can recognize the name of a fast-food restaurant long before they can identify individual letters or words.

1. Have each child create an environmental print book. Let the children collect letters, labels, and anything else that they can read.

2. They can paste these items on sheets of paper and insert them in plastic page protectors.

3. Assemble the pages all of the children have made into a three-ring binder.

4. It is also possible to make an electronic environmental print book by cutting and pasting images into a free software program such as VoiceThread, which allows the user to record the pronunciation of the word and a comment for each entry.

Level III: Beginning to Use Symbols

The second stage of word recognition is *alphabetic*: children pay attention to letters to try to figure out words.

1. Encourage play with letters by supplying alphabet books, blocks, foam or magnetic letters, and so on. For English language learners, gather environmental print examples in the child's first language as well as in English.

2. Using cut-out images from magazines, newspapers, and advertising, have each child make a set of environmental print cards on index cards.

3. Have a volunteer or classroom aide sit with an individual child and invent a simple story into which environmental print such as toys, cartoons, and restaurant or food logos can be inserted. For example, they could use the following prompts, from the 2008 study "Exploring Intentional Instructional Uses of Environmental Print in Preschool and Primary Grades" by Billie Enz, Jennifer Prior, Maureen Gerard, and Myae Han.

   Once upon a time, a _____ went _____. When she got to _____, she decided she wanted to eat _____. After she ate, she saw her friend _____. They played with _____. They had fun!

Extensions

Relate environmental print that children see on signs to the signs produced by protesting turkeys in *One Tough Turkey* by Steven Kroll. In this popular children's book, the turkeys petition against the traditional Thanksgiving meal, using signs to try to persuade others.

Picture Book Recommendations

T = Toddlers
(ages 1–2)

P = Preschool
(ages 3–5)

K = Kindergarten
(ages 5–6)

1st = First grade
(ages 6–7)

2nd = Second grade
(ages 7–8)

3rd = Third grade
(ages 8–9)

Cuyler, Margery. 2000. *Road Signs: A Harey Race with a Tortoise.* New York: Two Lions. **(K, 1st, 2nd, 3rd)**

This humorous retelling of the fable "The Tortoise and the Hare" includes familiar road signs and signs made by the spectators of the race. Emergent readers will enjoy trying to guess what each sign says by relying on their knowledge of environmental print, while older children can use their knowledge of the alphabet or sight vocabulary to read the signs.

Hill, Mary. 2003. *Signs at the Pool.* Danbury, CT: Children's Press. **(P, K)**

Part of a series featuring common signs within different environments, this book focuses on the signs at a swimming pool, such as the hours of operation, pool depth, and *no diving.* Other books in the series include *Signs at the Airport, Signs at School, Signs at the Park,* and *Signs on the Road.*

Kessler, Leonard. 2001. *Mr. Pine's Mixed-Up Signs.* Cynthiana, KY: Purple House. **(P, K, 1st, 2nd, 3rd)**

When Mr. Pine, the town sign maker, loses his glasses, he mixes up all of the town's signs! Young readers can use what they understand about environmental print to help to sort out where all of the signs belong.

Lehrhaupt, Adam. 2013. *Warning: Do Not Open This Book!* New York: Simon and Schuster. **(K, 1st, 2nd, 3rd)**

Monkeys, toucans, and alligators ignore signs with humorous results.

McCaughtry, Keith. 2012. *All about Street Signs and Laws.* Bloomington, IN: AuthorHouse. **(1st, 2nd)**

This book teaches about some common street signs to help children understand what they mean and how to correctly follow what they say.

Milich, Zoran. 2005. *City Signs.* Toronto: Kids Can Press. **(T, P, K)**

This book uses actual photographs of signs that children would likely see in an urban setting. The children may realize that they are already able to read some of these words.

Tepper, Yona. 2010. *Passing By.* La Jolla, CA: Kane Miller. **(T, P, K)**

As a toddler peers through the railings of a balcony, she hears and sees many different passersby. All of the signs are in Hebrew script.

Van Lieshout, Maria. 2012. *Backseat A-B-See.* San Francisco, CA: Chronicle. **(P, K, 1st)**

Street signs from *A* to *Z* appear as a child rides along in the back seat of the family car.

What Is It?

A song picture book consists of song lyrics that have been illustrated and published as a book. Song picture books are particularly useful for learning language because there are clear connections between language development and musical development in young children. After children have memorized the words to a song, even nonreaders are capable of "reading" a chart of the song's lyrics with their classmates. Therefore, song picture books are not only aesthetic objects but also very engaging tools for emergent literacy.

Song Picture Books that Support Emergent Reading

Why Is It Important?

Music throughout the school day supports literacy development. It is obvious that music affects memory—we can recall the lyrics of a song longer than other text, presumably because singing involves more areas of the brain simultaneously. Music often is used to motivate children to learn—for example, learning the alphabet by singing "The ABC Song." Music also creates a more relaxed emotional tone, supplies repetition, and invites joyful participation. These things may be particularly important when a child is reluctant to use English in public at first. Combining music with pictures and text is a good way to develop early literacy skills.

How Does It Work?

Try the following sequence for sharing song picture books with young children:

- **Play the music.** Play the song in the background during free play or art activities so children get familiar with the tune and lyrics. Take children on a picture walk through the book, and turn the pages in pace with the lyrics.
- **Begin small.** Have the children perform just the motions, insert just one word, learn one phrase, or sing only the chorus. Keep building until the whole song is familiar. Find versions of the song in different languages to support young children who are learning English.
- **Prepare a song chart.** Take children through the lyrics, using a pointer to indicate where they are in the text. You may want to produce a rebus song chart that illustrates some of the key words. Give children opportunities to be the director who leads the class by using the pointer.
- **Put the book and the recording in the listening center.** Provide a recorded version with an audible signal, such as a bell, to indicate when to turn the pages so that children do not lose their place. Have children play games with sight words from the song's lyrics. Invent new verses for the song with the children. Invite children to illustrate their own version of the song using a template that you provide.

Connections with the Common Core State Standards

Age	Category	Standard
Kindergarten	Vocabulary Acquisition and Use	L.K.6. Use words and phrases acquired through conversations, reading and being read to, and responding to texts.
First Grade	Vocabulary Acquisition and Use	L.1.6. Use words and phrases acquired through conversations, reading and being read to, and responding to texts including frequently occurring conjunctions to signal simple relationships.
Second Grade	Vocabulary Acquisition and Use	L.2.6. Use words and phrases acquired through conversations, reading and being read to, and responding to texts, including using adjectives and adverbs to describe.
Third Grade	Vocabulary Acquisition and Use	L.3.6. Acquire and use accurately grade-appropriate conversational, general academic, and domain-specific words and phrases, including those that signal spatial and temporal relationships.

Leveled Adaptations

Level I: Relying on Actions and Oral Language

1. Give children a set of toys and props to sing a song that is very familiar to them. It is important that the text be predictable; it should have a simple sequence of events, use repetition, rhyme, or familiar structures. A good example is the counting rhyme "Ten in the Bed." Share it numerous times, and consider using several different formats, such as a blanket on the floor with ten children, with a set of ten bean bags or other small toys, or with flannel-board or clip-art cutouts.

2. Two good song collections are *Children's Songs: A Collection of Childhood Favorites* by Susie Tallman and *Toddler Favorites*, a collection from Music for Little People. Toddlers and preschoolers often delight at hearing their names in stories or songs and seeing their names in print.

Level II: Relying on Visual Images

1. Introduce a song picture book for a song that is already familiar to the children, such as *Little White Duck* by Walt Whippo and Bernard Zaritsky, *Five Little Speckled Frogs* by Nikki Smith, or *Twinkle, Twinkle, Little Star* by Jerry Pinkney.

2. Develop the idea of making pictures to go along with the words of the song.

3. Read *You Are My Sunshine* by Jimmie Davis, and teach them the song. (To see and hear it in Spanish, visit YouTube.com. Type "Eres mi estrella Sunny Earth Academy" into the search bar.)

4. Make an illustrated song chart using clip art, and send home smaller copies of the song lyrics for children to sing for their families.

5. Teach the children new lyrics to a familiar tune, such as this one sung to the tune of "The Wheels on the Bus":

The Children on the Playground

The children go outside and run around, run around, run around. (children run in place)

The children go outside and run around on the playground.

The children on the swings go up and down, up and down, up and down. (children swing their arms)

The children on the swings go up and down on the playground.

The teacher tells the children come back in, come back in, come back in. (gesture with arm to come inside)

The teacher tells the children come back in, on the playground.

Level III: Beginning to Use Symbols

1. Introduce the children to different musical styles, such as the zydeco music of "They All Ask'd for You" by the Meters. To hear the tune and see a video that shows its Louisiana origins, visit YouTube.com. (Type "They All Ask'd for You by Enchanted Escape" into the search bar.)

2. Introduce two song picture books of reggae music, *One Love* by Cedella Marley and *Every Little Thing* by Bob Marley and Cedella Marley, to the children. Use clip art to make song charts for each one.

Extensions

1. Have the children learn longer, narrative songs, such as the following:
   - "The Big Rock Candy Mountain" (traditional)
   - "Over the Rainbow" by Harold Arlen and E. Y. Harburg
   - "The City of New Orleans" by Steve Goodman
   - "My Favorite Things" by Richard Rodgers and Oscar Hammerstein
   - "Puff the Magic Dragon" by Peter Yarrow and Leonard Lipton

2. Another intellectually challenging task for a child or small group is to convert a song picture book, such as *Down by the Bay* by Raffi, into a rebus song chart to share with the class.

3. Children who are gifted with language might try to produce new lyrics to a familiar tune. Begin with a very simple song picture book, such as *If You're Hoppy* by April Pulley Sayre and based on "If You're Happy and You Know It," that requires just changing the action. Or try a version of "The Wheels on the Bus," such as *The Seals on the Bus* by Lenny Hort or *The Babies on the Bus* by Karen Katz. *Jo MacDonald Saw a Pond* by Mary Quattlebaum is sung to the tune of "Old MacDonald Had a Farm," and *I Know a Wee Piggy* by Kim Norman is based on "I Know an Old Lady Who Swallowed a Fly."

Picture Book Recommendations

Davis, Jimmie. 2011. *You Are My Sunshine*. New York: Cartwheel Books. **(T, P, K)**
   Children follow a toddler and a teddy bear across the pages of this bright board-book version of the old hit song. Send home the lyrics so families can share in the fun.

Hort, Lenny. 2000. *The Seals on the Bus*. New York: Henry Holt. **(T, P, K)**
   More and more animals pile on the bus, each making a funny sound, in this reimagined version of "The Wheels on the Bus."

T = Toddlers (ages 1–2)

P = Preschool (ages 3–5)

K = Kindergarten (ages 5–6)

1st = First grade (ages 6–7)

2nd = Second grade (ages 7–8)

3rd = Third grade (ages 8–9)

Katz, Karen. 2011. *The Babies on the Bus.* New York: HarperCollins. **(T)**

Based on the song "The Wheels on the Bus," this version features babies as the stars. The book can also be used with older students as an example of creating new lyrics for a familiar tune.

Marley, Bob, and Cedella Marley. 2012. *Every Little Thing.* San Francisco, CA: Chronicle. **(T, P, K, 1st, 2nd, 3rd)**

Based on "Three Little Birds" by Bob Marley and the Wailers, this illustrated version of the favorite reggae song reminds children that "every little thing's gonna be all right." Children will enjoy chiming in on the chorus, so a typed version of the lyrics—with the repeated parts highlighted—can support practice with emergent reading.

Marley, Cedella. 2011. *One Love.* San Francisco, CA: Chronicle. **(T, P, K, 1st, 2nd, 3rd)**

Bob Marley's reggae song "One Love/People Get Ready" was the inspiration for this book, created by his daughter. Relate it to the song, "What a Wonderful World," written by Bob Thiele and George Weiss, and then ask students to think about how a small kindness can make a difference.

Pinkney, Jerry. 2011. *Twinkle, Twinkle, Little Star.* New York: Little, Brown. **(P, K, 1st, 2nd, 3rd)**

Dreamy illustrations complement the famous lullaby in this picture book. Relate it to other lullabies in picture-book form, such as *All the Pretty Horses* by Susan Jeffers and *Hush Little Baby* by Sylvia Long. Older students can work individually or in groups to choose a lullaby to illustrate and share with younger children.

Quattlebaum, Mary. 2011. *Jo MacDonald Saw a Pond.* Nevada City, CA: Dawn. **(K, P, 1st, 2nd)**

In this book that can be sung to the tune of "Old MacDonald," the inhabitants of a pond have each found a special sound—for example, the dragonflies go, "whir-whir."

Sayre, April. 2011. *If You're Hoppy.* New York: Greenwillow. **(P, K, 2nd, 3rd)**

A version of "If You're Happy and You Know It," this book invites children to connect movement with music and words. Make a set of cue cards that remind children about what physical action is expected for each verse in the book. Then, have the children work in small groups to create their own version of the song with accompanying cue cards so that the entire class can participate.

What Is It?

Coaching Parents to Become Reading Partners at Home

Research has found that a number of factors can affect whether or not a family reads at home with their children: educational beliefs; views of the purposes for reading; approaches to sharing, such as reading to teach versus interactive reading; and the parents' own literacy practices. Changing these factors requires a variety of approaches that will meet individual needs, activities that are engaging, effective role models, and opportunities for guided practice. Build families' confidence by teaching them how to read aloud expressively; ask open-ended, child-friendly questions; and invite the child to participate through approaches such as taking turns and echo reading.

Why Is It Important?

One of the most accurate predictors of children's achievement in literacy is the simple act of regularly sharing picture books. Yet, studies show that 39 percent of fathers report never reading to their children, and in families with incomes below the poverty line, only 39 percent of the families mention reading aloud as a favorite activity or report sharing books at bedtime. Deterrents to reading at home include time constraints, limited access to materials suitable for young children, and lack of understanding of exactly how to read to a young child. Encourage parents to:

- make reading a high priority and to be role models through reading for themselves,
- make reading aloud relaxed and enjoyable,
- involve all members of the family in reading with young children,
- show that people read for different purposes,
- give children access to a wide variety of books, and
- join a library.

How Does It Work?

Do not assume that families already know how to help at home. They may think that only professional teachers are qualified to read with children and may lack confidence in their abilities, particularly if their first language is not English. Offer family literacy events that coach parents and families in ways to support literacy learning. Researcher Catherine Cook-Cottone found that the materials and activities that are most appreciated by parents are erasable writing boards, parent handbooks, a presentation by a professional storyteller, modeled read alouds, literacy games that can be played by the whole family, a zoo visit that leads to a language experience story, and group trips to the library.

Coach the families in the following basic ways of talking about books:

- Point to pictured objects, and ask the child to name them: "What do you call this?"
- Link to a child's interests: "This book is about a boy who likes animals, just like you do."
- Demonstrate how to summarize: "So, she eats the porridge because she is hungry. Then, she falls asleep."

- Ask the child to make inferences: "How do you think he feels? How do you know?"
- Refer to the child's prior knowledge: "He is riding a bike, just like you do."
- Encourage a prediction: "What do you think will happen next?"
- Ask the child to suggest solutions: "How do you think she will find her way through the forest?"
- Invite the child to explain: "How does she get across the stream?"
- Discuss characters' actions and motives: "Why do you think he says that?"
- Invite the child to imagine beyond the story: "What do you think she did the next day?"

Connections with the Common Core State Standards		
Age	**Category**	**Standard**
Kindergarten	Range of Reading and Level of Text Complexity	RL.K.10. Actively engage in group reading activities with purpose and understanding.
First Grade	Integration of Knowledge and Ideas	RL.1.7. Use illustrations and details in a story to describe its characters, setting, or events.
Second Grade	Integration of Knowledge and Ideas	RL.2.7. Use information gained from the illustrations and words in a print or digital text to demonstrate understanding of its characters, setting, or plot.
Third Grade	Integration of Knowledge and Ideas	RL.3.7. Explain how specific aspects of a text's illustrations contribute to what is conveyed by the words in a story.

Leveled Adaptations

Level I: Relying on Actions and Oral Language

When families say that their child is not interested in books, it may be that the books they have selected are not developmentally appropriate. Participation books that have flaps to lift and textures to feel, such as the classic *Pat the Bunny* by Dorothy Kunhardt and *Riding in My Car* by Woody Guthrie, are interactive and more likely to capture children's attention. For a list of recommended books for toddlers, see Good Reads at http://www.goodreads.com/shelf/show/child-participation.

Level II: Relying on Visual Images

Set parents and families up to experience success. For example, you might send home a book with a note that reads, "Diego really likes this book. Ask him to show it to you. He probably will ask you to read it again!" If parents and families see their children enjoying books, they will be more inclined to make the time to read aloud.

Level III: Beginning to Use Symbols

As children begin reading, parents will continue to need support in locating suitable books for beginning readers. A common misconception is that books have to be workbook-like for children to learn from them. Try to break this barrier with families by modeling how to enjoy books with their children.

When their child makes mistakes in reading, parents may worry that this is an indicator of long-term reading difficulties. They may rush to correct the child, saying, "You should know that word—it's easy," rather than encouraging the child to figure it out: "That's a good guess, but the word begins with *w*, not *s*. Do you have another idea?" Remind families that mistakes are a natural part of learning to read.

Extensions:

As children become independent readers, some parents and families stop reading together and assume that the child no longer needs support. Children continue to need models of fluent reading and encouragement for their efforts. Some books that are really interesting to a child may be beyond his independent reading level, so this can be an opportunity to truly read together. For example, take turns reading the pages, or have the child read until she gets stuck and then chime in. Beginning chapter books can be useful at this stage. Encourage families to read one or two chapters each night to build suspense.

Picture Book Recommendations

Henkes, Kevin. 2013. *Penny and Her Marble*. New York: Greenwillow. **(2nd, 3rd)**

In this chapter book, Penny finds a beautiful marble in her neighbor's yard that she wants to keep. Older children can create a storyline for the plot of this engaging story.

Hoberman, Mary Ann. 2002. *You Read to Me, I'll Read to You: Very Short Stories to Read Together*. **(1st, 2nd, 3rd)**

Part of a series of books designed for reading by two people—read some parts individually and others in unison.

Kimura, Ken. 2011. *999 Tadpoles*. New York: North-South. **(K, 1st, 2nd)**

A mother frog and father frog lead nearly a thousand children as they search for a new home. The humor, danger, and illustrations will encourage conversation. There are two sequels, *999 Tadpoles Find a Home* and *999 Frogs Wake Up*.

Lobel, Anita. 2008. *Hello, Day!* New York: Greenwillow. **(T, P, K)**

A group of farm animals greet the day out in the country with their characteristic sounds in this picture book with minimal text.

Logue, Mary. 2012. *Sleep like a Tiger*. Boston, MA: HMM. **(P, K)**

Parents tackle the perennial problem of a child who resists going to sleep with baby steps—just putting on pajamas, just getting on the bed, and so forth. She wants to know about animals' bedtime routines and eventually decides to curl up like a tiger.

McBratney, Sam. 2012. *You're All My Favorites*. Somerville, MA: Candlewick. **(T, P, K)**

How can all three children be the favorites of Mom and Dad Bear? As their parents explain, the oldest is the "most perfect first bear," the middle is the "most perfect second bear," and so forth.

Sadler, Judy Ann. 2011. *Reaching*. Tonawanda: Kids Can Press. **(T, P)**

In rhyming text, this lovely book with soft watercolors shows an infant growing into a toddler and all of the loving family members eager to support that process.

Willems, Mo. 2006. *Don't Let the Pigeon Stay Up Late!* New York: Hyperion. **(K, 1st, 2nd)**

What parent has not dealt with a child who is reluctant to go to bed? The pigeon is full of funny diversionary tactics.

| **T** = **Toddlers** (ages 1–2) |
| **P** = **Preschool** (ages 3–5) |
| **K** = **Kindergarten** (ages 5–6) |
| **1st** = **First grade** (ages 6–7) |
| **2nd** = **Second grade** (ages 7–8) |
| **3rd** = **Third grade** (ages 8–9) |

Daily Journal Drawing and Writing to Foster Self-Expression

What Is It?

Learning to write is a developmental process. Young children's journals are daily entries of early drawing and writing efforts. Their entries can be scribbles, shapes, attempts to write their names, text copied from another piece of print, or lists of words that they know or want to try to spell. Invented spelling refers to the child's attempts to represent oral language in written form, such as *hpy* for *happy* or *strz* for *stars*, and is an essential part of learning to spell words correctly. Attempting to spell and getting feedback on correct spelling is more intellectually challenging for students than tracing or copying correctly spelled words. Journals are most effective when they are used daily, include feedback from teachers and peers, are integrated into other classroom activities, provide opportunities for sharing in a supportive environment, and encourage home-school communication.

Why Is It Important?

When adults value children's drawings, make them part of daily routines, and respond to them as meaningful, this has a powerful effect on children's ideas about using drawing to communicate. Children first create various shapes and symbols to represent meaning, which eventually become letters and words. As they gain more experience with symbols, children begin to give their scribbles a name, such as, "It says *Mom.*" It is important that teachers and families support emergent drawing and writing as equally important ways of communicating.

How Does It Work?

Make writing and drawing time part of the daily schedule, provide the children with notebooks and various writing tools, and let them experiment. Some children can write better with a marker than with a crayon, for example, because a felt-tip marker drags on the paper more and can give greater control. Conversely, a child who has a physical condition that results in less hand strength might actually do better at writing with a ballpoint pen that glides on the paper. You can make a simple weekly journal as follows:

1. Staple together five pieces of paper (one page each for Monday through Friday) to make one journal. Make a journal for each child, and put it into his mailbox every Monday.

2. Allocate journal-writing time each day. For very young children, ten minutes may be sufficient. Children in second or third grade probably can use twenty to thirty minutes. Encourage the children to talk quietly throughout this time period. Meet with several children each day, and function as a listener or take dictation if a child wishes.

3. Consider a way of sharing just a couple of journal entries each day, making sure that everyone gets a turn during the week. Notify two children a day in advance that they will be sharing their work with the class. Designate a seat as a special "writer's chair," or let the child wear a special hat to signify that she is the one sharing. Encourage the other children

to practice giving positive feedback and posing open-ended questions, such as "How did you do that?" or "Why did you go there?"

4. Make the journals interactive by writing in the child's journal. A smiley face, an exclamation point, or *Wow* may be sufficient. Or, you might invest in some stamps and a stamp pad or stickers as a way to communicate your responses to the child's writing.

Connections with the Common Core State Standards		
Age	**Category**	**Standard**
Kindergarten	Text Types and Purposes	W.K.1. Use a combination of drawing, dictating, and writing to narrate a single event or several loosely linked events, tell about the events in the order in which they occurred, and provide a reaction to what happened.
First Grade	Text Types and Purposes	W.1.3. Write narratives in which they recount two or more appropriately sequenced events, include some details regarding what happened, use temporal words to signal event order, and provide some sense of closure.
Second Grade	Text Types and Purposes	W.2.3. Write narratives in which they recount a well-elaborated event or short sequence of events; include details to describe actions, thoughts, and feelings; use temporal words to signal event order; and provide a sense of closure.
Third Grade	Text Types and Purposes	W.3.3. Write narratives to develop real or imagined experiences or events using effective technique, descriptive details, and clear event sequences.

Leveled Adaptations

Level I: Relying on Actions and Oral Language

Teachers sometimes think that materials such as fingerpaint and clay are strictly for art class, but these materials offer excellent ways to support children's early writing and drawing efforts. Fingerpainting enables very young children to explore making marks on paper because it does not require managing a writing implement. It frees the child to practice the types of finger, hand, and arm movements made later during writing. For a different texture and feel, try a plastic dishpan partially filled with colored sand or cornmeal. Children can use the sand to make simple graphic symbols and can change them at will. Touch-screen devices, such as tablet computers, are an important breakthrough for young children.

Level II: Relying on Visual Images

Model how to combine drawing and writing for children. Think out loud, and say, for example, "Today when I went outside, I saw lots of snow. I'm going to draw something that I saw in my front yard—a snowman that my children made. I'm going to put my children's names next to the snowman. Now, I'm going to write *S* for snow. My children want to play in the snow tonight. I'm going to draw lots of snowballs and a sled. I'll put those words that start with *S*—*snowballs* and *sled*—right on my picture."

Level III: Beginning to Use Symbols

Use an old briefcase or suitcase as a container for a collection of writing papers and implements that a child can check out and take home at night or over the weekend. You may wish to include materials that stimulate writing, such as pictures of story characters, commercially available as story cards or blocks, and copies of pictures of storybook characters read about in school.

Extensions

Technology is a natural medium for enabling children to publish their work and share it with a larger, perhaps even international, audience. The online publishing option offers special opportunities for English language learners because they may be capable of publishing and reading in their first language and then translating a text into English. See "15 Ways to Publish Student Writing" by Jill Olthouse, available at http://tinyurl.com/k5jyd3j, for ideas about how to publish children's work.

T = Toddlers
(ages 1–2)

P = Preschool
(ages 3–5)

K = Kindergarten
(ages 5–6)

1st = First grade
(ages 6–7)

2nd = Second grade
(ages 7–8)

3rd = Third grade
(ages 8–9)

Picture Book Recommendations

Alexander, Claire. 2012. *Back to Front and Upside Down!* Grand Rapids, MI: Eerdmans. **(1st, 2nd)**
Children are learning to write but the letters do not turn out right, until the teacher steps in to help in this introduction to formal instruction in writing.

Cronin, Doreen. 2013. *Diary of a Worm.* New York: HarperCollins. **(K, 1st, 2nd, 3rd)**
This worm attends school, but instead of doing his homework, he eats it! Combine with *Diary of a Fly* and *Diary of a Spider* to inspire older students to write diaries for unusual creatures.

Moss, Marissa. 2006. *Amelia's Notebook.* New York: Simon and Schuster. **(1st, 2nd, 3rd)**
Amelia uses a journal to chronicle her experiences with moving. Her journal includes text, drawings, and postcards that older children might want to emulate in their own journals.

Portis, Antoinette. 2010. *Kindergarten Diary.* New York: Harper. **(K, 1st)**
A child who enjoyed preschool but was reluctant to go to kindergarten has now settled in and describes what happens over the course of a month. A good introduction to keeping a journal in kindergarten.

Reynolds, Peter. 2003. *The Dot.* Somerville, MA: Candlewick. **(P, K, 1st, 2nd)**
What to do when you cannot think of what to draw? This book advises children to "just make a mark" and get the process started. Pair it with *Ish* by the same author and *Begin at the Beginning* by Amy Schwartz to encourage discussions about making art.

Watt, Melanie. 2009. *Chester.* Toronto, ON: Kids Can Press. **(K, P)**
An author and illustrator produces a story about a mouse, only to have Chester, her cat, take over the work, red marker in hand. A humorous way to discuss creative differences among writing and drawing teams. Other books in the series are *Chester's Masterpiece* and *Chester's Back!*

What Is It?

Encouraging Extended Conversations to Develop Oral Language

The secret to conversing with a young child is to step back and listen. Conversing with a young child is an important skill that will require you to

- show genuine interest in what the child has to say;
- identify with the child's needs, interests, and perspectives;
- follow the child's lead and make all of your statements related to what the child just said;
- support the child as he moves back and forth between thinking and speaking; and
- ask questions about things that the child knows more about than the adult, rather than expecting the child to guess what is in the adult's mind.

Why Is It Important?

Beginning at about age three, most young children learn several new words per day. When classroom conversations are limited to teacher directives and questions that require one-word responses from children, this is a missed opportunity to build facility with oral language. So, it is particularly important to plan times for children to talk to one another and their teachers. Likewise, families may overlook naturally occurring opportunities for children to practice oral language at home. Provide parents and families with suggestions on how to make mealtimes the basis for talk about a variety of topics, including favorite meals and reasons for liking particular food items; vocabulary for utensils, foods, and colors; and how foods were selected, purchased, and prepared.

How Does It Work?

Some basic strategies for encouraging conversation:

- **Repeating**—echoing what the child says
- **Narrating**—labeling things in the environment and giving a play-by-play description as the child is doing something
- **Expanding**—elaborating on what the child has to say
- **Extending**—adding new information to the conversation
- **Answering questions**—listening between the lines to respond to the child

	Connections with the Common Core State Standards	
Age	**Category**	**Standard**
Kindergarten	Comprehension and Collaboration	SL.K.1. Participate in collaborative conversations with diverse partners about kindergarten topics and texts with peers and adults in small and larger groups.
First Grade	Comprehension and Collaboration	SL.1.1. Participate in collaborative conversations with diverse partners about first-grade topics and texts with peers and adults in small and larger groups.
Second Grade	Comprehension and Collaboration	SL.2.1. Participate in collaborative conversations with diverse partners about second-grade topics and texts with peers and adults in small and larger groups.
Third Grade	Comprehension and Collaboration	SL.3.1. Engage effectively in a range of collaborative discussions (one-on-one, in groups, and teacher-led) with diverse partners on third-grade topics and texts, building on others' ideas and expressing their own clearly.

Leveled Adaptations

Level I: Relying on Actions and Oral Language

Put some interesting toys, such as a plastic dinosaur, a plastic construction vehicle, or a toy that represents a character from a familiar picture book, inside a pillowcase or a large tote bag. Conduct the activity individually or with no more than four children at one time. Pass the bag around so that each child can pull out one item. Ask the child to show the other children how to play with the toy. As she does, model how to narrate out loud what the child is doing. After they become familiar with providing a play-by-play description, let the children try narrating as other children play with toys.

Level II: Relying on Visual Images

On the program *Sesame Street*, a silly character called Mr. Noodle often does the wrong thing with an object, such as an umbrella. As the character makes these mistakes, the children talk about it and suggest how to remedy the errors. The book *Oh, Daddy!* by Bob Shea has a similar theme in which a baby hippo has to lend a hand when Daddy makes mistakes. Try something such as this with your students. Show them, for example, a group of pictures all out of sequence. As you rearrange them, make some deliberate mistakes to see if the children notice the error. Ask them what needs to be corrected—and why.

Level III: Beginning to Use Symbols

Assign children to small groups, and have them bring along a book that they have read and want to recommend to classmates. When it is a child's turn to lead the conversation, he begins by showing the cover of the book, reading the title, and saying something about the book that would encourage others to read it. The remaining members of the group may ask one question each about the book, and the child who has read it can supply the answer.

Extensions

Try a conversation station, a learning center for no more than two or three children and one adult who encourages the children to talk. Post a sign: "Let's talk about . . ." and offer materials suitable for the discussion, such as a tabletop pocket chart, theme props, and a familiar book. Using concrete materials is particularly important for English language learners.

Connections with the Common Core State Standards		
Age	**Category**	**Standard**
Kindergarten	Text Type and Purposes	W.K.3. Use a combination of drawing, dictating, and writing to narrate a single event or several loosely linked events, tell about the events in the order in which they occurred, and provide a reaction to what happened.
First Grade	Key Ideas and Details	RL.1.2. Retell stories, including key details, and demonstrate understanding of their central message or lesson.
Second Grade	Presentation of Knowledge and Ideas	SL.2.4. Tell a story or recount an experience with appropriate facts and relevant, descriptive details, speaking audibly in coherent sentences.
Third Grade	Presentation of Knowledge and Ideas	SL.3.5. Create engaging audio recordings of stories or poems that demonstrate fluid reading at an understandable pace; add visual displays when appropriate to emphasize or enhance certain facts or details.

Picture Book Recommendations

T = Toddlers
(ages 1–2)

P = Preschool
(ages 3–5)

K = Kindergarten
(ages 5–6)

1st = First grade
(ages 6–7)

2nd = Second grade
(ages 7–8)

3rd = Third grade
(ages 8–9)

Aylesworth, Jim. 2012. *Cock-a-Doodle-Doo, Creak, Pop-Pop, Moo.* New York: Holiday House. **(T)**

A day on a farm, told in rhyme that invites "repeat after me" story book sharing.

Beaumont, Karen. 2004. *Baby Danced the Polka.* New York: Dial. **(T)**

This baby can dance, whether it is the boogie-woogie with a goat, the cha-cha with a cow, or the shooby-dooby with a sheep. The lilting rhythm, rhyme, and repetition of the book—combined with demonstrating the different types of dancing—encourage toddlers to join in. It also teaches the concept of dynamics in music as the characters move rapidly during the dance sequences and slow down when the baby is put to bed.

Carle, Eric. 2005. *Ten Little Rubber Ducks.* New York: Harper Festival. **(T, P, K)**

Rubber ducks are assembled at a factory, and a box of ten ends up in the ocean for big adventures. Use a set of ten little plastic ducks, available at dollar stores and party-supply stores, to encourage the children to talk and use the props to retell the story.

Cook, Julia. 2013. *Tease Monster: A Book about Teasing vs. Bullying.* Boys Town, NE: Boys Town Press. **(P, K, 1st, 2nd)**

A group of monsters learns the difference between good-natured teasing and hurtful bullying. They learn that it is okay to laugh *with* someone but not okay to laugh *at* a fellow monster named One-of-a-Kind. Children can discuss how friends behave and the behaviors that are not acceptable from others.

Hodgman, Ann. 2012. *Uh-Oh! Oh No!* Wilton, CT: Tiger Tales. **(T)**

Mealtime creates spills and cleanup in this book that invites toddlers to join in on the refrain from the title.

Isadora, Rachel. 2008. *Uh-Oh!* New York: Harcourt. **(T)**

In this child's introduction to slapstick comedy, all sorts of entertaining mistakes sustain a toddler's interest.

Macken, JoAnn. 2011. *Baby Says "Moo!"* New York: Hyperion. **(T, P)**

This colorful rhyming book is appealing to babies and young children who are learning the sounds that animals (and babies) make.

Patricelli, Leslie. 2012. *Faster! Faster!* Somerville, MA: Candlewick. **(T)**

A ride on Daddy's back at the park turns into an imaginative adventure for a baby.

Rubin, Adam. 2012. *Dragons Love Tacos.* New York: Dial. **(K, 1st, 2nd)**

Dragons come to the party prepared to eat any type of taco; however, when they pour on the hot salsa, it makes their fiery breath even hotter. This humorous book about a familiar food invites conversation.

Shea, Bob. 2010. *Oh, Daddy!* New York: HarperCollins. **(T, P, K)**

A clever preschool hippo has to help out as his dad makes mistakes when doing everyday tasks, such as watering the garden or getting dressed.

What Is It?

Rhyming Words to Build Phonemic Awareness

Phonemic awareness—the ability to hear and discriminate among different sounds of language—does not rely on recognizing letters or reading print. Researchers have found that even a four-week-old baby can detect the difference between the letter sounds of *g* and *k*, for example. Most two-year-olds can detect the subtle differences among the words *hot, not,* and *lot,* or among *cat, cut,* and *cot.* Activities such as listening to and chiming in on nursery rhymes are ways of building phonological awareness. Children's phonological sensitivity and recognition of rhyme affects later literacy development; it is a good predictor of who will master phonics later on and become a successful reader.

Why Is It Important?

Preschool children's phonemic awareness is a good predictor of who will succeed in reading later on. Phonemic awareness is one of the pillars of early literacy instruction identified by the National Reading Panel. Unlike phonics, in which the child needs to know letters and their sounds, phonemic awareness can be demonstrated with eyes closed because it relies on what the child hears. The most common cause of early reading difficulty is weakness in children's ability to apprehend, manipulate, and use the sound structure of spoken language to crack the alphabetic code.

How Does It Work?

Clusters of words can be used to assess children's ability to detect rhyming words. A teacher might begin by asking children to find the words that match, saying, "*Tree, bee.* Do they sound alike?" "*Tree, sock.* Do they sound alike?" "*Tree, duck.* Do they sound alike?" Following some practice, use clip art to make illustrated matches, such as *box/fox, star/car, moon/spoon, bat/cat, sock/clock, run/sun,* and *pig/wig.*

Connections with the Common Core State Standards		
Age	**Category**	**Standard**
Kindergarten	Knowledge of Language	LK.5. With guidance and support from adults, explore word relationships and nuances in word meanings.
First Grade	Phonics and Word Recognition	RF.1.3. Know and apply grade-level phonics and word-analysis skills in decoding words.
Second Grade	Phonics and Word Recognition	RF.2.3. Know and apply grade-level phonics and word-analysis skills in decoding words.
Third Grade	Phonics and Word Recognition	RF.3.3. Know and apply grade-level phonics and word-analysis skills in decoding words. Identify and know the meaning of the most common prefixes and derivational suffixes.

Leveled Adaptations

Level I: Relying on Actions and Oral Language

1. Watch the video of author Mem Fox reading *Hello Baby!* on YouTube.com. (Type "Mem Fox reads from Hello Baby" in the search bar.)
2. Make a list of the rhyming word pair from each page, then make several pairs of words that do not rhyme.
3. Have the children use listening only and clap when the words sound alike or rhyme. When the word pair does not sound alike, the children do not clap.
4. Nursery rhymes are another way to build phonological awareness, teach children cultural traditions, support speaking and listening skills, and encourage creative expression. Include the nursery rhymes of lots of cultures, and, if possible, share them in the original language to preserve alliteration, rhythm, rhyme, and repetition. Volunteers and tutors who speak a child's first language can share nursery rhymes in this authentic way and point out the words that rhyme.

Level II: Relying on Visual Images

1. Long before children can read and say rhyming words, they can hear words that match. Introduce the concept of a dust bunny—a nice way of saying that there is so much dust, fuzz, and hair on the floor that it starts to collect and move around. Read *Rhyming Dust Bunnies* by Jan Thomas. In this story, three dust bunnies, Ed, Ned, and Ted, rhyme, but not Bob. He is a rugged individualist and does not like sounds that "match." When a broom and sweeper threaten to break up the happy group, Bob comes to the rescue.
2. The book contains rhyming word groups, and for each group, there is also a word that does not rhyme. Have the children listen to the words in random order and stand up when they hear the word that does not match the others.
   car, far, jar, tar, look
   bug, rug, hug, mug, out
   dog, hog, log, fog, monster
   cat, sat, pat, rat, help

3. To make the game more active, make a box labeled *same/rhyming* and a box labeled *different/not rhyming*. The *same/rhyming* box should show four identical white dust bunnies, while the *different/not rhyming* box should show a blue bunny. Use five nylon net body scrubber poufs, available at the dollar store—four of the same color and one that is different. When a child takes a turn, she will listen to a series of five words—some that rhyme and one that does not. If a word sounds like the others, she can toss a white scrubber into the *same/rhyming* box. If a word sounds different, she can toss the different-colored scrubber into the *different/not rhyming* box. Then, go back through and review the five words.

    bear, chair, hair, pear, cow

    duck, truck, cluck, yuck, mouse

    dog, frog, log, hog, cat

    bed, head, said, fed, cow

    run, sun, fun, bun, play

    bee, knee, tree, see, cloud

    big, pig, wig, dig, leaf

    sad, mad, bad, dad, desk

    hen, pen, den, men, chair

4. Practice all of the rhymes that children can hear together. Children will see that the one word that does not "match" is also a different color. When this concept is in place, you can line up the "dust bunnies" and practice with other five-word/picture sets. For each set that you invent, one word should be dramatically different in sound.

Level III: Beginning to Use Symbols

1. The book *Dig!* by Andrea Zimmerman and David Clemesha has a text and picture clues that make it a good choice for beginning readers. Read it with the children.

2. Using clip art, make images of all the rhyming pairs that describe the things on Mr. Rally's to-do list. Let the children match the pictures of the rhyming pairs.

Extensions

Phonemic awareness is difficult because the child needs to recognize *phonemes*, the smallest units of sound in language. For example, the word *cat* has three phonemes: c/a/t. Generally speaking, children recognize beginning sounds, then ending sounds, and, finally, sounds in the middle. They hear consonants before they hear vowels; for example, a child attempting to spell the word *picture* might write it first as *pr*, later as *pktr*, later still as *picter*, and finally, write it as *picture*. Knowing this general progression will help you to plan activities suited to the children's skills in detecting the sounds of language.

Begin with two units of sound that can be converted into different words by changing the first letter only; for example, *-an* can become *fan, tan, man*, and *pan*. Teach the *-an* sound, then have children build new words and put them on the word wall. Try *-at, -un, -up*, and so on. After children have mastered these, try some four-letter words, such as *-ick, -ack*, and *-ook*. To make the task more difficult, try letter combinations such as *st-, fl-*, and *tr-*. Harder yet is changing the ending of the word; hardest of all is changing the vowel or vowel combination.

Picture Book Recommendations

T = Toddlers (ages 1–2)

P = Preschool (ages 3–5)

K = Kindergarten (ages 5–6)

1st = First grade (ages 6–7)

2nd = Second grade (ages 7–8)

3rd = Third grade (ages 8–9)

Ada, Alma, Isabel Campoy, and Alice Schertle, eds. 2003. *¡Pío Peep! Traditional Spanish Nursery Rhymes/Rimas Tradicionales en Español.* New York: HarperCollins. **(T, P, K)**
A collection of traditional nursery rhymes in Spanish.

Ashburn, Boni, and Sergio De Giorgi. 2013. *Builder Goose: It's Construction Rhyme Time!* New York: Sterling. **(T, P)**
These nursery rhymes are all based on popular Mother Goose rhymes but feature a construction theme. Fun illustrations and silly rhymes allow children to see exciting building happening with the different construction equipment.

Beaton, Clare. 2012. *Clare Beaton's Farmyard Rhymes.* Cambridge, MA: Barefoot. **(T, P, K)**
Familiar nursery rhymes—illustrated in folk-art style with fabric, buttons, stitches, and sequins—focus on the animal kingdom. See also *Clare Beaton's Nursery Rhymes* and *Clare Beaton's Action Rhymes.*

Bunting, Eve. 2013. *Have You Seen My New Blue Socks?* Boston, MA: Clarion. **(P, K, 1st, 2nd, 3rd)**
A duck searches the countryside for his new blue socks, using words that rhyme: *socks, box, fox,* and *ox.*

Fox, Mem. 2013. *Good Night, Sleep Tight.* New York: Orchard. **(T, P, K)**
Skinny Doug, a very entertaining babysitter, recites all of the nursery rhymes he knows to get two rambunctious children ready for bed. Included are "This Little Piggy," "Pat-a-Cake," and others, both familiar and new.

Minor, Wendell. 2013. *My Farm Friends.* New York: Nancy Paulsen. **(P, K, 1st)**
Engaging rhymes provide interesting animal facts in this farm story—for example: "Pigs can't sweat/ Or jump in a pool/ So they roll in the mud/ That's how they stay cool."

Park, Linda. 2013. *Xander's Panda Party.* Boston, MA: Clarion. **(P, K, 1st, 2nd, 3rd)**
This humorous story, told in rhyme, answers the question "How do you plan a party and generate the perfect guest list?"

Thomas, Jan. 2009. *Rhyming Dust Bunnies.* New York: Beach Lane. **(P, K)**
A zany group of four dust bunnies—Ed, Ned, and Ted, who always rhyme, and Bob, who does not like rhyming—meet the challenge of a broom and a vacuum sweeper.

Tiger Tales. 2012. *Hey, Diddle, Diddle and Other Favorite Nursery Rhymes.* Wilton, CT: Tiger Tales. **(T, P, K)**
A board book version of the simple, traditional folk rhymes.

Zimmerman, Andrea, and David Clemesha. 2013. *Dig!* Boston, MA: HMH. **(P, K)**
Pairs of rhyming words and counting off his to-do list help Mr. Rally and his dog to manage an eventful day of moving soil with heavy equipment.

What Is It?

A wordless book is a picture book that relies on the illustrations to tell the story. Wordless books have no text at all or, in some instances, a single word or phrase.

Why Is It Important?

Contemporary children live in a very visual culture. They can share images instantly; locate images online; and encounter all kinds of visually appealing materials in their homes, schools, communities, and beyond. Working with a sequential set of images is the precursor to understanding plot in the written text of a book after they begin to read. Although it may seem counterintuitive, books that tell a story without words or with very few words are a great support for learning to read. Studies show that when children invent stories to accompany wordless books, they produce longer stories with more varied vocabulary.

How Does It Work?

The procedure for using wordless books to teach sequence is as follows:

1. Select a variety of wordless books that are suitable for very young children. The concepts presented should be concrete rather than abstract.
2. Choose one book to share with the children. Take them through a "picture walk" of the entire book before you share some text to go along with the pictures.
3. Model dictating captions or the text of a story to accompany each page.
4. Have the children work with a partner or a small group to generate text to go with a wordless book of their choice.
5. Record their words, either by having a volunteer take dictation or using some type of recording equipment.
6. Produce a page-by-page transcript so that each child's version can be cut apart, positioned on the page, and shared with the class.

Connections with the Common Core State Standards		
Age	**Category**	**Standard**
Kindergarten	Integration of Knowledge and Ideas	RL.K.7. With prompting and support, describe the relationship between illustrations and the story in which they appear, such as what moment in a story an illustration depicts.
First Grade	Integration of Knowledge and Ideas	RL.1.7. Use illustrations and details in a story to describe its characters, setting, or events.
Second Grade	Integration of Knowledge and Ideas	RL.2.7. Use information gained from the illustrations and words in a print or digital text to demonstrate understanding of its characters, setting, or plot.
Third Grade	Comprehension and Collaboration	SL.3.2. Determine the main ideas and supporting details of a text read aloud or information presented in diverse media and formats, including visually, quantitatively, and orally.

Leveled Adaptations

Level I: Relying on Actions and Oral Language

1. Use this activity to introduce the idea of a book that tells the story entirely through pictures, then share a very simple wordless book. The book *All of Baby Nose to Toes* by Victoria Adler, for example, shows the different body parts, including the eyes, ears, nose, tummy, legs, and toes.
2. On the second reading, demonstrate how you can communicate without the word for each body part by pointing.
3. Have the children do likewise on their own bodies or on a toy.

Level II: Relying on Visual Images

1. Read a version of the fable "The Lion and the Mouse" such as *Mouse and Lion* by Rand Burkert and Nancy Burkert or *The Lion and the Mouse* by Jerry Pinkney, which has beautiful illustrations in an African setting.
2. After viewing all of the pictures, go back through and model how to invent words or dialogue to go along with the images.
3. Give the children a sequence of images, and have them dictate a story to go along with it. Be sure to let them see all of the pictures first.

Level III: Beginning to Use Symbols

1. Read a wordless book such as *A Boy, a Dog, and a Frog* by Mercer Mayer.
2. Model for the children how to invent dialogue for characters that goes along with the pictures. If you like, you can have the children watch an example for this book on YouTube.com. (Type "a boy a dog and frog caftw11" in the search bar.) Watch the entire film, then go back, and have the children invent text to go along with the pictures.
3. Give the children a variety of wordless books to choose from, and let them work in small groups to dictate or compose a text for each page.

Extensions

1. Wordless books are not simple just because they do not have text; in fact, they frequently include abstract concepts. Encourage the children to make their own wordless books that imitate some of the interesting devices used in wordless books. For example, the book *Home* by Jeannie Baker shows a community's transformation as viewed through one window. *Mr. Wuffles* by David Weisner uses the frames of a comic book.

2. The children might also try their hand at a high-fantasy wordless book such as *Chalk* by Bill Thomson, *Journey* by Aaron Becker, or *Museum Trip* by Barbara Lehman.

Picture Book Recommendations

Aruego, Jose, and Ariane Dewey. 2006. *The Last Laugh*. New York: Dial. **(K, 1st, 2nd)**

   A wordless story with bright illustrations in which a clever duck outwits a bullying snake to illustrate the concept that what goes around, comes around.

Baker, Jeannie. 2004. *Home*. New York: Greenwillow. **(K, 1st, 2nd, 3rd)**

   Detailed collages demonstrate how a community can change their neighborhood for the better. All the action is seen through one window.

Becker, Aaron. 2013. *Journey*. Somerville, MA: Candlewick. **(P, K, 1st, 2nd, 3rd)**

   After drawing a door on her bedroom wall, a young girl enters a magical world where things she draws can come to life.

Burkert, Rand, and Nancy Burkert. 2011. *Mouse and Lion*. New York: Scholastic. **(P, K, 1st, 2nd, 3rd)**

   In this retelling of the fable by Aesop, a mouse asks for—and is granted—his freedom from a lion. Later, the mouse returns the favor by gnawing through the ropes of a hunter's net to free the lion.

Geisert, Arthur. 2012. *The Giant Seed: Stories without Words*. Brooklyn: Enchanted Lion. **(P, K, 1st, 2nd, 3rd)**

   A group of pigs has their home destroyed by a volcano, but fortunately they planted a huge seed before the disaster that turns out to offer a solution to their housing crisis.

Geisert, Arthur. 2011. *Ice*. Brooklyn: Enchanted Lion. **(P, K, 1st, 2nd)**

   A group of pigs bring an iceberg to their island to bring the temperature down in this surprising adventure story told completely in pictures.

Henkes, Kevin. 2011. *Little White Rabbit*. New York: Greenwillow. **(T, P, K)**

   A bunny wonders what it would be like to be the different things he sees in nature, whether it is the grass or a butterfly. Finally, he encounters a cat and runs back home.

Lehman, Barbara. 2006. *Museum Trip*. Boston, MA: HMH Books. **(K, 1st, 2nd)**

   In this wordless picture book, a boy imagines himself inside some of the exhibits when he goes on a field trip to a museum.

Lehman, Barbara. 2004. *The Red Book*. Boston, MA: HMH Books. **(K, 1st, 2nd)**

   A magical red book transports a girl on many adventures with each turn of the page.

Newgarden, Mark, and Megan Cash. 2007. *Bow-Wow Bugs a Bug*. Boston, MA: HMH. **(P, K, 1st, 2nd)**

   A wordless picture book about a persistent terrier who spends a day following a bug through his neighborhood. Make a story map of the dog's travels.

T = Toddlers (ages 1–2)

P = Preschool (ages 3–5)

K = Kindergarten (ages 5–6)

1st = First grade (ages 6–7)

2nd = Second grade (ages 7–8)

3rd = Third grade (ages 8–9)

Pinkney, Jerry. 2009. *The Lion and the Mouse*. New York: Little, Brown. **(P, K, 1st)**

> This book won the Caldecott medal, with good reason. It is a gorgeous version of Aesop's fable in which a mighty lion spares a mouse that later comes to his rescue. The message that all can make a difference, from the smallest to the mightiest, comes through beautifully.

Pinkney, Jerry. 2013. *The Tortoise and the Hare*. New York: Little, Brown. **(P, K, 1st)**

> The familiar fable by Aesop gets a southwestern U.S. treatment with an almost wordless text and earth-tone illustrations.

Sis, Peter. 2005. *Dinosaur!* New York: Greenwillow. **(T, P, K)**

> While taking a bath, a young boy is joined by all sorts of dinosaurs that lead him on a magical journey.

Thomson, Bill. 2010. *Chalk*. Tarrytown, NY: Marshall Cavendish. **(P, K, 1st, 2nd)**

> Imagine what might happen if children find a bag of sidewalk chalk that turns out to be magical. The pictures drawn come to life, which proves problematic when one of the drawings was a dinosaur! Relate this to the children's classic book *Harold and the Purple Crayon* by Crockett Johnson.

Weisner, David. 2013. *Mr. Wuffles!* Boston, MA: Clarion. **(P, K, 1st, 2nd, 3rd)**

> In this almost wordless tale presented in comic-book format, a cat finds a spaceship and lots of adventures.

What Is It?

Literacy-Enriched Play to Develop Vocabulary

Young children's language skills develop best in natural settings, such as in play-based experiences. Repeated readings of children's books, accompanied by props and literacy materials, are ways to enrich and extend young children's understandings of picture books. Activities such as these build a bridge between play and language and provide varied opportunities for children to demonstrate their learning.

Why Is It Important?

Children's active participation is a key to supporting literacy growth. There Is a strong link between a play-based environment and the development of literacy skills in young children. Children's play is particularly useful in acquiring new vocabulary because they use the words in meaningful contexts.

How Does It Work?

Literacy-enriched play is adding print materials to children's play; for example, rather than simply riding around on their bikes, you can set up traffic signs, and a police officer with a book of "tickets" can stop those who ignore the road signs. Rather than just watching a film of a children's book, you can set up a movie theater with a ticket booth, snack bar, drink and food containers, cash register, play money, movie posters, and a marquee with lights. Adding these materials not only encourages dramatic play but also builds emergent literacy skills.

Connections with the Common Core State Standards		
Age	**Category**	**Standard**
Kindergarten	Vocabulary Acquisition and Use	LK.4. Determine or clarify the meaning of unknown and multiple-meaning words and phrases based on kindergarten reading and content.
First Grade	Vocabulary Acquisition and Use	L.1.4. Determine or clarify the meaning of unknown and multiple-meaning words and phrases based on first-grade reading and content.
Second Grade	Vocabulary Acquisition and Use	L.2.4. Determine or clarify the meaning of unknown and multiple-meaning words and phrases based on second-grade reading and content, choosing flexibility from an array of strategies.
Third Grade	Vocabulary Acquisition and Use	L.3.4. Determine or clarify the meaning of unknown and multiple-meaning [words] and phrases based on third-grade reading and content, choosing flexibly from a range of strategies.

Leveled Adaptations

Level I: Relying on Actions and Oral Language

1. Have the children watch an episode of the television program *Martha Speaks* called "Shelter Blues" (available at the PBS website http://www.pbs.org).
2. Read books about shelter dogs, such as *Buddy Unchained* by Daisy Bix, *"Let's Get a Pup!" Said Kate* by Bob Graham, and *The Stray Dog* by Marc Simont.
3. Supply a large stuffed toy dog, a collar, a leash, a bed and basket, a plastic bowl, a dog toy, a dog brush, and a cardboard-box dog house so that the children can dramatize scenes from these books, retell the stories, or invent stories of their own.

Level II: Relying on Visual Images

1. Create prop boxes—collections of items related to a theme—to stimulate dramatic play. These collections can focus on a familiar story, such as "Little Red Riding Hood," and include such things as a piece of furry fabric to tie on for the wolf's tail, a hat to represent Grandma, a cap to represent the wood cutter, and a basket and red hoodie for Little Red.
2. Create other types of prop boxes for experiences that children might have, such as attending a community-sponsored event at a public park. Be sure to include literacy materials that go along with the theme—for example, a sign about the event, tickets, a menu, a cash register, play money, and a map of the park.

Level III: Beginning to Use Symbols

1. One way to inspire literacy-based play is through readers' theater. Choose a predictable book that children can memorize with some practice and learn to read in unison, such as *Mrs. Wishy-Washy* by Joy Cowley.
2. Have a small group of children use some simple props to dramatize actions from the story. Store the props in a themed prop box so that the children can use it again and again.

Extensions

Have the children use the computer to make literacy materials for use in play, such as signs for their pretend grocery store, a menu for their restaurant, a poster for their theater, placards for their zoo of stuffed toys, or a picture book. Word processing, clip art, and print-shop software can be used to explore shapes; make pictures; and paint, draw, or otherwise illustrate a wide array of literacy materials.

Picture Book Recommendations

Bell, Babs. 2004. *The Bridge Is Up!* New York: HarperCollins. **(T, P)**

> In this cumulative tale about a drawbridge, a series of vehicles has to wait when the bridge goes up, and then each gets to cross. Great for inspiring new play themes with wheeled toys in the block area.

Bix, Daisy. 2002. *Buddy Unchained.* Edina, MN: The Gryphon Press. **(K, 1st, 2nd)**

> After hearing this story of an abandoned dog who gets adopted, children can engage in dramatic play about animal rescue.

Choung, Eun-Hee. 2008. *Minji's Salon.* La Jolla, CA: Kane/Miller. **(P, K, 1st)**

> A South Korean girl pretends, with her dog as a customer, to have a salon just like the one her mother visits. Use this book to inspire dramatic play themes about different businesses in children's neighborhoods. Add signs, a cash register, an appointment book, and a cell phone.

Clanton, Ben. 2013. *The Table Sets Itself.* London, UK: Walker Children's. **(P, K, 1st, 2nd)**

> This book would be a great way to introduce words such as *dish, table, fork, knife*, and so on. Children can use plastic items to set their own tables and can let their imaginations take them home or to their favorite place to eat.

Graham, Bob. 2003. *"Let's Get a Pup!" Said Kate.* Somerville, MA: Candlewick. **(P, K, 1st, 2nd)**

> Kate and her parents go to the animal shelter but have trouble picking a dog because they fall in love with a puppy as well as a senior dog. Set up a dog-shelter theme in the play area after sharing this book.

James, Simon. 2013. *Nurse Clementine.* Somerville, MA: Candlewick Press. **(T, P, K)**

> A young child gets a nurse costume and a first-aid kit. Although Mom and Dad will play along, her little brother will not cooperate. Children will enjoy enacting the behaviors as this book is read aloud and, later, in a medical-office play theme.

McQuinn, Anna. 2010. *Lola Loves Stories.* Watertown, MA: Charlesbridge. **(T, P, K)**

> A young girl's play themes and creative thinking are influenced by the stories that she loves to hear. Use this book to introduce prop boxes related to favorite stories.

Oxenbury, Helen. 2014. *Eating Out.* Somerville, MA: Candlewick. **(P, K, 1st, 2nd)**

> After reading about going to a restaurant, children can pretend to take on different roles such as waiter, waitress, and cashier, and can practice taking orders and preparing food.

Rylant, Cynthia. 2012. *Brownie and Pearl Get Dolled Up.* New York: Simon Spotlight. **(P, K, 1st, 2nd)**

> The dynamic duo of a girl and her kitten play dress up in this easy reader that inspires dramatic play.

Simont, Marc. 2003. *The Stray Dog.* New York: HarperCollins. **(P, K, 1st, 2nd, 3rd)**

> After a dog appears at the family picnic, they cannot stop thinking about his fate. They return to the site and, just as the dog is about to be picked up by animal control, a quick-witted girl uses her hair ribbon to claim the dog. This book was inspired by a true story.

Wells, Rosemary. 2004. *Ruby's Beauty Shop.* New York: Puffin. **(P, K, 1st, 2nd)**

> Ruby and her friend Louise want to play beauty shop with her brother Max, including wigs and makeup, but Max wants to play beauty shop his own way. Young readers can create their own beauty shop and learn the vocabulary and actions involved with running a salon.

Alphabet Recognition with Books and Technology

What Is It?

There are many different levels of knowing the alphabet. A child may be able to sing "The Alphabet Song," for example, without being able to correctly identify any letters of the alphabet. Most tests of alphabet knowledge require children to identify letters of the alphabet, both uppercase and lowercase. Many other readiness tests and early literacy assessments require them to discriminate among letters—for example, directing the child to "Circle the letter *b*" when the three choices are *d, b,* and *a.*

Why Is It Important?

According to the National Center for Education Statistics, at the start of kindergarten, 26 percent of children who were read to three or four times in the last week by a family member recognized all letters of the alphabet, while only 14 percent of children read to less frequently could do this. When they begin kindergarten, two out of three children know the alphabet. Knowledge of the alphabet is one of the most powerful predictors of success with early reading.

How Does It Work?

Teachers of young children need many different ways to teach and review the alphabet. Technology is a great support because it provides hundreds of activities at various levels of difficulty that are free and ready to use. It is important, however, to preview these activities first to make sure that they are not confusing. For example, some activities with letters convert the letters into characters with eyes, arms, and feet; this actually can make it harder for children to identify the letter. Differences among letters can be subtle—for example, *l* and *t*—so adults need to draw children's attention to these differences. As children get more familiar with letters, researcher Jonda McNair suggests pointing out how some letters have short sticks, long sticks, circles, tails, and so on, and then having the children sort letters, and later on words, into categories. They might sort letters that have long sticks or classmates' names that have tails. This encourages them to pay attention to specific features of letters of the alphabet and learn to recognize letters more quickly.

Connections with the Common Core State Standards		
Age	**Category**	**Standard**
Kindergarten	Conventions of Standard English	L.K.1. Print many upper- and lowercase letters. L.K.2. Spell simple words phonetically, drawing on knowledge of sound-letter relationships.
First Grade	Conventions of Standard English	L.1.1. Print all upper- and lowercase letters.
Second Grade	Conventions of Standard English	L.2.1. Demonstrate command of the conventions of standard English grammar and usage when writing or speaking.
Third Grade	Conventions of Standard English	L.3.1. Demonstrate command of the conventions of standard English grammar and usage when writing or speaking.

Leveled Adaptations

Level I: Relying on Actions and Oral Language

1. Have the children physically build letters with long sticks, short sticks, circles, tails, and dots in puzzle-type activities. Give each child flexible sticks, such as Wikki sticks or pipe cleaners, and have them try to replicate the letter that you hold up or write on a whiteboard.

2. To make a lowercase *j*, they will need a dot, a short stick, and a tail. Making the letters in this way encourages children to pay attention to the formation of the letters.

3. For free, printable templates, see Activity Mom at http://activity-mom.com/2009/11/17/printable-build-letter-puzzles or Build a Letter Templates, second edition, at http://www.scribd.com/doc/31419788/build-a-letter-templates-2nd-edition.

4. It also is possible to purchase a letter-building kit, such as the Letter Instruction Activity Set from Learning Resources. Alphabet lacing cards also can help children to physically form the shapes of letters.

Level II: Relying on Visual Images

1. Watch Ruben Studdard, winner of *American Idol*, and Elmo sing "The Alphabet Song" on YouTube.com. (Search for "Ruben Studdard Elmo ABC".) As they sing, each uppercase letter of the alphabet appears on screen.

2. To review the lowercase letters, watch India Arie and Elmo sing the song, also on YouTube.com.

3. In a third video, the group Tilly and the Wall sing a jazzy version and dance to the song.

4. Using the very popular children's book *Chicka Chicka Boom Boom* by Bill Martin, Jr., and John Archambault, make an interactive bulletin board with the coconut tree and cutouts for all of the letters of the alphabet. Store a set of alphabet letters nearby, and have the children match and attach each letter to its outline using magnets or Velcro.

Level III: Beginning to Use Symbols

1. Post the alphabet, upper- and lowercase, and pictures to represent each letter. To find examples, type "images for alphabet cards" into your browser, then select "printable."

2. You can make a set of alphabet flashcards so that children begin to recognize specific letters. Begin with ones that are very distinctive, such as *Ss* or *Oo* or letters that begin the children's names.

3. Gradually add the letter sounds to the discussion by making cards that have a picture to represent each letter sound. A site called ESL-Kids.com has many free printable variations of flashcards. Visit http://esl-kids.com/flashcards/alphabet.html.

Extensions

1. As children become familiar with upper- and lowercase letters, they can begin linking letters with the sounds that the letters typically make. View "Phonics Song 2 (new ZED version)" on YouTube.com. It features an alphabet song that shows capital and small letters, pronounces the letters correctly, and matches them with pictures that begin with that letter.

2. The PBS site http://pbskids.org has many different alphabet games at different levels of difficulty, including ones in which children build words.

3. Another site called The Classroom Creative at http://www.theclassroomcreative.com offers twenty-five ready-to-print alphabet activities.

Picture Book Recommendations

Baker, Keith. 2010. *LMNO Peas*. New York: Beach Lane. **(T, P, K)**
> This entertaining book presents the alphabet through a cast of pea characters dressed for a variety of occupations and activities.

Bingham, Kelly. 2012. *Z Is for Moose*. New York: Greenwillow. **(K, 1st, 2nd)**
> Animals parade by, from *A* to *Z*, but Moose has a meltdown when Mouse gets the *M*. Fortunately, a solution is found.

Cabatingan, Erin. 2012. *A Is for Musk Ox*. New York: Roaring Brook. **(1st, 2nd)**
> A musk ox takes children through a tour of the alphabet using himself as the theme. Suitable for older children who already know the alphabet, this book reviews *A* to *Z* with a humorous twist.

DK Publishing. 2012. *Touch and Feel ABC*. New York: Dorling Kindersley. **(P, K)**
> This board book offers a way for children to feel their way to alphabet recognition.

Heder, Thyra. 2013. *Fraidyzoo*. New York: Harry N. Abrams. **(P, K, 1st, 2nd, 3rd)**
> Little T and her family romp through the alphabet creating zoo animals from paper, using scissors and glue. This book bursts with energy and encourages creativity.

Jay, Alison. 2005. *ABC: A Child's First Alphabet Book*. New York: Dutton Juvenile. **(T, P)**
> Bright illustrations highlight many words that begin with each letter of the alphabet.

Martin, Bill, Jr., and John Archambault. 2012. *Chicka Chicka Boom Boom*. New York: Little Simon. **(T, P, K)**
> This alphabet chant presents the letters through fun, rhythmic text in this board-book reissue of the 1989 classic.

Pallotta, Jerry. 2006. *The Construction Alphabet Book*. Watertown, MA: Charlesbridge. **(P, K, 1st, 2nd, 3rd)**
> This book explores construction equipment starting with each of the letters of the alphabet.

Trasler, Janee. 2011. *Caveman: A. B. C. Story*. New York: Sterling. **(K, 1st, 2nd)**
> Children who are already familiar with the alphabet will get the humor of this prehistoric *A* to *Z* story.

Wood, Audrey. 2001. *Alphabet Adventure*. New York: Blue Sky. **(P, K, 1st, 2nd, 3rd)**
> A comical story of the letters of the alphabet on their way to the first day of school.

T = Toddlers (ages 1–2)
P = Preschool (ages 3–5)
K = Kindergarten (ages 5–6)
1st = First grade (ages 6–7)
2nd = Second grade (ages 7–8)
3rd = Third grade (ages 8–9)

Learning to Formulate Questions and Answers

What Is It?

Researchers have found that when an adult is doing the asking, young children are expected to give a one-word answer most of the time. So, children may not be getting much practice with questions that require further information. Many of the questions that adults pose to children are *yes/no* and do not require additional information—for example, "Do you want some juice?" However, when children enter school, they are asked more sophisticated questions, and they are expected to answer. Children who do not have much experience answering questions may be puzzled by these new expectations. Unfortunately, they also may be seen as less intelligent and not ready for school.

Why Is It Important?

Young children tend to be curious and ask lots of questions. They also are asked many different questions, such as "How old are you?" "What's your sister's name?" or "How is your grandma doing?" A question uses specific words—*who, what, when, where, why, how*—and changes the typical sequence of words in English. Questions can be particularly troublesome for second language learners. For example, "¿Cómo te llamas?" would be translated literally as "How do you call yourself?" but "What is your name?" is a better way to ask the question in English. Even within English, we usually change the word order when asking a question—for example, "Are you sleeping?" rather than "You are sleeping?" The ability to ask and answer questions is developmental, so young children may use an incorrect word order with rising intonation.

How Does It Work?

The general developmental sequence begins with questions that start with *what, where,* and *who.* Next, children learn to ask and answer questions that begin with *is* and *do.* Finally, children learn to ask and answer questions using *when, why,* and *how.*

Connections with the Common Core State Standards

Age	Category	Standard
Kindergarten	Key Ideas and Details	RL.K.1. With prompting and support, ask and answer questions about key details in a text.
First Grade	Comprehension and Collaboration	SL.1.3. Ask and answer questions about what a speaker says to gather additional information or clarify something that is not understood.
Second Grade	Key Ideas and Details Comprehension and Collaboration	RL.2.1. Ask and answer questions such as *who, what, where, when, why,* and *how* to demonstrate understanding of key details in a text. SL.2.3. Ask and answer questions about what a speaker says to clarify comprehension, gather additional information, or deepen understanding of a topic or issue.
Third Grade	Key Ideas and Details	RL.3.1. Ask and answer questions to demonstrate understanding of a text, referring explicitly to the text as the basis for the answers.

Leveled Adaptations

Level I: Relying on Actions and Oral Language

1. Use question-and-answer format books such as *I Went Walking* by Sue Williams, and make a path for the children to walk along. You can make a path with masking tape or with carpet squares on the floor.
2. Post clip art or position stuffed toys along the path to represent what the book describes: black cat, brown horse, red cow, green duck, pink pig, and yellow duck.
3. Listen to Lee Ecco's version of *I Went Walking*, sung to the tune of "Frère Jacques" and posted on YouTube.com. (Type "Lee Ecco I Went Walking" into the search bar.) To help the children remember the lyrics, show them the pages as you sing together.
4. Let the children sing the song as they walk the path again. You might try making a numbered card of each animal for the child to pick up as he walks along.
5. When they return to the circle, let the children arrange their cards in the same order as the book, and then sing the song again.

Level II: Relying on Visual Images

1. Many popular children's books use a question-and-answer format, such as Bill Martin, Jr., and Eric Carle's *Brown Bear, Brown Bear, What Do You See?* and *Polar Bear, Polar Bear What Do You Hear?* Read these with the children.
2. Consider using Eric Carle's book *From Head to Toe* and the accompanying song posted on YouTube.com. (Type "Eric Carle From Head to Toe song" in the search bar.) Have the children perform the actions from the book. When you ask, "Can you do it?" have them answer in unison, "I can do it!" as they demonstrate the actions.

You can find videos of authors or teachers reading favorite children's books on YouTube.com. Search the name of the book or the author's name to find a suitable video to share with the children in your class.

Level III: Beginning to Use Symbols

1. On YouTube.com, watch a video of *Where's Spot?* read aloud in English, and watch *¿Dónde está Spot?* in Spanish. In this book, which uses a question-and-answer format, a mother dog searches throughout the house for her puppy.

2. Use clip art to make a set of cards that correspond to the incidents in the story; for example, the text reads, "Is he in the closet?" and the answer is "No." Make cartoon speech bubbles for what various animals say in response to the questions.

3. Let the children hold up the appropriate card or speech bubble to ask and answer the questions as you read together.

Extensions

1. Read the question-and-answer book *I Want My Hat Back* by Jon Klassen.

2. Watch a video that shows children with stick puppets telling the story at http://www.teachingideas.co.uk/library/books/iwantmyhatback.htm.

3. In this story, a bear searches for his hat by asking, "Have you seen my hat?" Nine different animals answer the question: fox, mouse, rabbit, frog, turtle, snake, beaver, deer, and squirrel. Using clip art, create image cards for each animal. Make each image 8.5" x 11", type the animal's name on the paper, and insert the appropriate numeral (1–9) at the top of each page. Glue the images to cardboard or cover them with contact paper for durability.

4. Give out the images, and arrange the students in the sequence of the story. Read the story together. Before you get to each page, ask them to look to see what animal comes next.

5. Have the children invent their own lift-the-flap books with a question-and-answer format. Demonstrate how to construct flaps: show how one side of the square or rectangle has to be connected to create a hinge for the flap. Let them practice with recycled paper, tape, and scissors before actually constructing the final book. They can plan their books by choosing a character to be lost and another character to search for the lost one. Then, they can make a list of places to hide and an animal to hide in each location. They can decide where the animal will be found.

Picture Book Recommendations

Beaumont, Karen. 2009. *Who Ate All the Cookie Dough?* New York: Henry Holt. **(P, K)**

> Use this rhyming chant to model asking and answering questions that begin with *who*.

Eastman, P. D. 1998. *Are You My Mother?* 2nd ed. New York: Random House. **(T, P, K)**

> This classic book uses patterned dialogue as a baby animal searches for its mother. The familiar story is just right for homemade books that follow a similar question-and-answer format and could be written for younger children by children in the primary grades.

Gibbs, Edward. 2011. *I Spy with My Little Eye.* Somerville, MA: Candlewick. **(K, 1st, 2nd)**

> A question-and-answer game with die-cut pages that reveal just a portion of a photograph. Children need to use their visual literacy skills to identify the animal.

Hill, Eric. 2003. *¿Dónde está Spot?* New York: Putnam. **(T, P)**

> A Spanish version of the much-loved book, *Where's Spot?*

Hill, Eric. 2003. *Where's Spot?* New York: Putnam. **(T, P)**

This lift-the-flap edition allows young readers to ask questions about where Spot can be. For thirty years, children have been enjoying this lift-the-flap book.

Hulbert, Laura. 2011. *Who Has These Feet?* New York: Henry Holt. **(P, K, 1st)**

In guessing-game format, an animal's feet are shown on one page, and the child discovers the correct answer on the next two-page spread.

Klassen, Jon. 2011. *I Want My Hat Back.* Somerville, MA: Candlewick. **(P, K, 1st, 2nd, 3rd)**

When the bear's hat disappears, he questions all of the other animals to see if they know where it is. When a deer comes along and asks the bear a question, it helps him remember something that leads to a continued investigation.

Laden, Nina. 2000. *Peek-a-Who?* San Francisco, CA: Chronicle. **(T, P)**

Young readers will have fun guessing who is peeking at them through the cutouts in this rhyming book that is full of surprises.

Martin, Bill, Jr., and Eric Carle. 1996. *Brown Bear, Brown Bear, What Do You See?* New York: Henry Holt. **(P, K, 1st)**

This classic book follows a bear as he meets all sorts of different animals with sometimes surprising colors.

Miller, Virginia. 2002. *Where Is Little Black Kitten?* Somerville, MA: Candlewick. **(T, P, K)**

A personified bear and his teddy bear search around the house for their pet kitten in this lift-the-flap book.

Portis, Antoinette. 2011. *Not a Box.* New York: HarperCollins. **(P, K, 1st)**

Through a series of paired questions and answers, the rabbit is asked why he is sitting in, standing on, spraying, or wearing a box. Each time, he insists, "It's not a box!" The opposite page reveals the many things a small child's imagination can make of one box: a race car, a mountain, a burning building, a robot.

Schaefer, Lola. 2002. *Hermit Crabs.* Portsmouth, NH: Heinemann. **(P, K, 1st)**

Each page of this science book that is illustrated with photographs begins with a question about these intriguing animals and then supplies the answer.

Swinburne, Stephen. 2010. *Whose Shoes? A Shoe for Every Job.* Boyds Mills. **(P, K)**

Photographs of different shoes and feet ask children to guess whom they belong to—and offer some surprises along the way.

Symes, Sally. 2012. *Whose Toes Are Those?* Somerville, MA: Candlewick. **(T, P)**

This book links pictures of animals with their physical attributes and the sounds that they make.

T = Toddlers (ages 1–2)

P = Preschool (ages 3–5)

K = Kindergarten (ages 5–6)

1st = First grade (ages 6–7)

2nd = Second grade (ages 7–8)

3rd = Third grade (ages 8–9)

Opposites to Increase Vocabulary

What Is It?

Opposites, also called antonyms, are pairs of words that represent concepts at different extremes—*up/down, fast/slow, happy/sad, sink/float* and so forth. Synonyms are words that are similar in meaning, such as *nice, kind, thoughtful,* and *simpático.*

Why Is It Important?

Studies show that many children can begin getting the concept of opposites around three years of age. The first opposites that they learn should be rooted in their actual experience, such as *hot* soup and *cold* milk. It is not until the child understands opposites that she can deal with finer-grained distinctions and the words for them, such as *warm* or *cool.* Learning pairs of opposites is a good way to build vocabulary, particularly when a child is learning a new language, because knowledge of one word is reinforced by understanding the antonym and synonyms for that word.

How Does It Work?

To develop a concept, you need to understand not only what it is, but also what it is not. A child will not fully understand the word *soft* until she understands what is not soft, the concept of *hard.* Often, such concepts are formed by beginning with dramatic examples. Many traditional children's stories and activities incorporate opposites; for example, the story of *The Three Bears* uses the structure, "but it was too hard," "but it was too soft," and "it was just right."

Connections with the Common Core State Standards		
Age	**Category**	**Standard**
Kindergarten	Vocabulary Acquisition and Use	L.K.5. Demonstrate understanding of frequently occurring verbs and adjectives by relating them to their opposites (antonyms).
First Grade	Vocabulary Acquisition and Use	L.1.5. Distinguish shades of meaning among verbs differing in manner and adjectives differing in intensity by defining or choosing them or by acting out the meanings.
Second Grade	Vocabulary Acquisition and Use	L.2.5. Distinguish shades of meaning among closely related verbs and closely related adjectives.
Third Grade	Vocabulary Acquisition and Use	L.3.5. Demonstrate understanding of figurative language, word relationships, and nuances in word meanings.

Leveled Adaptations

Level I: Relying on Actions and Oral Language

Make opposites visible to the children using items around the classroom, such as the following:

- Use two containers to show *empty* and *full*.
- Put two toys side by side to show *big* and *little*.
- Choose two children to show *curly* and *straight* hair.
- Choose two objects, such as a rock and a feather, to show *heavy* and *light*.
- Use an old, sharpened pencil and a brand new pencil to show *short* and *long*.
- Use two containers with lids to show *open* and *closed*.
- Use two paper towels to show *wet* and *dry*.

Level II: Relying on Visual Images

1. Type the words "images for teaching opposites preschool" into your browser. Select some images to teach the concept.
2. Make some opposites games, such as the one posted at http://www.meddybemps.com/opposites/BigLittle.html.
3. Share the Learning for Kids Opposite Train videos with children; they are posted on YouTube.com. (Just type "opposites trains learning for kids" in the search bar.)

Level III: Beginning to Use Symbols

Encourage the children to construct their own word walls with pairs of opposites in the languages that they know—for example: *dirty/clean* and *sucio/limpio*. Do the same for synonyms; see http://www.teachingideas.co.uk/english/synonympairs.htm.

Extensions

1. Have the children play a challenging synonym and antonym game after watching the instructional video on YouTube.com (Just type "synonym antonym jumping game" in the search bar.)
2. Send home an opposites book that includes some more challenging opposites. Children can draw and label one half of the page while their families draw and label the other. If you need ideas, see http://www.spellingcity.com/antonyms.html (the site is free to join).

Picture Book Recommendations

T = Toddlers
(ages 1–2)

P = Preschool
(ages 3–5)

K = Kindergarten
(ages 5–6)

1st = First grade
(ages 6–7)

2nd = Second grade
(ages 7–8)

3rd = Third grade
(ages 8–9)

Carle, Eric. 2007. *Opposites.* New York: Grosset and Dunlap. **(T, P)**

Unfolding the full-page flaps in this book will reveal illustrated opposites.

Coat, Janik. 2012. *Hippopposites.* New York: Abrams. **(T, P, K)**

A hippo is the basis for introducing opposites, from the simple, such as *large* and *small*, to the more sophisticated, such as *opaque* and *transparent.*

Deneux, Xavier. 2013. *Opposites.* San Francisco, CA: Chronicle. **(1st, 2nd)**

An inventive approach to opposites, this thick volume includes some challenging concepts, such as *caged* and *free.*

Gurth, Per-Henrik. 2010. *Hockey Opposites.* Toronto, CA: Kids Can Press. **(P, K, 1st)**

In this book set in Canada, opposites are brought to the hockey rink.

Hills, Tad. 2008. *What's Up, Duck? A Book of Opposites.* New York: Schwartz and Wade. **(T, P, K)**

This board book, part of a series about Duck and Goose, is a good introduction to the concept of opposites for toddlers.

Horacek, Petr. 2013. *Animal Opposites.* Somerville, MA: Candlewick. **(P, K, 1st, 2nd)**

The pop-up images and flaps in this exciting book show opposites through the characteristics of animals.

MacRae, Tom. 2006. *The Opposite.* Atlanta, GA: Peachtree. **(K, 1st, 2nd, 3rd)**

This clever story depicts opposites through the character of The Opposite. The Opposite keeps making opposites happen to Nate, but Nate devises a plan to trick The Opposite. This book gives older children a chance to engage in opposites again.

Patricelli, Leslie. 2010. *No No Yes Yes.* Somerville, MA: Candlewick. **(T, P)**

Toddlers are fascinated by good and bad behavior. In this board book, a rambunctious baby tries out behaviors—both acceptable and unacceptable to adults—with interesting results.

Patricelli, Leslie. 2003. *Quiet LOUD.* Somerville, MA: Candlewick. **(T, P)**

Things that are quiet and things that are loud are recounted in this humorous board book. After sharing the book, make a list of the quiet and loud things mentioned. Then, have the children add to each list to build the concept of contrasting two things.

Seeger, Laura. 2006. *Black? White! Day? Night! A Book of Opposites.* New York: Roaring Brook. **(P, K, 1st)**

Die-cut pages change what appears to be one thing to be the opposite in eighteen different pairs of words. Readers can see the first word and can guess the opposite before it is revealed in the book.

Stickland, Paul. 2010. *Big Bug, Little Bug: A Book of Opposites.* New York: Scholastic. **(T, P, K)**.

A bevy of bugs illustrate simple opposites in this colorful book. The last page is a pop-up!

Yoon, Salina. 2009. *Opposnakes: A Lift-the-Flap Book about Opposites.* New York: Little Simon. **(P, K, 1st)**

Lifting the large flaps in this book reveals snakes with opposite characteristics. One is dirty while another is clean; one is quiet while another is loud.

What Is It?

Talking Drawings to Further Listening Comprehension

The talking drawings strategy begins with listening to a short, nonfiction passage. Children are then called upon to demonstrate their listening comprehension by labeling a picture of something that was described in what they heard. So, after listening to a brief passage about fish, for example, children would label a picture of the fish with some of the new words they learned such as *fin* or *gills*. Children can participate as a large group, in small groups, with a partner, or individually. Children who are English language learners can be paired with children who are more fluent in English, and they can label the drawings in both languages. The goal of the activity is to support listening comprehension, which is the precursor of reading comprehension.

Why Is It Important?

Young children's skill in hearing and understanding spoken language typically is far more advanced than their ability to speak, read, or write. Teachers are often advised to begin "where the child is," so starting with listening activities often is a good place to begin with preschoolers. Many studies have shown that helping children to link actions and images with their own drawings, words, and attempts to write represent a giant step in literacy.

How Does It Work?

Approach the talking drawings with an "I do, we do, you do" sequence. For the "I do" part, begin with numerous examples of diagrams that you have found or created that are labeled with words. Because the strategy typically is used with nonfiction, locate some information books or download a simple diagram from a site called Enchanted Learning (http://www.enchantedlearning.com). Point out how the illustrator has used specialized vocabulary to label the various parts and draws a line connecting it to the drawing.

For the "we do" part, use clip art, photos, posters, or actual items in the classroom to create a labeled diagram together. For example, if the classroom has a pet rabbit, you could read a short passage that you wrote about the rabbit and then have the children position labels you have made for the parts of the rabbit's body that were mentioned, such as *ears, tail, feet,* and *whiskers* on a clip art image or photo of the rabbit.

For the "you do" part, children work on this in teams or in small groups. Choose a short passage that describes something factual, such as the parts of a plant, and ask the children to imagine what a diagram might look like. Make a list of the vocabulary that they might use. Distribute a drawing or have the children draw a plant and write the words on the drawing next to the correct part.

Connections with the Common Core State Standards

Age	Category	Standard
Kindergarten	Text Types and Purposes Comprehension and Collaboration	W.K.2. Use a combination of drawing, dictating, and writing to compose informative or explanatory texts in which they name what they are writing about and supply some information about the topic. SL.K.5. Add drawings or other visual displays to descriptions as desired to provide additional detail.
First Grade	Presentation of Knowledge and Ideas	SL.2.5. Create audio recordings of stories or poems; add drawings or other visual displays to stories or recounts of experiences when appropriate to clarify ideas, thoughts, and feelings.
Second Grade	Presentation of Knowledge and Ideas	SL.3.5. Create engaging audio recordings of stories or poems that demonstrate fluid reading at an understandable pace; add visual displays when appropriate to emphasize or enhance certain facts or details.
Third Grade	Presentation of Knowledge and Ideas	RL.3.7 Explain how specific aspects of a text's illustrations contribute to what is conveyed by the words in a story.

Leveled Adaptations

Level I: Relying on Actions and Oral Language

1. If children are not drawing representationally, provide them with an image to label. Be certain to select something that all of the students have experienced directly as a starting point. For example, take a photo of the play area, and make labels for the names of the items pictured.
2. Talk about the picture with the children, and ask them what the various items are called.
3. Work with them to locate the appropriate labels. Even if children are not yet reading, some may be able to use their knowledge of the initial consonant or word clues (such as the length or shape of the word) to locate the correct label.
4. Link the words to the picture with string, yarn, or ribbon.

Level II: Relying on Visual Images

1. Put children into pairs in which one child is more proficient with language than her partner. For example, pair a child who is learning English with a partner who knows English well or an emergent reader with a child who is reading independently. Working with a partner supports peer interaction and careful listening.
2. Begin by showing the children examples of labeled diagrams so that they get the concept.
3. Ask them to draw something and attempt to label it before reading a short passage about the subject. They might, for example, draw and label a spider.
4. Watch a short video or read a nonfiction passage that provides more information about spiders.
5. Let them label their drawing or make a new drawing with words, such as lines for the eight legs and the words *eight legs*.

6. Have the children revisit their drawings and add details, such as eyes, legs, fangs, and abdomen. For emergent readers, labels can be made by referring to an illustrated vocabulary chart or with the child's invented spelling.

7. Try another technique called directed drawing. For example, the children can draw the weather on a whiteboard or Smart Board. Simply make a picture of a window pane, and let the child depict and label the weather conditions, such as sunny, cloudy, windy, or snowy.

Level III: Beginning to Use Symbols

1. After children have begun to draw items that "look like" something and have begun to write letters, try more of a pretest/posttest approach. Begin by sharing several different, accurately labeled diagrams. Locate dozens of them by typing "Diagram of a ___" into your browser online. Be sure to select one that is not too complicated.

2. Select a short text on a relevant topic that you can read aloud to the children.

3. Before sharing the book or passage, ask the children to work with partners to create a labeled drawing that represents their prior knowledge of the topic—for example, an octopus.

4. Share the text and, after children have heard the material, have them return to their drawings and redraw or revise, adding all of the new terminology and features they now know about. Researchers have found that, when this was done with a passage on the octopus, for example, older children's prelearning drawings were like cartoons. After hearing about the octopus, however, their drawings were much more detailed, and they labeled such things as tentacles and the ink sack. From an assessment standpoint, talking drawings are exceptionally easy to evaluate—look at the "before" and "after" drawings, and identify the advances in the students' reading and listening comprehension for a particular topic.

Extensions

1. Although the talking drawings strategy has been used primarily with factual information, it can be used with fiction as well. For example, children can label a diagram of an imaginary creature or its habitat. The children can label images of storybook characters, such as Winnie the Pooh, his tree, and honey.

2. Try making an interactive bulletin board that children can use to match labels with the correct part of a diagram using magnets.

Picture Book Recommendations

T = Toddlers
(ages 1–2)

P = Preschool
(ages 3–5)

K = Kindergarten
(ages 5–6)

1st = First grade
(ages 6–7)

2nd = Second grade
(ages 7–8)

3rd = Third grade
(ages 8–9)

Adler, Victoria. 2009. *All of Baby Nose to Toes*. New York: Dial. **(T, P)**

This book takes a tour of babies' body parts—including eyes, ears, nose, tummy, legs and toes—so that the youngest listeners can participate. Have toddlers hold a toy or doll and point to each part. Then use clip art to make a labeled diagram.

Bloom, Suzanne. 2001. *The Bus for Us*. Honesdale, PA: Boyds Mills Press. **(P, K, 1st)**

Many children are captivated by the sight of the big, yellow school bus. Make two oversized images of a bus. Cut one of them into pieces so that children can affix the components—wheels, wipers, and so on—to the completed image with magnets. Add labels with the words. Children with some knowledge of word configuration and initial alphabet sounds can practice placing the word labels on the picture.

Davies, Nicola. 2012. *Just Ducks!* Somerville, MA: Candlewick. **(P, K, 1st, 2nd)**

In this story illustrated with watercolor images of mallard ducks, a young girl learns about their unique physical characteristics. Type "diagram of a mallard duck" into your browser to get a photograph or drawing that illustrates these parts. Have the children attempt to label it before and after hearing the book. Tie this book in with the Robert McCloskey classic *Make Way for Ducklings* and early childhood songs about ducks, such as "Six Little Ducks."

Davies, Nicola. 2008. *Surprising Sharks*. Somerville, MA: Candlewick. **(K, 1st, 2nd)**

This book is full of interesting facts about sharks. Have the children label a diagram of a shark before and after listening to or reading the book.

Rustad, Martha. 2009. *Animals in Winter*. North Mankato, MN: Capstone Press. **(P, K, 1st)**

Lovely photographs and spare text explain how animals prepare for the cold weather. Make a winter-scene bulletin board, and have the children represent what they have learned in pictures and words.

Tafolla, Carmen. 2009. *What Can You Do with a Paleta?* New York: Tricycle Press. **(P, K, 1st)**

Popsicles (*paletas*) get a bilingual treatment in this story about waiting for the ice cream truck to arrive. Draw or use clip art of some frozen-treat favorites, and involve the children in identifying the parts: stick, cone, and so on. Then make a self-correcting matching game of colors and flavors, such as purple/grape, red/cherry or strawberry, in multiple languages for children to use at a learning center or in small groups.

Waters, Jo. 2006. *A Walk on the Beach*. North Mankato, MN: Raintree. **(T, P, K)**

Beautiful photographs and a simple text introduce children to the treasures that wash up on shore. Have children make a diagram of the water line and draw what they might find. Have them revisit their drawings after sharing the book.

What Is It?

A story map is a type of graphic organizer that reflects the structure of the text, the events in the plot, or the sequence of steps in a process. Reading Rockets offers more information about story maps at http://www.readingrockets.org/strategies/story_maps.

Why Is It Important?

One of the driving questions in reading is "what happens next?" An understanding of sequence is essential to comprehending stories, processes, and procedures. Teaching children to make predictions is fundamental to their understanding of sequence.

How Does It Work?

To introduce these ideas to children, choose something that is very familiar to all of the students as the focal point—for example, brushing their teeth. Begin by having a child demonstrate how this is done while you narrate the behavior: "First, she is picking up the toothbrush. Now she's getting the toothpaste. She's taking off the cap. Now she's putting some on the toothbrush," and so on. Use the book *Brush, Brush, Brush!* by Alicia Padron to reinforce the steps. When first introducing these sequencing activities, provide prompts and text cues that guide children in understanding the organization of the material. Use clip art or provide pictures that illustrate the steps. Have children arrange the images in the correct order on the floor, a clothesline, or a magnetic board.

STRATEGY 17

Story Maps and Process Charts to Teach Sequence

Connections with the Common Core State Standards

Age	Category	Standard
Kindergarten	Key Ideas and Details	RI.K.1. With prompting and support, ask and answer questions about key details in a text.
	Key Ideas and Details	RI.K.2. With prompting and support, identify the main topic and retell key details of a text.
First Grade	Key Ideas and Details	RI.1.1. Ask and answer questions about key details in a text.
	Key Ideas and Details	RI.1.2. Identify the main topic and retell key details of a text.
Second Grade	Integration of Knowledge and Ideas	RL.2.7. Use information gained from the illustrations and words in a print or digital text to demonstrate understanding of its characters, setting, or plot.
Third Grade	Integration of Knowledge and Ideas	RL.3.7. Use information gained from the illustrations and words in a print or digital text to demonstrate understanding of its characters, setting, or plot.

Leveled Adaptations

Level I: Relying on Actions and Oral Language

1. Begin with a very simple story, such as Pat Hutchins's book *Rosie's Walk*. It is the story of a little hen that is oblivious to her pursuit by a hungry fox as she walks through the barnyard. The fox has many slapstick-humor types of mishaps along the way, such as falling into the pond, stepping on a rake and getting hit in the head, and so forth.

2. Make a story line on the floor with pictures to represent each incident in the book. Make a large image of a hen and a fox using clip art, and glue them onto heavy paper or card stock. Punch holes in the corners and use a length of ribbon or yarn so that one child can play the hen and another, the fox.

3. Read the story aloud as the children walk on the story line. Have children take turns walking the story line and using whatever vocabulary they have to talk about each incident.

4. Select a book with a very simple plot, such as Eric Carle's *The Very Hungry Caterpillar,* to read with the children.

5. After the children have heard the book a couple of times, provide images to represent the events in the book. Use a clothesline and clothespins or magnets on a board, and arrange the images in random order. Have the children come up, one at a time, to choose the image that comes next in the book and place it in the sequence of the story. This is a good opportunity to use ordinal-number vocabulary with questions such as, "What is the first thing that the caterpillar eats?" or "What is the last thing that happens?"

Level II: Relying on Visual Images

1. Use a story with six main events, such as *The Cow Who Clucked* by Denise Fleming, to make a paper-plate sequence activity. Divide the paper plate into six equal sections. Place a picture and caption of each main story event in each segment.

2. Divide a second paper plate into six sections, and cut out one of the six segments. Affix the second plate on top of the illustrated paper plate with a metal brad.

3. Have the child illustrate the top paper plate and write the title of the book. As they turn the top plate, they will reveal one section of the plate underneath (and one main event in the story). The child can then use this to tell the story.

4. Try the activity with other books, such as Eric Carle's *The Grouchy Ladybug* or the series of books by Laura Joffe Numeroff that begins with *If You Give a Mouse a Cookie*.

Level III: Beginning to Use Symbols

To make a process chart, focus on character perspectives, motives, and reactions to events. A good choice for this activity is *Too Many Tamales* by Gary Soto and the Spanish equivalent, *¡Qué montón de Tamales!* In this story, a young girl tries on her mother's engagement ring while they are cooking, and it is lost. She assumes that the ring is inside one of the many tamales that they prepared and enlists the help of her siblings and cousins to eat them all to find the ring. Try a process chart that has four sections:

● Setting: making tamales for a party
● Problem: ring is lost and appears to have been cooked into the food
● Solution: carefully search through all of the tamales to find it
● Surprise: the ring was not really lost

See more activities related to the book at http://www.rif.org/documents/us/Too-Many-Tamales-All.pdf

Extensions

1. Children can use a free software program such as VoiceThread to create a version of *If You Give a Mouse a Cookie*. To get the children started thinking, share Numeroff's variants of her book, such as *If You Give Pig a Pancake* and *If You Give a Moose a Muffin*.

2. Ask the children to identify an animal and something that they give it to eat.

3. Ask them to imagine a series of demands by that same animal and a way to get back to the beginning again. This is an excellent activity for a small group of children with gifts and talents in language that can be shared with everyone in the class. VoiceThread is flexible because the children can rearrange images easily. In addition, others can view the VoiceThread and embed verbal comments about the presentation that can be played by clicking on that person's uploaded picture.

Picture Book Recommendations

Barton, Byron. 2014. *My Bus.* New York: HarperCollins. **(T, P, K)**
    A bus driver picks up passengers and delivers them to their destinations in this simple book that lends itself to a story map. Resources are available at: http://readcommoncore.com/book/hardcover/my-bus/9780062287366.

Beaumont, Karen. 2006. *Move Over, Rover!* Boston, MA: HMH Books. **(T, P, K)**
    On a rainy day, Rover is warm and dry inside his dog house. Several other animals decide to join him—until skunk appears on the scene and clears the area. Invite children to join in on the refrain, "Move over, Rover!" Relate to other tales that challenge the idea that there's always room for one more, such as *The Mitten* by Jan Brett or *Mushroom in the Rain* by Mirra Ginsburg.

Beaumont, Karen. 2012. *No Sleep for the Sheep!* New York: Scholastic. **(T, P, K)**

In this cumulative tale, other residents of the farm make their characteristic noises—and also make it impossible for the sheep to get any rest. After each disruptive incident, the sheep says, "Shhh, not a peep. Go to sleep!"

Chaconas, Dori. 2010. *Please Don't Slam the Door!* Somerville, MA: Candlewick. **(T, P, K)**

A rhyming circular story with lots of humor and a refrain for children to repeat.

Costello, David. 2010. *I Can Help.* New York: Farrar, Straus, and Giroux. **(P, K, 1st, 2nd)**

This circular story about passing on kindnesses lends itself to a process chart.

Fleming, Candace. 2012. *Oh, No!* New York: Schwartz and Wade. **(T, P, K, 1st)**

In this cumulative, repetitive tale, a mouse is chased by a tiger and falls into a hole. When a series of other animals try to help, they fall in, too—"Oh, no!" A surprise ending adds to the fun.

Hutchins, Pat. 1971. *Rosie's Walk.* New York: Aladdin. **(P, K, 1st, 2nd, 3rd)**

A little hen flies the coop and goes for a walk around the barnyard, oblivious to the fox that is pursuing her. Each of the fox's failed attempts to catch Rosie—such as stepping on a rake and being hit in the head—give the story humor and action.

Lester, Alison. 2005. *Are We There Yet? A Journey around Australia.* LaJolla, CA: Kane Miller. **(1st, 2nd, 3rd)**

A family goes on a three-month camping trip throughout Australia. Older children can follow the maps that show the route for the trip and points of interest.

Milway, Katie. 2008. *One Hen.* Toronto, CA: Kids Can Press. **(1st, 2nd, 3rd)**

In this story set in Ghana, children get a lesson in economics as Kojo turns one hen and a microloan into a thriving business. The cumulative text is written in a "This Is the House that Jack Built" style.

Nelson, Kadir. 2013. *Baby Bear.* New York: HarperCollins. **(T, P, K)**

Baby Bear gets lost, but a series of encounters with other animals puts him safely on the path home in this gentle story. Draw a story map as you share the book, and demonstrate using it to retell the story.

Numeroff, Laura. 2008. *If You Give a Cat a Cupcake.* New York: HarperCollins. **(T, P, K, 1st, 2nd)**

After receiving the cupcake, the cat asks for sprinkles, spills them, has to clean up, and needs a bath afterward. These books can lead to many activities related to plot and sequence—they also can inspire children's original cyclical stories.

Numeroff, Laura. 2011. *If You Give a Dog a Doughnut.* New York: HarperCollins. **(P, K, 1st, 2nd)**

Use story maps to show the flow of events and to see the cause and effect.

Stein, David. 2012. *Because Amelia Smiled.* Somerville, MA: Candlewick Press. **(P, K, 1st)**

This story originates in New York City when a happy child starts a sequence of positive events. The girl's smile causes her neighbor to send cookies to her grandson in Mexico, and a chain reaction of small kindnesses is put into motion.

Wilson, Karma. 2012. *Bear Says Thanks.* New York: Margaret McElderry. **(P, K, 1st, 2nd, 3rd)**

This book and others in the series include a sequence of events, each followed by a refrain.

What Is It?

Digital Language Experience Approach with VoiceThread

The language experience approach (LEA) begins with a concrete experience the children use to dictate a story, which is then transcribed by the teacher as reading material. The advantage to an LEA is that the texts produced are relevant and in the children's own words. The LEA is designed to make children aware of the conventions of print, encourage social interactions, involve children in practical uses of written language, and build on their familiarity with spoken language to move into reading. Traditionally, the LEA is written on chart paper and children's names are placed after the sentences that they contribute. In a digital LEA, teachers can use digital photography and Web 2.0 tools, such as VoiceThread, to enhance the experience and make it more interactive. An individual child, a small group, or a larger group can produce an LEA. The LEA stories then become reading-practice material for the students.

Why Is It Important?

It is a common misconception that children need to be accomplished readers before they become writers; actually, reading and writing are learned simultaneously most of the time. The texts that children have written themselves may be easier for them to read because they are familiar with the experience and recall some of their words. Therefore, these dictated sentences provide a sort of scaffold for early reading. Dictated stories or story charts may be particularly helpful in reading instruction with English language learners because they begin with what they know—their own experiences. The concrete experience helps to make the words more understandable because they are used in context and focus on children's home cultures.

How Does It Work?

Meaningful group experiences are a good starting point for the LEA. The LEA has four steps:

- **Experience**—Children participate in a group activity, such as preparing food, taking a walking field trip, examining an unusual object, participating in an arts experience, or learning a simple game from another culture.
- **Description**—Children describe the activity in their own words, and the teacher guides them in producing a detailed account by helping them consider sequence: What did we do first? After that, what happened? Now what should we include?
- **Transcription**—The teacher takes dictation in the children's words so that they can see their ideas converted into print. The teacher labels each contribution with the child's name.
- **Reading**—The teacher reads the text aloud to familiarize the children with it. Each child reads what she has contributed. After practicing it several times, children can then attempt to read the entire text of the LEA in unison. The teacher can use the text for reading instruction by asking the children to find their names, search for particular vocabulary words, identify words with the same initial consonant, or look for punctuation marks.

Connections with the Common Core State Standards

Age	Category	Standard
Kindergarten	Comprehension and Collaboration	SL.K.1. Participate in collaborative conversations with diverse partners about kindergarten topics and texts with peers and adults in small and larger groups.
First Grade	Comprehension and Collaboration	SL.1.1. Participate in collaborative conversations with diverse partners about first-grade topics and texts with peers and adults in small and larger groups.
Second Grade	Comprehension and Collaboration	SL.2.1. Participate in collaborative conversations with diverse partners about second-grade topics and texts with peers and adults in small and larger groups.
Third Grade	Comprehension and Collaboration	SL.3.1. Engage effectively in a range of collaborative discussions (one-on-one, in groups, and teacher-led) with diverse partners on third-grade topics and texts, building on another's ideas and expressing their own clearly.

Leveled Adaptations

Level I: Relying on Actions and Oral Language

1. Children often are capable of composing stories orally before they have the fine motor skills and knowledge of print to produce writing. In these circumstances, a teacher, volunteer, tutor, or technology can be used to take dictation and produce a written text. The LEA begins with an experience, so try taking the children outdoors to play and produce an LEA of -ing verbs that describe what they are doing.

2. Use the format of "[Child's name] is _____ing ." This will produce lines such as, "Marisol is swinging." "Carlos is running." "Rashid is jumping."

3. Take digital photographs of each action for use in an electronic class book. Using a tool such as VoiceThread, upload and label each photo so the children can connect the verb to the image.

4. Share the book with the children and their families. Using VoiceThread to produce the book makes it possible for families who view the book to upload an image of themselves and embed comments about particular pages or the entire book.

Level II: Relying on Visual Images

1. Consider different ways to present an LEA, such as a class book, bulletin board, individual photo album, or illustrated poster. For example, create an illustrated bulletin board of a class visit to a fire station.

2. Use photos taken on the field trip. Work with the children to put the photos in sequence on the bulletin board.

3. Take dictation of the children's descriptions of the trip, and put these quotations on the bulletin board along with the name of the child who offered each description.

4. Revisit the board frequently with the children.

Level III: Beginning to Use Symbols

1. Create an LEA story chart of a shared experience, taking the children's dictation and incorporating their words into the chart. Then, try the following ideas for using the story chart to scaffold the children's early reading.

2. Try cutting the story into sentence strips and having the children reassemble it in sequence.

3. When you read the story with the children, cover key words with sticky notes and try rereading the sentences, asking the children to fill in the missing words.

4. Make a small version of the story for a child to take home and read.

5. Try exchanging LEA charts with another class and asking the other class to respond to what your class wrote.

6. Draw attention to certain features, such as rhyming words or punctuation, with highlighter markers or highlight tape (transparent fluorescent tape).

7. Use a series of pictures, digital photographs, or children's drawings to create a common experience and produce a class big book.

Extensions

VoiceThread (http://voicethread.com) can be especially helpful at increasing student engagement and motivation while activating learning. This computer tool allows students to participate and collaborate in making narrated slide shows, similar to PowerPoint for adults. VoiceThread also has many applications for student self-assessment. A child can review his original stories written throughout the year, select the best one, and refer to a checklist to evaluate his own story.

Story Evaluation Checklist			
My story had a good title.	🙂	😐	☹️
It had a cover page.	🙂	😐	☹️
The pictures and text went together.	🙂	😐	☹️
It included information about the author.	🙂	😐	☹️

Picture Book Recommendations

T = Toddlers
(ages 1–2)

P = Preschool
(ages 3–5)

K = Kindergarten
(ages 5–6)

1st = First grade
(ages 6–7)

2nd = Second grade
(ages 7–8)

3rd = Third grade
(ages 8–9)

Hapka, Catherine. 2013. *Sophia Makes a Friend.* New York: Disney Press. **(P, K)**

Sophia attracts lots of playmates, so the challenge is pleasing all concerned. Have the children dictate, draw, or write about a time when conflict arose over play.

Laminack, Lester. 2010. *Snow Day!* Atlanta, GA: Peachtree. **(K, 1st, 2nd, 3rd)**

After the forecast predicts a major snow storm, the characters in his book imagine what they'll do during their day off. Use the book to inspire a "What We Did on Our Snow Day" slideshow illustrated with digital photographs.

Murkoff, Heidi. 2003. *What to Expect at Preschool.* New York: Harper Festival. **(P, K, 1st, 2nd)**

The transition to preschool is an important one. Ask children to dictate a story about their first day of a new experience.

Parish, Herman. 2011. *Amelia Bedelia's First Field Trip.* New York: Greenwillow. **(P, K, 1st, 2nd)**

Amelia Bedelia is notorious for mixing up words with humorous results.

Park, Laura Sue. 2005. *Bee-Bim Bop!* Boston, MA: Clarion. **(T, P, K)**

A Korean mom and her child prepare dinner in this book about a common experience. Use it to inspire children's food-preparation stories.

Penn, Audrey. 2007. *The Kissing Hand.* Terre Haute, IN: Tanglewood. **(P, K, 1st, 2nd)**

A little raccoon is anxious about leaving his mom for the first time to go to school, so she sends him off with a kiss on his hand. Have the children produce a class LEA about first experiences.

Rylant, Cynthia. 2004. *The Relatives Came.* Pine Plains, NY: Live Oak Media. **(K, 1st, 2nd, 3rd)**

An extended family gathers for a summertime reunion in this story that could inspire children's original books about diverse families.

Stead, Philip. 2012. *Bear Has a Story to Tell.* New York: Roaring Brook. **(P, K, 1st, 2nd)**

Invite children to predict what sort of story Bear is so eager to tell. Have children sit with a partner and share a favorite story of their own.

What Is It?

A mystery box is a guessing game. You will need a sturdy box with a lid or with a cut-out flap covered by a piece of cloth. Decorate it with colorful wrapping paper or question marks. Identify several small objects that will become the secret items placed inside. As they ask questions to try to determine what the hidden object is, the children will practice their listening, speaking, and critical thinking skills.

Why Is It Important?

Learning to make inferences is a critical thinking skill. Asking children to guess on the basis of clues builds their logical thinking skills. When a familiar object is hidden from their view and they can use questions to identify it, they develop a strategy for raising questions, receive guidance from the teacher in making inferences, and build skills in oral expression.

How Does It Work?

Seat a small group of children in a circle on the carpet. Show them the mystery box, and tell them that there is a secret object inside. Try some easy ones at first, such as, "It's something you would find at school." Give each child a chance to ask one question that has a yes-or-no answer. Children will learn that the best use of their question is to narrow the category down. For example, if the children begin with broad categories, such as, "Can you write with it?" or "Can you read it?" they will be more successful at guessing than if they jump right into specific questions, such as "Is it a pencil?" or "Is it an eraser?" Children also will learn to listen more carefully. Gradually, they will begin to realize that if they ask, "Is it a crayon?" after the teacher has already answered no to "Can you write with it?" then they are wasting one of their questions.

Connections with the Common Core State Standards		
Age	**Category**	**Standard**
Kindergarten	Comprehension and Collaboration	SLK.3. Ask and answer questions in order to seek help, get information, or clarify something that is not understood
First Grade	Comprehension and Collaboration	SL1.2. Ask and answer questions about key details in a text read aloud or information presented orally or through other media.
Second Grade	Comprehension and Collaboration	SL2.3. Ask and answer questions about what a speaker says in order to clarify comprehension, gather additional information, or deepen understanding of a topic or issue.
Third Grade	Comprehension and Collaboration	SL.3.3. Ask and answer questions about what a speaker says in order to clarify comprehension, gather additional information, or deepen understanding of a topic or issue.

Leveled Adaptations

Level I: Relying on Actions and Oral Language

1. Develop the concept of guessing with *Spots, Feathers, and Curly Tails* by Nancy Tafuri. As you read this book, the children can guess the name of a farm animal after looking at a visual clue.

2. On YouTube.com, watch a video on the construction and use of science mystery boxes in which children use their sense of touch to describe an object. (To find it, type "preschool kids science mystery boxes" into the search bar.)

3. To introduce the idea of guessing, make the task very simple at first. For instance, you might place a small stuffed toy inside a box and give every child a chance to touch it.

4. Ask a few questions that children can respond to in a physical way, such as, "Stand up if you think it is something to eat," "Sit down if you think it is something to play with," or "Clap two times if you think it is something to read."

Level II: Relying on Visual Images

1. Make guessing more concrete by using picture cards and making a themed mystery box. Be certain to select items that are part of children's everyday experience. For example, post images of fruits, labeled with their names in English and other languages spoken by children in the class.

2. Have the children reach inside the box to touch a plastic food replica then select the card that they think it is—banana, apple, orange, grapes, pineapple, cherries, and so on. Guide them with questions, such as, "Is it round?" "Is it smooth or bumpy?" "Is it one shape or lots of little shapes?" and "What color do you think it is?"

3. When they make a selection, have them say why they chose that answer.

4. Other themes might be school supplies, such as a crayon, child-safe scissors, a pencil, or an eraser, or replicas of farm and wild animals.

Level III: Beginning to Use Symbols

1. Put an object inside a mystery box.

2. As the children touch the object inside, have them generate lists of descriptive words. Write down the words as they say them.

3. Make a poster that includes a picture of the item inside the box, along with the words the children used to describe each item. If you like, you can make posters on edu.glogster.com.

4. Have the children select a favorite object and produce their own posters, either on paper or using Glogster.

5. Revisit the posters frequently to support the children's early reading.

Extensions

1. As children gain experience, one of them can be in charge of selecting a secret object to put in a mystery box and answering questions about it.

2. Children with gifts and talents in language can develop more mysteries for the boxes by choosing everyday items and preparing several clues to help classmates guess. They can lead the discussion after they have seen the teacher model this behavior several times.

3. Another is for children to create a literacy mystery box based on a favorite story, information book, poem, song, or film. They can use the items in the box to build interest, to follow the sequence of the text, or as a comprehension check for independent readers.

Picture Book Recommendations

Butler, John. 2003. *Who Says Woof?* New York: Viking. **(T)**

Each page introduces an animal by the sound it makes. Then, the child can guess which baby animal is on the next page. For silly fun, try using it with the funny song by the Norwegian group, Ylvis, "What Does the Fox Say?" (available on YouTube.com)

Falwell, Cathryn. 2009. *Mystery Vine: A Pumpkin Surprise.* New York: Greenwillow. **(K, 1st, 2nd)**

Young children plant a garden but do not know what will be produced by a vine that grows. Use this book to develop the concept of guessing.

Laden, Nina. 2014. *Peek-a-Zoo!* San Francisco, CA: Chronicle. **(T, P)**

A book that gives children a clue to what animal is peering from the cut-out section. They can then turn the page to see if their guess was correct. Use it to introduce the concept of a clue.

Marzollo, Jean. 2011. *I Spy Spectacular: A Book of Picture Riddles.* New York: Cartwheel. **(P, K, 1st, 2nd, 3rd)**

Children can use their observation skills to match the objects in the rhymes of this book with the pictures.

Perrin, Martine. 2012. *Cock-a-Doodle Who?* Chicago, IL: Whitman. **(T)**

Black-and-white silhouettes and a simple rhyming text turn this book into a guessing game for babies.

Saltzberg, Barney. 2002. *Peekaboo Kisses.* Boston, MA: HMH. **(T, P)**

Uses the peekaboo game to give clues to a hidden animal's identity; for example, "It's something woolly, something fluffy, something fuzzy, and something squeaky."

Tafuri, Nancy. 1988. *Spots, Feathers, and Curly Tails.* New York: Greenwillow. **(T, P)**

This simple guessing-game book invites children to figure out which farm animal will be pictured next after seeing a distinctive clue, such as the pig's curly tail.

Timmerman, Gayla. 2012. *Charlie and the Mystery in the Box.* Mustang, OK: Tate. **(P, K, 1st)**

Charlie the cat finds a mysterious box in his favorite alley and wants to discover what is inside. Readers can guess along with Charlie before the box's contents are revealed.

T = Toddlers (ages 1–2)

P = Preschool (ages 3–5)

K = Kindergarten (ages 5–6)

1st = First grade (ages 6–7)

2nd = Second grade (ages 7–8)

3rd = Third grade (ages 8–9)

Rebus Recipes to Learn Specialized Vocabulary

What Is It?

A rebus is an image that represents entire words or parts of words. It can be a photo, a picture, a geometric shape, or an abstract symbol that represents an entity, such as a logo for a corporation.

Why Is It Important?

Experts recommend embedded teaching or using familiar contexts as a support for making language more understandable. For instance, it is more understandable to the child to learn words associated with foods and meals if they are discussed during snack or lunchtime. Actually preparing a simple, healthful food by following a rebus recipe not only promotes proper nutrition but also reinforces visual literacy and literacy with print.

How Does It Work?

According to researcher Kathy Kalmar, food-preparation activities may be particularly helpful in developing vocabulary because they teach words in meaningful context, involve all of the senses, are highly motivating, and connect literacy with math and science concepts. When you add rebus recipes to the activity, children can link pictures and oral vocabulary with printed words and physical actions. Doing this makes the cooking experience a way to support the literacy learning of children at very different levels.

Connections with the Common Core State Standards		
Age	**Category**	**Standard**
Kindergarten	Vocabulary Acquisition and Use	L.K.4. Determine or clarify the meaning of unknown and multiple-meaning words and phrases based on kindergarten reading and content.
First Grade	Vocabulary Acquisition and Use	L.1.4. Determine or clarify the meaning of unknown and multiple-meaning words and phrases based on first-grade reading and content.
Second Grade	Vocabulary Acquisition and Use	L.2.4. Determine or clarify the meaning of unknown and multiple-meaning words and phrases based on second-grade reading and content, choosing flexibly from an array of strategies. Use sentence-level context as a clue to the meaning of a word or phrase.
Third Grade	Vocabulary Acquisition and Use	L.3.4. Determine or clarify the meaning of unknown and multiple-meaning words and phrases based on third-grade reading and content, choosing flexibly from an array of strategies. Use sentence-level context as a clue to the meaning of a word or phrase.

Leveled Adaptations

Level I: Relying on Actions and Oral Language

1. Listening to an audio recording of a simple, no-bake recipe is a highly motivating listening activity. Make a center with all of the ingredients, a rebus recipe (arranged in the correct sequence), and recorded instructions (in more than one language, if possible).

2. Explain the three roles for the children. They will need an equipment operator, a director, and a cook. Send three children at a time to the center and assign each to a role. The equipment operator will operate the recording. The director will use a pointer to point to the correct step in the process. The cook will make the snack.

3. When they finish with one snack, they can switch roles and the other two can make their snacks.

4. Assign a new group of three to the center to make their snacks.

5. As the children prepare the food, take digital photos or let children make drawings of the activity to put into a class scrapbook with captions and comments.

Level II: Relying on Visual Images

1. William Steig's book *Pete's a Pizza* tells the story of pretend play in which a young boy's dad pretends to turn him into a pizza. Read the book, then dramatize the story in class.

2. Check out a list of other rebus books at: http://www.readwritethink.org/files/resources/lesson-docs/RebusBookList.pdf

Level III: Beginning to Use Symbols

1. Print out rebus puzzles, and send them home with the children to share with their families. Examples are available at Scholastic's Mini-Books page, http://minibooks.scholastic.com.

2. Visit the Nick Jr. site at http://www.nickjr.com, and type "rebus" into the search box to find rebus songs and books for the popular children's television programs, *Wonder Pets* and *Dora the Explorer*. Practice the rebus with the children and then send home a copy.

Extensions

1. Have children create a simple rebus recipe for a healthful snack, such as bugs on a log (a stick of celery with cream cheese or peanut butter topped with raisins). As with any food, be sure to check about children's allergies first.

2. Post the rebus recipe at the cooking center, and have students use the ingredients to prepare their own snack.

Picture Book Recommendations

Argueta, Jorge. 2010. *Arroz con leche/Rice Pudding.* Toronto: Groundwood. **(P, K, 1st, 2nd, 3rd)**

Argueta, Jorge. 2010. *Guacamole: Un Poema para cocinar/A Cooking Poem.* Toronto: Groundwood. **(P, K, 1st, 2nd, 3rd)**

These two bilingual books describe the preparation of two foods that are popular in Latin America: rice pudding and guacamole. More than just recipes, both books have charming illustrations and language worth savoring. Use them to inspire children's rebus recipes about a favorite dish from their families.

Bailey, Linda. 2012. *Toads on Toast.* Toronto: Kids Can Press. **(P, K, 1st)**

A toad introduces a fox to a recipe that is completely toad free: toad in a hole, which is an egg cooked in a piece of toast. Suggest to parents that they and their children might try making this recipe at home. It can be converted to a rebus recipe by children who can draw representationally, or you can do this with clip art.

Bauer, Marion. 2004. *A Recipe for Valentine's Day: A Rebus Lift-the-Flap Story.* New York: Little Simon. **(T, P, K, 1st, 2nd)**

This book is a "recipe" for the perfect valentine. Readers lift the flaps to find out the ingredients that are represented in pictures. Use it to inspire other types of recipes that are not for food but for a concept.

Calmenson, Stephanie, ed. 2005. *Kindergarten Kids: Riddles, Rebuses, Wiggles, Giggles, and More!* New York: HarperCollins. **(P, K, 1st)**

This collection will get young children thinking about clever ways to combine pictures with words and word play.

Christensen, Bonnie. 1997. *Rebus Riot.* New York: Dial. **(1st, 2nd, 3rd)**

Poetry and rebuses make a great combination. The children will love figuring out the riddles to get the jokes.

Hillenbrand, Will. 2011. *Mother Goose Picture Puzzles.* New York: Two Lions. **(P, K, 1st)**

This book features twenty familiar Mother Goose rhymes converted into rebus versions. Use this story to demonstrate how a picture can take the place of a word—for example, in "Little Boy Blue," the word *horn* is replaced with a drawing of a horn.

Marzollo, Jean. 2000. *I Love You: A Rebus Poem.* New York: Scholastic. **(P, K, 1st)**

In this I Spy book designed to encourage children to look closely at details, the adult reads the words while the child interprets the pictures.

Sierra, Judy. 2011. *We Love Our School! A Read-Together Rebus Story.* New York: Knopf. **(P, K, 1st, 2nd)**

Perfect for not-yet-readers, this book is about the first day of school. It will give the children an opportunity to join in the reading on day one as they supply the names of the pictures as the teacher reads the text. Use it to inspire older students to work on a rebus book that can be read with a partner.

What Is It?

Volunteer Tutors to Practice Reading Aloud

Volunteer tutors—defined as individuals who do not have professional teaching credentials but who focus on supporting children's literacy—can exert a powerful and positive effect on children's reading. Researchers have identified important aspects of a successful volunteer tutoring program:

- The program must align with classroom instruction and be well-implemented.
- The tutors must be well-trained and supervised.
- The tutoring should occur on a regular schedule and provide sufficient time.
- The tutors and students need to build rapport so that the experience is enjoyable for both.
- The tutor should consider each reader's choices, interests, motivation, literacy level, general self-esteem, and self-confidence as a literacy learner.
- The program's effectiveness must be evaluated.

Why Is It Important?

Volunteer tutors can provide individual support for students and can assist with differentiating instruction. It is often the children who struggle the most with reading who benefit the most, so individual tutoring is well worth the effort. For the child who has a short attention span, is learning English, or has limited support for schoolwork at home, volunteer tutors can be very beneficial in helping a child maintain focus, providing language support, and assisting with homework. In their review of twenty-one studies of the effectiveness of volunteer tutoring programs, researchers Gary Ritter, Joshua Barnett, George Denny, and Ginger Albin concluded that "students who work with volunteer tutors are likely to earn higher scores on assessments related to letters and words, oral fluency, and writing as compared to peers who are not tutored."

How Does It Work?

Tutors can be identified in many different ways. College students who are studying to be teachers, the national Foster Grandparents Program (http://www.nationalservice.gov/programs/senior-corps/foster-grandparents), Reach Out and Read volunteers (http://www.reachoutandread.org/get-involved), and local community volunteers can participate. It is important that all of these individuals meet the criteria for working in a public school. This typically includes a negative TB test, a criminal-record check, and a child-abuse-history clearance.

The following is a list of recommended tutorial strategies:

- Review work that the child has learned in the regular classroom program.
- Discuss the child's family, pets, school, and so forth to motivate drawing and writing.
- Play structured games to motivate interest in acquiring literacy skills.

- Read stories from classroom materials to provide reinforcement.
- Work with phonics.
- Do both oral and silent reading.
- Expand vocabulary and use context clues to figure out words.
- Predict outcomes in stories.
- Summarize the stories read.
- Use leveled books to provide students with appropriate reading materials.
- Provide high-interest reading materials for the child.
- Encourage the child to write and draw in a journal each day.
- Talk with the child about what she has written or wants to write.
- Keep a list of words to enhance vocabulary development and sight vocabulary.
- Offer support and encouragement.

Connections with the Common Core State Standards		
Age	**Category**	**Standard**
Kindergarten	Range of Reading and Level of Text Complexity	RL.K.10. Actively engage in group reading activities with purpose and understanding.
First Grade	Comprehension and Collaboration	SL.1.2. Recount or describe key ideas or details from a text read aloud or information presented orally or through other media.
Second Grade	Comprehension and Collaboration	SL.2.2. Recount or describe key ideas or details from a text read aloud or information presented orally or through other media.
Third Grade	Range of Reading and Level of Text Complexity	RL.3.10. By the end of the year, read and comprehend literature, including stories, dramas, and poetry.

Leveled Adaptations

Level I: Relying on Actions and Oral Language

Tutors may need coaching on how to work with a child who knows very little English, no letters, and no letter sounds. Use a picture-book version of a song that calls upon children to perform various actions, such as *Clap Your Hands* by Lorinda Cauley. Practice the motions first, then sing it together.

Level II: Relying on Visual Images

1. Read *I Went Walking* by Sue Williams.
2. Have the children watch a YouTube video in which Lee Ecco turns the text of the book into a song to the tune of "Frère Jacques." (Type "Lee Ecco I went walking" into the search bar.)
3. Show them how to use the images in the book to support predictions of what will happen next in the story, an important skill in reading. The pages of the book give a hint about which animal will join the walk next, so draw children's attention to those clues.

Level III: Beginning to Use Symbols

1. Read *I Went Walking* by Sue Williams.
2. Download the free printables for use with *I Went Walking* from http://www.wiseowlfactory.com/BookaDay/archives/3859.
3. Have the children fill in the name and color of each animal that appears in the book.

Extensions

1. Take the children on a short trip, perhaps to visit the library or the schoolyard.
2. Afterward, let them work in small groups to create original books using the format, "I went walking. What did you see? I saw a (color) (living thing) looking at me." So, after a tour of the schoolyard, they might write: "I went walking. What did you see? I saw a red swing looking at me."
3. Let the children decorate their books and share them with their friends and families.

Picture Book Recommendations

Cousins, Lucy. 2005. *Hooray for Fish!* Somerville, MA: Candlewick. **(T, P, K)**

This story celebrates individual differences through little fish of different sizes and colors. The illustrations help children to figure out unfamiliar words.

Holub, Joan. 2013. *Pumpkin Countdown.* New York: Scholastic. **(P, K, 1st, 2nd)**

In this rhyming counting book, children take a field trip to the pumpkin patch and count up to twenty and back down again.

Martin, Bill, Jr., and Michael Sampson. 2013. *Kitty Cat, Kitty Cat, Are You Going to School?* New York: Henry Holt. **(P, K, 1st)**

This book series presents an adorable kitten who is getting accustomed to routines. In this one, she plays, has a snack, paints, sings a song, listens to a story, and shares something special during show-and-tell at her preschool. The repetition and picture cues support struggling readers, and the school setting gives it appeal as a choice for tutors.

Meisel, Paul. 2011. *See Me Run.* New York: Holiday. **(P, K, 1st, 2nd)**

An adventurous dog leads his friends of many different breeds to the park where they start digging and unearth—a dinosaur! This easy reader uses simple words, repetition, and brief text to support struggling readers.

Raschka, Chris. 2011. *A Ball for Daisy.* New York: Schwartz and Wade. **(P, K, 1st, 2nd)**

In this simple tale, a dog's favorite toy is ruined—a situation with which children can relate.

Schneider, Josh. 2011. *Tales for Very Picky Eaters.* New York: Clarion Books. (1st, 2nd, 3rd)

A boy who refuses to eat ordinary foods is offered disgusting alternatives by his dad in this humorous book.

Sullivan, Mary. 2013. *Ball.* New York: Houghton Mifflin Books for Children. **(K, 1st)**

A ball-obsessed pup desperately waits for his owner to return to continue their play.

Williams, Sue. 1992. *I Went Walking.* San Diego, CA: Harcourt Brace. **(T, P, K)**

This book follows the pattern: "I went walking. What did you see? I saw a (color) (animal) looking at me."

Williams, Sue. 2000. *Let's Go Visiting.* San Diego, CA: Harcourt Brace. **(T, P, K)**

This board book is similar in format to *I Went Walking* by the same author. The predictable text and animal pictures make it easier for a child to read.

T = Toddlers (ages 1–2)
P = Preschool (ages 3–5)
K = Kindergarten (ages 5–6)
1st = First grade (ages 6–7)
2nd = Second grade (ages 7–8)
3rd = Third grade (ages 8–9)

How to Share Picture Books with ELLs

What Is It?

Simply pulling a picture book off the shelf is not effective in supporting children's literacy learning when reading aloud. According to researcher Renee Neu, young children—particularly those for whom English is not their first language—need opportunities for talk in smaller, relaxed groups that lessen fear of making a mistake. Book sharing can be a scaffold for talk because it focuses on a familiar topic in a more controlled context.

Why Is It Important?

Oral language and written language are fundamentally different. So, even though most young children without disabilities learn to speak or listen, not all become fluent readers and writers. The oral language skills of listening and speaking—both in a child's first language and in her second—are linked to literacy with print. Researchers have found that, for ELLs with a solid foundation in their first language, experiencing books in their home language first can be a great boost to comprehension.

How Does It Work?

Researchers Cristina Gillanders and Dina Castro suggest the following procedure when sharing picture books with dual language learners:

1. Select a book written in both the child's first language and English that has some predictable qualities to it, such as a repetitive phrase, a cumulative structure, or that is organized by familiar sequences such as counting or by the days of the week.

2. Assemble props, picture cards, and simple puppets, and make several of the centers in the classroom relate to the theme. For example, you could place a recording of the story in the listening center and theme-related information books in the reading center.

3. Go through the book and identify core vocabulary.

4. Choose a repetitive phrase or refrain.

5. Plan ways to teach the core vocabulary and repetitive phrase before sharing the book. For example, before you read *Pete the Cat and His Four Groovy Buttons* by Eric Litwin, explain the meaning of the words *groovy* and *colorful*. The book has a chant, "My buttons, my buttons, my four groovy buttons!"

6. Begin with a picture walk through the book. Look at the illustrations with the children and talk about what they contain.

7. Read the book in the child's first language, then read it in English.

8. Let the children retell the story using props and puppets, and act it out for their friends.

Connections with the Common Core State Standards

Age	Category	Standard
Kindergarten	Comprehension and Collaboration	SL.K.2. Confirm understanding of a text read aloud or information presented orally or through other media by asking and answering questions about key details and requesting clarification if something is not understood.
First Grade	Comprehension and Collaboration	SL.1.2. Ask and answer questions about key details in a text read aloud or information presented orally or through other media.
Second Grade	Comprehension and Collaboration	SL.2.2. Recount or describe key ideas or details from a text read aloud or information presented orally or through other media.
Third Grade	Comprehension and Collaboration	SL.3.2. Determine the main ideas and supporting details of a text read aloud or information presented in diverse media and formats, including visually, quantitatively, and orally.

Leveled Adaptations

Level I: Relying on Actions and Oral Language

1. Teach the song "Five Little Monkeys Jumping on the Bed" to the children.
2. Share with them the video on YouTube.com. (Type "Five Little Monkeys kidstv123" into the search bar.)
3. Select seven children to participate: five to play the monkeys, one to play the mother, and one to play the doctor. Designate an area on the carpet where five children can jump and one at a time can "stop, drop, and roll" off. Provide two toy telephones so that the mother can call the doctor. The rest of the class can sing the song while the action takes place. Be sure to keep track of who gets a turn with each role; children will want to sing and act out this rhyme again and again.

Level II: Relying on Visual Images

1. Make a game that children can play with a partner. If they do not already know it, teach the children the song or chant of "Five Little Monkeys Jumping on the Bed."
2. Cut out five monkey shapes, and number them one through five. Cut out X shapes that are made to look like bandages.
3. Pair the children, and let them sing the song and place a "bandage" on each monkey that drops out of the rhyme, until there are "no more monkeys jumping on the bed."

Level III: Beginning to Use Symbols

1. Read Eileen Christelow's picture book that was inspired by this chant.
2. Ask the children to compare and contrast the song or chant with this longer, more detailed version. How are they alike? How do they differ?

Extensions

1. Eileen Christelow has an entire series of books about the five little monkeys in which they go shopping, bake a birthday cake, play hide and seek, read in bed, and jump in the bath. Let the children read several of these books.

2. Give them an opportunity to plan a different type of adventure for the lively group of monkeys, such as coming to the children's school, center, cafeteria, or playground.

3. Ask them to create a story about the new adventure.

Picture Book Recommendations

T = Toddlers (ages 1–2)
P = Preschool (ages 3–5)
K = Kindergarten (ages 5–6)
1st = First grade (ages 6–7)
2nd = Second grade (ages 7–8)
3rd = Third grade (ages 8–9)

Church, Caroline. 2014. *Ten Tiny Toes.* New York: Cartwheel. **(T)**

In this rhyming text, a baby recounts body parts, including "mouth, ears, eyes, nose, and a love that grows and grows." Before you share the book, have the children practice pointing to the body parts and making a heart shape with their hands on the refrain.

Janovitz, Marilyn. 2012. *Play Baby Play!* Naperville, IL: Source-books. **(T)**

Babies in a playgroup enjoy participating in all of the activities that include rolling around, ringing bells, and listening to stories. Before you share the book, have the children perform or mime all of the actions.

Savage, Stephen. 2013. *Ten Orange Pumpkins: A Counting Book.* New York: Dial. **(T, P, K)**

A little bit scary and a whole lot of fun, ten orange pumpkins disappear one by one in this Halloween-themed picture book.

Tafolla, Carmen. 2010. *Fiesta Babies.* Berkeley, CA: Tricycle Press. **(T, P)**

Babies participate in a Latino festival in this charming book that includes words in Spanish. Try combining it with homemade maracas so that children can shake along with the rhythm of the text. To make your own, use plastic eggs with barley or rice inside that are securely shut and glued with hot glue.

Tafuri, Nancy. 2012. *All Kinds of Kisses.* New York: Little, Brown. **(T, P)**

A sequence of baby animals gets different types of kisses from their moms in this brightly colored picture book. Very young children will get the humor of a chick that loves cluck kisses, a calf that loves moo kisses, a kid that loves baah kisses, and so forth. Show children the pictures and have them practice the animal sounds before you read the book.

Thomas, Jan. 2009. *Can You Make a Scary Face?* San Diego, CA: Beach Lane. **(T, P, K)**

This story challenges listeners to make a face, wiggle, and dance to chase away a pesky bug. Use plastic bugs as props to get the children involved in pantomiming the actions to repel an insect pest.

Ward, Jennifer, and T. J. Marsh. 2000. *Somewhere in the Ocean.* New York: Cooper Square. **(P, K, 1st, 2nd)**

Show the children images of the animals in the book, such as octopus, clown fish, and sea turtles. Teach them the song "Over in the Meadow." (To find it on YouTube.com, type "Over in the Meadow" in the search bar.) Take a picture walk through the book to see all of the images. Then, read the book. Make a bulletin board with a photo of each animal and its name, and discuss it with the children.

Storytelling with Props to Build Comprehension

What Is It?

Storytelling with props uses real or representative objects to introduce a character, underscore a key concept, build suspense, or surprise listeners. Researchers have found that when children practice telling stories with props, they tend to:

- include more key incidents from the stories,
- describe different scenarios from the original stories,
- show more confidence in the oral storytelling activity, and
- write higher-quality stories of their own.

Why Is It Important?

Many ethnic and cultural groups have strong oral storytelling traditions. One way of demonstrating respect for other cultures is to include distinctive community storytelling styles in the curriculum. When children use props to tell and retell stories, they practice, recall, and understand the story better and retell the story with more detail.

How Does It Work?

There are lots of different ways to model storytelling with props, such as the following:

- **Draw and Tell:** Use drawing to supplement the story. For example, in reading and retelling the story *The Maid, the Mouse, and the Odd-Shaped House* by Paul Zelinsky, you can make simple drawings of each character and setting as you tell the story. To see a video example of draw and tell on YouTube.com, type "Curious Little Mouse Heidi Butkus" into the search bar.

- **Cut and Tell:** These are stories in which the final result is a surprising shape. The site Notes from the Story Room has many examples: http://meusenotes.blogspot.ca/p/cut-and-tell-stories.html.

- **Storytelling Apron:** Sew multiple pockets onto an apron. Fill the pockets with the storybook, models of characters, and practical objects from the story. Use these props to retell the story.

Connections with the Common Core State Standards

Age	Category	Standard
Kindergarten	Comprehension and Collaboration	SL.K.2. Confirm understanding of a text read aloud or information presented orally or through other media by asking and answering questions about key details and requesting clarification if something is not understood.
First Grade	Comprehension and Collaboration	SL.1.2. Ask and answer questions about key details in a text read aloud or information presented orally or through other media.
Second Grade	Comprehension and Collaboration	SL.2.2. Recount or describe key ideas or details from a text read aloud or information presented orally or through other media.
Third Grade	Comprehension and Collaboration	SL.3.2. Determine the main ideas and supporting details of a text read aloud or information presented in diverse media and formats, including visually, quantitatively, and orally.

Leveled Adaptations

Level I: Relying on Actions and Oral Language

1. Teach the children the counting song "Ten in the Bed":

    There were ten in the bed,

    and the little one said, "Roll over! Roll over!"

    So they all rolled over, and one fell out.

    Continue in this manner, counting down in each stanza until you get to one.

    There was one in the bed,

    and the little one said, "Good night!"

2. The children can take turns acting out the song using a blanket and ten children at a time. Spread the blanket out on the floor. Tape a large, laminated numeral on each child so they are numbered one to ten.

3. Arrange the children from high number to low, and place the highest-numbered child at the blanket's edge. Practice having everyone roll in the same direction simultaneously, and the child on the end "falls out."

4. Sing the song together, and let the ten children act out the story. Let groups of children take turns rolling, until everyone has had a chance.

5. To facilitate retelling later, gather some small toys, such as bean bag toys, and make a card for each one with a numeral on it. Use a hole punch and hang the numeral from the toy's neck. Arrange the animals on a large box to represent the bed. Show the children how to recite the rhyme and retell the story in a small group.

Level II: Relying on Visual Images

1. Fill the pockets of a storytelling apron with the characters from Merle Peek's illustrated picture book *Roll Over! A Counting Song*: a bear, a snake, a cat, a bunny, a boy, a raccoon, a dog, a parrot, a kangaroo, and a monkey. The pockets can serve as a "headboard" for the bed as you tell the story.

2. As you sing the song, remove one character per verse from a pocket to "fall out" of the bed.

Level III: Beginning to Use Symbols

1. Tell the children the traditional folktale "The Tailor." A printable version is available at http://region1rttt.ncdpi.wikispaces.net/file/view/The+Tailor.pdf.

2. Have the children practice it until they can retell it, using the props in sequence to prompt their recollection of the story.

3. Read *Pete the Cat and His Four Groovy Buttons* by Eric Litwin. Make an image of Pete and attach four big buttons with Velcro or magnets to the image. Print Pete's chant on the whiteboard or a piece of paper and display the words as you share the book.

4. Count down when his buttons are lost, and remove each one. Use a pointer to point to the words of the chant so that the children can read and chant along with you.

5. To hear more of Pete the Cat's favorite songs, visit http://www.harpercollinschildrens.com/feature/petethecat.

Extensions

Visit The Story Sack website http://www.storysack.com to get ideas about the types of props that you can collect to create a story sack. You can build your own with the children's help and some visits to the toy section of thrift stores.

Picture Book Recommendations

Fleming, Candace. 2010. *Clever Jack Takes the Cake*. New York: Schwartz and Wade. **(K, 1st, 2nd)**

Jack wants to give the princess a present, but he has no money. He trades all of his resources to make a cake, but encounters with a troll, blackbirds, a spooky forest, a dancing bear, and a castle guard destroy the cake. Empty handed, he decides to share his adventure, and this turns out to be the princess's favorite gift!

Fleming, Denise. 1991. *In the Tall, Tall Grass*. New York: Henry Holt. **(P, K, 1st, 2nd, 3rd)**

In this caterpillar's-eye view of the world, everything is tall. Use props such as a piece of green shag carpet for the grass, rubber insects, a snake, a toy rabbit, toad, bat, and mole.

Foley, Greg. 2012. *Thank You Bear*. New York: Viking. **(P, K, 1st)**

Bear is a subdued, thoughtful character in this series that includes *Don't Worry Bear, Good Luck Bear*, and *I Miss You Mouse*. In this story, Bear finds a small, empty box and thinks it is "the greatest thing ever!" until Monkey, Owl, Fox, Elephant, Squirrel, and Rabbit fail to see its potential. Fortunately, Mouse agrees wholeheartedly that it is a fabulous find and uses it as a bed. Great for retelling with props.

Ketteman, Helen. 2010. *Goodnight, Little Monster*. New York: Two Lions. **(P, K, 1st)**

The bedtime rituals of monsters are surprising and funny, such as brushing fangs and picking off bugs. Supply children with props, such as toothbrushes and plastic bugs, so that they can retell the story after they are familiar with it.

Litwin, Eric. 2012. *Pete the Cat and His Four Groovy Buttons*. New York: HarperCollins. **(P, K, 1st, 2nd)**

One very cool cat pops all four buttons off his favorite shirt until no buttons—but his belly button—are left. Consider making the text of the book into a story chart that shows the parts the children are to chime in on displayed in a different color. Use a pointer to lead them through their parts.

T = Toddlers (ages 1–2)	
P = Preschool (ages 3–5)	
K = Kindergarten (ages 5–6)	
1st = First grade (ages 6–7)	
2nd = Second grade (ages 7–8)	
3rd = Third grade (ages 8–9)	

McPhail, David. 2013. *Ben Loves Bear.* New York: Abrams Appleseed. **(T, P)**

> This story shows the joys of a young boy spending a quiet day with a beloved teddy bear. The same favorite-toy theme can be found in *Bella Loves Bunny* by the same author.

McNaughton, Colin. 2002. *Good News! Bad News!* New York: HarperCollins. **(P, K, 1st, 2nd, 3rd)**

> The day begins with the good news that school is canceled for the day; however, bad news follows during a trip to the dentist. A boy encounters a mean teacher, aliens, a dinosaur, and a witch. Retell the story using simple stick puppets for each character.

Pinkwater, Daniel. 2012. *Bear in Love.* Somerville, MA: Candlewick. **(P, K, 1st)**

> Food surprises appear on Bear's doorstep each day, and he wonders about the identity of his secret friend. He tries placing the best food he can think of—a honeycomb—on a rock. The next day, it is replaced by a flower. Then, he sets out blueberries, and they are replaced by a cookie. Finally, Bear meets his admirer—a shy little bunny. This book lends itself to storytelling with simple props—a rock, an empty plastic honey bottle, a fabric flower, a can of blueberries or a pint container, and a box of animal crackers.

K-W-L-S to Assess Prior Knowledge

What Is It?

The K-W-L-S strategy, originally developed by Donna Ogle as the K-W-L strategy, gets children involved in identifying and building background knowledge and reading intentionally to find information. The columns are titled "What We KNOW," "What We WANT to Know," "What we LEARNED," and "What We STILL Want to Know." Type "Images for KWLS Chart" into your browser to see dozens of variations on this technique, ranging from simple to complex.

Why Is It Important?

The importance of building background knowledge before attempting to read texts is frequently overlooked in reading instruction and assessment. For example, a child who actually plays baseball is much better prepared to listen to or read a story about the sport than a person who is entirely unfamiliar with it.

How Does It Work?

1. Choose a book that has sparked the children's interest. Preview it, identifying several stopping points where a particular concept will require elaboration or terminology will need clarification.

2. Make a chart with four columns headed as follows: *K, W, L,* and *S.*

3. Assess the children's prior knowledge on the book's topic before reading. In the *K* column of the chart, make a list of what the children think they know about the topic, even ideas that are incorrect. You can complete this step as a whole group, with small groups, or by pairs of students. Take dictation for not-yet-writers, pair independent writers with partners who cannot write, or have pairs of child writers take turns writing.

4. Fill the *W* column of the chart with questions generated by the students. This gives the children purposes for listening to the story or reading it independently. Seeing these questions appear in print as they are asked can provide additional support for children who struggle with reading and for English language learners.

5. Read the book aloud as the students listen for words and phrases that answer their questions. Record these in the *L* column, or have children who are writing independently record them. As you read, the students are also free to add more questions to the *W* column.

6. When you have finished reading the book, go over and summarize with the children which questions were answered and which were not.

7. In the *S* column, fill in the questions that the children still want to know. You can use this list to guide the children in searching online for authoritative answers to their questions.

8. You can follow up with a graphic organizer that organizes all of the information into meaningful categories.

Connections with the Common Core State Standards		
Age	**Category**	**Standard**
Kindergarten	Key Ideas and Details	RL.K.1. With prompting and support, ask and answer questions about key details in a text.
First Grade	Key Ideas and Details	RL.1.1. Ask and answer questions about key details in a text.
Second Grade	Key Ideas and Details	RL.2.1. Ask and answer such questions as who, what, where, when, why, and how to demonstrate understanding of key details in a text.
Third Grade	Key Ideas and Details	RL.3.1. Ask and answer questions to demonstrate understanding of a text, referring explicitly to the text as the basis for the answers.

Leveled Adaptations

Level I: Relying on Actions and Oral Language

1. With the children, complete a modified version of the K-W-L-S chart that focuses on physical abilities. In the *K* column, list some physical actions that the children know how to do already, such as clapping, running, hopping, and stretching.
2. In the *W* column, list of some things they want to know how to do, such as skipping, whistling, and riding a bicycle.
3. In the *L* column, list what they hope to learn this year.
4. Revisit the chart later in the school year to update with the children's newly acquired skills.

Level II: Relying on Visual Images

1. This activity with a small group models how to use resources to locate information. Based on what you know about the children's interests, put together a collection of picture books focusing on a topic.
2. Post a large, blank K-W-L-S chart. Take dictation as the children provide information for the first column—what they already know or think that they know.
3. Take dictation as they tell you what they want to know.
4. Use picture books that will address their questions. Read with the children to find information.
5. Briefly discuss what they have found, and then take dictation to fill in the *L* column.
6. Have the children identify questions that were not answered, and place those in the *S* column.

Level III: Beginning to Use Symbols

1. Pair the children and give each pair an information book about an animal.
2. In *K* column, have the partners draw or write some things that they know about the animal.
3. In the *W* column, have them draw or write some of the things that they want to find out.
4. Have the partners look at the pictures in the books and then complete *the L* column, what they have learned.

5. In the *S* column, have them write or draw questions they still have.

6. As a culminating activity, have them produce a book that tells all about what they know and have learned about the animal.

Extensions

1. For students with extensive knowledge of a particular topic, have them participate in several K-W-L-S activities on that topic.

2. Use print and nonprint media to get more interesting facts about the topic using a book, such as *What Is Taste?* by Jennifer Boothroyd, as a model.

3. After hearing the book, have the children add to their K-W-L-S charts. They can do additional research online to get answers to what they still want to know.

Picture Book Recommendations

Boothroyd, Jennifer. 2010. *What Is Taste?* New York: Lerner. **(K, 1st, 2nd, 3rd)**

Part of a series on the senses, this book explains the sense of taste through photographs and interesting facts.

Kondonassis, Yolanda. 2012. *Our House Is Round: A Kid's Book about Why Protecting Our Earth Matters.* New York: Sky Pony. **(1st, 2nd, 3rd)**

This book encourages children to explore environmental issues such as recycling, planting trees, and global warming.

Levine, Ellen. 2012. *Seababy: A Little Otter Returns Home.* London, UK: Walker Childrens. **(P, K, 1st, 2nd, 3rd)**

When a baby otter is separated from his mother, a human rescues him and prepares him to be released back into the wild. Use information from the Monterey Bay Aquarium website to answer questions about sea otters.

Lyon, George. 2011. *All the Water in the World.* New York: Atheneum. **(2nd, 3rd)**

Begin this book with some science questions. This beautifully illustrated book explains the water cycle in terms that children can understand.

Ray, Mary Lyn. 2011. *Stars.* New York: Beach Lane. **(P, K, 1st, 2nd)**

What do children know about stars? This book with lovely illustrations and text will stimulate children's questions as they fill out the K-W-L-S.

Sayre, April. 2013. *Let's Go Nuts! Seeds We Eat.* New York: Simon and Schuster. **(2nd, 3rd)**

Children are sure to be surprised by the many interesting facts about foods from nuts and seeds, including beans, coconuts, cacao, nut butters, and beverages. The book even includes information about allergies. Let children choose a favorite and investigate it further.

Sweet, Melissa. 2011. *Balloons over Broadway: The True Story of the Puppeteer of Macy's Parade.* Boston, MA: HMH. **(K, 1st, 2nd)**

This picture book biography explains how Tony Sarg invented the huge helium balloon puppets that are featured in the Macy's Thanksgiving Day Parade. Watch a film clip of the parade and fill out the Know and Want to Know columns of a K-W-L-S chart. Then, read the book and fill in the Learned and Still Want to Learn columns.

T = **Toddlers (ages 1–2)**

P = **Preschool (ages 3–5)**

K = **Kindergarten (ages 5–6)**

1st = **First grade (ages 6–7)**

2nd = **Second grade (ages 7–8)**

3rd = **Third grade (ages 8–9)**

Guided Imagery and Puppetry to Teach Visual Literacy Skills

What Is It?

Guided imagery involves coaching the children in how to create "pictures in their heads." The advantage to visualization activities is that they stimulate children's prior knowledge about a topic and provide a bridge between the new and the known.

Why Is It Important?

Young children live in a visual culture, immersed in fleeting images on the screens of television sets, smartphones, and computers. As a result, visual literacy—the ability to process, interpret, and generate—mental images is important because it is the precursor to listening comprehension and reading comprehension. Before, during, and after sharing a text, encourage children to build mental images. Imagery thinking helps listeners and readers to go beyond literal information and tap into thoughts and emotions. Puppets speak a universal language and invite children to create mental images; therefore, puppets can be particularly helpful for guided imagery and with English language learners.

How Does It Work?

According to researcher David Whitehead, there are three basic ways to stimulate imagery thinking:

- Still images, such as a collection of photographs
- Moving images that show a progression, such as puppies being let outside and romping around in the yard
- Melting images that represent changes in state, such as a melting ice cube or a person's change in mood

With still images, children can scan, change their point of view, or zoom in and out. Moving imagery responses include making predictions, reversing, moving forward, and fast forward. Melting images stimulate changes in state, such as a seed progressing to a flower or a sad character becoming happy.

Connections with the Common Core State Standards

Age	Category	Standard
Kindergarten	Integration of Knowledge and Ideas	RL.K.7. With prompting and support, describe the relationship between illustrations and the story in which they appear.
First Grade	Integration of Knowledge and Ideas	RL.1.7. Use illustrations and details in a story to describe its characters, setting, or events.
Second Grade	Integration of Knowledge and Ideas	RL.2.7. Use information gained from the illustrations and words in a print or digital text to demonstrate understanding of its characters, setting, or plot.
Third Grade	Integration of Knowledge and Ideas	RL.3.7 Explain how specific aspects of a text's illustrations contribute to what is conveyed by the words in a story.

Leveled Adaptations

Level I: Relying on Actions and Oral Language

1. Toddlers are sometimes frightened by puppets, so introduce a puppet slowly and give the child time to adjust to its motion. With very young children, consider using a puppet to interact with a child individually, and make the conversation all about that child. This will encourage the child to respond.

2. After the child interacts with the puppet, put the puppet inside a container that is its "house."

3. Ask the child to imagine and tell you about what the house looks like inside; this would be still-image thinking.

Level II: Relying on Visual Images

1. Give the children the experience of a simple puppet show. Inquire at the library about who would be willing to do this, or use a video such as the Edmonton Public Library's puppet show of "The Three Little Pigs" on YouTube.com. (To find it, type "Three Little Pigs Edmonton Public Library" into the search bar.)

2. Ask the children to imagine the progression of events in the story, and guide them in making a story line or map.

Level III: Beginning to Use Symbols

1. Assess children's prior knowledge by asking them how a butterfly is born.

2. Watch the progression from an egg to a butterfly on YouTube.com. (Type "amazing life cycle monarch butterfly" in the search bar to find the video.)

3. After they watch, have the children make a list of the stages of the life cycle and draw or write each one.

4. To let the children check the accuracy of their lists, let them watch a one-minute video on YouTube.com. (Type "butterfly life cycle video for kids" into the search bar.)

Extensions

Puppets can give children an opportunity to take on a different role. Give children an opportunity to experiment with the free apps Sock Puppets and Puppet Pals (see the Technology Supports for Strategy 25, available online) to produce a puppet show and share it with their classmates.

Picture Book Recommendations

T = Toddlers (ages 1–2)
P = Preschool (ages 3–5)
K = Kindergarten (ages 5–6)
1st = First grade (ages 6–7)
2nd = Second grade (ages 7–8)
3rd = Third grade (ages 8–9)

Barnett, Mac. 2013. *Count the Monkeys.* New York: Hyperion. **(P, K, 1st)**

In this interactive counting book, children can search for the ten monkeys.

Doner, Kim. 2008. *On a Road in Africa.* Berkley, CA: Tricycle Press. **(K, 1st, 2nd, 3rd)**

Illustrations with different perspectives above, alongside, and inside the car and a rhyming text tell the story of Mama O, who is spotted in her Land Rover. The question in the refrain, "Where you gonna go, Mama O, Mama O?" is finally answered when readers realize that she works at an animal orphanage in Nairobi.

George, Lindsay. 2011. *That Pup!* New York: Greenwillow. **(T, P, K)**

A mischievous yellow lab puppy digs his way through the fall. Children will enjoy using their visual literacy skills to locate the acorn and a squirrel hiding on each page.

Handford, Martin. 2007. *Where's Waldo?* Somerville, MA: Candlewick. **(K, 1st, 2nd, 3rd)**

This special edition about the popular character who travels the world encourages children to search for Waldo and his friends.

LaRochelle, David. 2012. *It's a Tiger!* San Francisco, CA: Chronicle. **(T, P, K)**

This interactive book keeps showing just a piece of a tiger that suggests an entirely different animal—until the page is turned. For example, what looks like an orange and black pillow turns out to be a close-up of the tiger's fur. Each time the tiger is revealed, the refrain "Run!" is repeated.

Litwin, Eric. 2010. *Pete the Cat: I Love My White Shoes.* New York: HarperCollins. **(P, K, 1st)**

Cool cat Pete starts out with white shoes, but every time he walks through different substances, the color of his shoes changes accordingly. The e-book version includes a download of the song that the group can sing as a set of stick puppets of Pete with different colored shoes are used to illustrate what is happening in the story.

Matheson, Christie. 2013. *Tap the Magic Tree.* New York: HarperCollins. **(K, 1st, 2nd)**

This lovely book depicts how a tree changes through the seasons. It surely will stimulate children's mental imagery of the process of transformation.

Parot, Annelore. 2011. *Kimonos.* San Francisco, CA: Chronicle. **(P, K, 1st, 2nd)**

This story from Japan is illustrated with five characters who represent the traditional hand-painted wooden *kokeshi* dolls. Each is dressed in a kimono that has the fabric pattern associated with the family's heritage. Readers need to look very closely to identify the patterns that match.

Schlitz, Laura Amy. 2011. *The Night Fairy.* Somerville, MA: Candlewick. **(1st, 2nd, 3rd)**

In this story, a fairy loses her wings and has to figure out a solution. Before you share the book, have the children use their imaginations to describe what a fairy's world might look like. Then, go through the pictures, page by page, so that children can see what the author imagined.

What Is It?

Retelling Folktales to Demonstrate Understanding

Retelling a story relies on the child's memory, familiarity with the story, and ability to use expressive language. Inviting children to retell is an open-ended activity that allows for differentiation; children's versions of the story can range from simple to complex and therefore adjust to their developmental levels. Children often have heard a folktale told and retold many times, so this aids in the retelling.

Why Is It Important?

When children know a story well, they can retell it in their own words. Research suggests that story retelling is particularly effective with children who come from cultures with rich oral traditions, and retelling is a good test of a child's memory of details, plot sequence, and story comprehension. Researcher Lesley Morrow has found that multiple retellings with adult guidance appear to yield the most positive effects. Folktales lend themselves to retelling because they have been perfected over time, have predictable elements that assist in retelling, and have simple plots.

How Does It Work?

Retellings are a good check on comprehension of a story. If you are working with a group, try this procedure:

- Select a simple, familiar, and predictable story with several characters. Make sure that the children have heard the story many times. Stories that are cumulative, such as *Move Over, Rover* by Karen Beaumont, are a good choice.
- Make a list of the main characters, and ask the children to use puppets to represent each character. Puppets can be commercially made or you can make simple puppets.
- Put the children in a line that corresponds to the story sequence, read the story aloud, and have the children step forward and move their puppets when the character's name is mentioned. Model for the children how the puppet can invent dialogue, based on the story.
- Pose questions from the story, and give children turns to answer back in the character of their puppets.
- Progress to dramatizing short scenes and eventually to enacting the entire story using their puppets and retelling skills. For more ideas on story retelling, see *The Complete Learning Center Book*, rev.ed., by Rebecca Isbell.

		Connections with the Common Core State Standards	
Age	**Category**	**Standard**
Kindergarten	Key Ideas and Details	RL.K.2. With prompting and support, retell familiar stories, including key details.
First Grade	Key Ideas and Details	RL.1.2. Retell stories, including key details, and demonstrate understanding of their central message or lesson.
Second Grade	Key Ideas and Details Key Ideas and Details	RL.2.2. Recount stories, including fables and folktales from diverse cultures, and determine their central message, lesson, or moral. RL.2.3. Describe how characters in a story respond to major events and challenges.
Third Grade	Key Ideas and Details Key Ideas and Details	RL.3.2. Recount stories, including fables, folktales, and myths from diverse cultures; determine the central message, lesson, or moral and explain how it is conveyed through key details in the text. RL.3.3. Describe characters in a story, such as their traits, motivations, or feelings, and explain how their actions contribute to the sequence of events.

Leveled Adaptations

Level I: Relying on Actions and Oral Language

1. Read and retell a story with the children several times so that they become familiar with it. Jan Brett's version of *The Mitten,* a Ukrainian folktale, is a good one to try.
2. Give the children a set of toys and props to use to retell the story. For example, if you are retelling *The Mitten,* they can use a cloth to represent the mitten. Different children can play the roles of the animals that crawl inside.
3. Have the children act out the parts as you read the story aloud.

Level II: Relying on Visual Images

1. Choose a folktale, such as Demi's *The Empty Pot.* Show the children an animated version of the story on YouTube.com. (Type "the empty pot" in the search bar.)
2. Read the story to the children. In this story, the emperor is looking for a successor. He gives seeds to all the children in the land and asks them to tend them and then bring the plants that they grew back to the palace. Other children arrive with beautiful flowers, but Ping— who actually has a green thumb—is honest and reports that his seed did not grow. The emperor explains that the seeds were cooked and would not have sprouted. The child with the empty pot is both honest and courageous, so he is the one who is rewarded.
3. Tell the story to the children using some plastic plants and flowerpots or clip art as props.

Level III: Beginning to Use Symbols

1. Show the children the video "I Bought Me a Cat" on YouTube.com. (To find it, type "I Bought Me a Cat musicK8" in the search bar.)
2. Let the children play a matching game in which they match a puppet, toy, or clip-art animal featured in the song to speech bubbles that represent the sounds that the animals make. Try using the app Doodle Text to create the speech bubbles.

Extensions

1. Introduce the children to retellings of familiar folktales, such as Nina Crews's *Jack and the Beanstalk* that changes the setting to modern-day New York City.

2. Have them experiment with changing the setting for a familiar tale and think about how that would modify the original. Use folktales such as *The Greedy Sparrow: An Armenian Tale* by Lucine Kasbarian and *Martina the Beautiful Cockroach: A Cuban Folktale* by Carmen Deedy to extend the children's repertoire of stories.

3. Encourage the children to compare and contrast variants of popular tales from other countries, such as different versions of Cinderella. John Steptoe's *Mufaro's Beautiful Daughters* is a good one to try. To see a video of the book, visit http://video.nhptv.org/video/1688033680.

Picture Book Recommendations

Cohn, Amy, ed. 1993. *From Sea to Shining Sea: A Treasury of American Folklore and Folk Songs*. New York: Scholastic. **(P, K, 1st, 2nd, 3rd)**

A classic collection of illustrated folktales.

Crews, Nina. 2011. *Jack and the Beanstalk*. New York: Holt. **(1st, 2nd, 3rd)**

Children who are familiar with the traditional tale will enjoy this retelling in a Brooklyn, New York, contemporary setting. Use it to inspire children's modern-day versions of familiar tales.

Deedy, Carmen. 2007. *Martina the Beautiful Cockroach: A Cuban Folktale*. Atlanta, GA: Peachtree. **(1st, 2nd, 3rd)**

A cockroach reaches marrying age in this book interspersed with Spanish words. Find out how the coffee spill test is used to decide which of her suitors is kind. Hear it read expressively by librarians at http://vimeo.com/44832855.

Emberley, Rebecca, and Ed Emberley. 2009. *Chicken Little*. New York: Roaring Brook. **(K, 1st, 2nd)**

The classic tale retold with wit is ideal for older children.

Emberley, Rebecca, and Ed Emberley. 2010. *The Red Hen*. New York: Roaring Brook. **(K, 1st, 2nd)**

In this modern spin on "The Little Red Hen," a chicken finds a cake recipe and tries to get Dog, Rat, and Frog to mix, bake, and frost it. But, as with the original story, they are not interested in the work, only in the payoff. The book concludes with a cake recipe.

Isadora, Rachel. 2008. *The Fisherman and His Wife*. New York: Putnam. **(1st, 2nd, 3rd)**

The classic story is about ever-escalating expectations after a first wish is granted. This version is retold in an African setting.

Marshall, James. 2000. *The Three Little Pigs*. New York: Grosset and Dunlap. **(P, K, 1st, 2nd, 3rd)**

Reading a familiar story together allows parents to help children to predict what will happen next. This version of the classic story of the three pigs features some new dialogue and vocabulary for young readers to learn and relate to the words in the story that they already know.

Legend
T = Toddlers (ages 1–2)
P = Preschool (ages 3–5)
K = Kindergarten (ages 5–6)
1st = First grade (ages 6–7)
2nd = Second grade (ages 7–8)
3rd = Third grade (ages 8–9)

McDermott, Gerald. 2011. *Monkey: A Trickster Tale from India*. New York: Harcourt. **(K, 1st, 2nd, 3rd)**

Monkey and Crocodile are pitted against one another in a battle of wits versus strength in this folktale from India. Relate it to other trickster tales, such as the African story *Anansi and the Moss-Covered Rock* by Eric Kimmell.

Norman, Kim. 2012. *I Know a Wee Piggy*. New York: Dial. **(P, K, 1st)**

Similar in style to "I Know an Old Lady Who Swallowed a Fly," this book, told in rhyme, introduces colors as a pig takes a romp through the state fair.

O'Malley, Kevin. 2010. *Animal Crackers Fly the Coop*. New York: Walker. **(1st, 2nd, 3rd)**

Children who are already familiar with "The Bremen Town Musicians" will see the similarities in this fractured folktale. A group of animals wants to form a comedy club but runs into obstacles that are described with humor and puns.

Pinkney, Jerry. 2012. *Puss in Boots*. New York: Dial. **(K, 1st, 2nd)**

This version of the French trickster tale features a clever cat that helps his master succeed. Older children will enjoy comparing and contrasting this story with the Disney movie version.

Willems, Mo. 2013. *Goldilocks and the Three Dinosaurs*. New York: HarperCollins. **(K, 1st, 2nd)**

This creative and funny version of the folktale will encourage children to consider how they might put a different spin on the stories that they know well.

What Is It?

The Talking Circle to Develop Oral Language

The talking circle gives all children a chance to contribute but does not pressure them to do so. Sit together in a small group, and use an object, such as a magic wand, a decorated stick, or a special hat, to indicate who is the speaker. The teacher's role is to encourage talk and interaction, identify interesting objects to spark discussion, follow the children's interests, and invite imaginative thinking with statements such as, "I wonder," or "I wish," rather than quizzing the speaker.

Why Is It Important?

Oral language is the place to begin for most typically developing young children, because their listening and speaking is more advanced than their literacy with print. Yet, many teachers report that they have difficulty guiding discussions with young children. Common challenges include getting children to listen to one another, speak loudly enough for others to hear, focus attention, and ask questions rather than making comments.

Abandon the old show-and-tell with the total group; this often puts a focus on what children own and may lead to conflict over treasured toys. Instead, conduct discussions, or talking circles, with a small group. Joanne Hendrick and Patricia Weissman, authors of *The Whole Child: Developmental Education for the Early Years*, suggest that teachers model the behaviors that they want to see in children, such as paying attention, conveying enthusiasm, making supportive comments, minimizing distractions, and asking open-ended questions.

How Does It Work?

One way to get children oriented to the talking circle, suggested by speech and language therapists Evi Typadi and Karen Hayon, is to place a large piece of paper in the center and tape it to the floor. Model making a scribble and then talking about what it could be. Give each child a marker, and let each of them make a scribble and talk about what it suggests to them. Another good warm-up activity is to place a mirror inside a box, have each child look inside, and then talk about some of the things that the children see.

Following this, the teacher can bring a variety of interesting objects that are relatively durable, clean, and can fit in a child's hand to discuss:

- Items that have action: a small car, a top, or a music box
- Natural item: a lovely stone, a seashell, or a brightly colored leaf
- Objects that transform: masks, jewels, a kaleidoscope, a magnifying glass, a hat, or a piece of colored cellophane
- Items associated with power: a key, a magnet, play money, or a telephone
- Items associated with travel and adventure: a map or a ticket
- Mementos of celebrations: a birthday candle, a wedding favor, or gift wrap
- Objects associated with the care of children: a baby doll with a bed, blanket, and bottle

The teacher can wear an apron with pockets or a hoodie with a pouch to store the objects.

Connections with the Common Core State Standards

Age	Category	Standard
Kindergarten	Presentation of Knowledge and Ideas	SL.K.6. Speak audibly and express thoughts, feelings, and ideas clearly.
First Grade	Presentation of Knowledge and Ideas	SL.1.4. Describe people, places, things, and events with relevant details, expressing ideas and feeling clearly.
Second Grade	Presentation of Knowledge and Ideas	SL.2.4. Tell a story or recount an experience with appropriate facts and relevant, descriptive details, speaking audibly in coherent sentences.
Third Grade	Presentation of Knowledge and Ideas	SL.3.4. Report on a topic or text, tell a story, or recount an experience with appropriate facts and relevant, descriptive details, speaking clearly at an understandable pace.

Leveled Adaptations

Level I: Relying on Actions and Oral Language

1. Play a circle game called Doggie, Doggie, Where's Your Bone? adapted from an activity in *A Year in the Story Room* by Dawn Roginski. Choose one child to search for the "dog."

2. Without letting the searcher see, choose another child to be the "dog" and hold a small bone shape behind his back.

3. Other than the searcher, all children sit in a circle with their hands behind their backs; just one holds the bone.

4. Everyone says in unison:

   Doggie, doggie, where's your bone?
   Someone took it from your home.
   Guess who! Maybe you!

5. The searcher has three guesses to find out who the "dog" is. If the searcher is right, the "dog" gets to be the searcher next; if the searcher is incorrect, give the bone to another child to hide.

Level II: Relying on Visual Images

1. Select a bendable, jointed toy or bean-bag toy that can be positioned into various poses as the item for discussion.

2. Make a set of picture cue cards for the actions the toy might perform: flipping over, sitting down, bowing, or rolling over. Label each card with the action verb: *flip, sit, bow, roll.*

3. Pass the toy around and say, "I wonder what else the _____ might do."

4. Use the talking circle to compose a group story. Suppose that the toy is an elephant. Pass the elephant around, and as each child gets a turn, say, "I wonder what an elephant might do."

5. Let each child demonstrate an action. As children give their ideas, make a new cue card for each idea, and label it with the child's name.

6. When you have collected the group's ideas, they become the basis for a story. Begin the story, saying, "Once upon a time, there was an elephant. That elephant could . . ." Hold up each card in turn and continue the story.

Level III: Beginning to Use Symbols

1. Read *Wilfrid Gordon McDonald Partridge* by Mem Fox to the children. To hear it read aloud, visit YouTube.com and type the book title in the search bar.
2. Locate real objects or photos of items that create memories for the story's elderly resident of a nursing home: seashells, a puppet on strings, a medal, a football, and an egg.
3. Invite the children to talk about how each item helped Miss Nancy remember something important.

Extensions

1. Develop the concept of mementos with children, using the book *The Matchbox Diary* by Paul Fleischman. Read the book with the children.
2. Have the children collect some items that represent their most fondly remembered experiences bring those items to class.
3. In a talking circle, let the children explain what each item represents.
4. Let the children write or dictate what the item is and why it is so special.
5. Create a museum-like display of the children's special items along with their stories.

Picture Book Recommendations

Fleischman, Paul. 2013. *The Matchbox Diary.* Somersville, MA: Candlewick. **(1st, 2nd, 3rd)**
   In this gentle story, a grandfather who came to the United States from Italy shares a group of matchboxes with his granddaughter, each of which contains a tiny remembrance of his new life. Ask children to discover immigration stories from their families and neighbors.

Fox, Mem. 1989. *Wilfrid Gordon McDonald Partridge.* La Jolla, CA: Kane Miller. **(P, K, 1st, 2nd, 3rd)**
   A young boy tries to bring back memories to his friend, a resident of a nursing home, in this gentle story illustrated by Julie Vivas.

Kalman, Maira. 2003. *What Pete Ate from A to Z.* London, UK: Puffin. **(P, K, 1st)**
   Pete the dog consumes twenty-six strange things in this zany alphabet book. Use it as a model for children to create their own stories during the talking circle.

Wilson, Karma. 2005. *Bear Snores On.* New York: Little Simon. **(T, P, K)**
   While the animals party, Bear continues to hibernate. Children can chime in on the refrain as it is read. Try composing a talking circle story using this book as a model.

T = Toddlers (ages 1–2)
P = Preschool (ages 3–5)
K = Kindergarten (ages 5–6)
1st = First grade (ages 6–7)
2nd = Second grade (ages 7–8)
3rd = Third grade (ages 8–9)

Reading with Companion Animals to Build Motivation

What Is It?

Librarians and educators have begun inviting registered, insured, highly trained, and carefully groomed dogs into schools and libraries as a way to motivate children to read. In such a program, the dog's handler serves as the literacy mentor, while the dog functions as the nonjudgmental listener. The dogs are referred to as *therapy dogs* because their purpose, unlike service dogs, is to supply a calming presence and offer stress-reducing benefits. Therapy dogs are not ordinary household pets; they are trained at a level well beyond basic obedience. If it is not feasible to bring dogs into the classroom, consider other companion animals that could serve as reading buddies, such as a litter-box trained rabbit or a gentle guinea pig. The children can take turns reading with the pet and an aide, older child, volunteer adult, or peer. If no live animals are a possibility, encourage children to practice reading at home with their pets.

Why Is It Important?

In the typical classroom, a child does not get more than a few moments of guided practice in reading aloud per day. Even when children do get more time, children who struggle with reading can be fearful of making mistakes and may develop anxiety about reading in front of peers and teachers. Building *situational interest*—offering a pleasant and surprising diversion to make a task more interesting and less daunting—can improve a child's motivation to read aloud. This is where companion animals come in. Researchers have found that having a dog in the classroom can increase children's motivation to read and to persist at reading.

How Does It Work?

Before the dogs arrive, collect permission slips from the children's parents or guardians to allow participation in the program. Identify a few books that are at the listening or reading level of each child, and make a schedule of fifteen-minute appointments for each child with one of the dogs. Before the reading begins, the handlers will introduce their dogs. The handlers can demonstrate the right way to sit with the dog and read. Next, the handlers position the dogs around the classroom, and the children follow the schedule to have their reading session. If time permits, the children can read with more than one of the dogs. Ideally, each child will have a card to indicate which book she read to which dog on each date, filled out by the handler. You can distribute to the children homemade stickers or bookmarks that have images of the dogs' faces. The children often are excited to collect these and share them at home.

Connections with the Common Core State Standards		
Age	**Category**	**Standard**
Kindergarten	Range of Reading and Level of Text Complexity	RL.K.10. Actively engage in group reading activities with purpose and understanding.
First Grade	Conventions of Standard English	L.1.1. Demonstrate command of the conventions of standard English grammar and usage when writing or speaking.
Second Grade	Phonics and Word Recognition	RF.2.3. Know and apply grade-level phonics and word analysis skills in decoding words.
Third Grade	Conventions of Standard English	L.3.1. Demonstrate command of the conventions of standard English grammar and usage when writing or speaking.

Leveled Adaptations

Level I: Relying on Actions and Oral Language

1. Before you bring a companion animal into the classroom, review with the children some basic rules on how to interact with dogs. Use a stuffed dog toy to demonstrate what dogs like: gentle stroking, soft voices, and slow and steady movements. Also review what dogs do not like: being squeezed, loud noises, and people jumping around.

2. Read a book such as *Tails Are Not for Pulling* by Elizabeth Verdick or a humorous book such as *Don't Lick the Dog! Making Friends with Dogs* by Wendy Wahman to reinforce ideas about interacting safely with dogs.

3. Have the handler bring in a dog, and let the reading and sharing begin!

Level II: Relying on Visual Images

1. Post a bulletin board that includes a picture of each dog, its name, age, gender, breed, and some interesting facts about the animal such as its favorite toy, food, or activity.

2. Plan an introduction session to let the children meet the dog handler or literacy volunteers and their animals. Ask each person to briefly tell her dog's story and bring some items that are used to care for the dog, such as a bowl, brush, collar, leash, ID tags, and blanket.

3. Set up a dog-grooming salon or veterinary office in the dramatic play area for children to dramatize dog-care routines.
4. Have the handler bring in a dog, and let the reading and sharing begin!

Level III: Beginning to Use Symbols

1. Introduce some vocabulary that is used specifically with dogs and symbols to represent each item—for example, *bark, wag, beg, sit,* and *fetch*.
2. Use clip art images to represent these words, or take digital photographs of the visiting dogs to illustrate some of the words.
3. Download diagrams of various breeds of dogs from http://www.enchantedlearning.com. With the actual dog, review the diagram with the children and point out the dog's features.
4. Have the handler bring in a dog, and let the reading and sharing begin!

Extensions

1. Have the children come up with questions about the dogs. For not-yet-writers, take dictation; for children who are using invented spelling or more conventional writing, they can produce their own questions.
2. Let the children submit their questions in a special box that is decorated with paw prints or in a gift bag with a dog theme.
3. Share the questions with the handler, and give the children an opportunity to interview each handler to have other questions answered and to learn the story of each dog.
4. Have the handler bring in a dog, and let the reading and sharing begin!
5. Ask the handlers to provide some digital photographs of the dogs so that the children can produce a picture book that tells each dog's story.
6. Let the children share the book with the handler before it is finished to make sure the information is correct and to get additional details.

Picture Book Recommendations

Christelow, Eileen. 2007. *Letters from a Desperate Dog*. New York: Schwartz and Wade. **(1st, 2nd, 3rd)**

Emma the pup writes to a newspaper advice column about her problems at home. After she is advised to pursue a career, she joins an acting troupe but cannot stop thinking about her home. Older children might be motivated to generate a dog advice column—either factual or fanciful.

Ehlert, Lois. 2011. *Rrralph*. New York: Beach Lane. **(P, K, 1st, 2nd)**

Ralph the dog can talk! This question-and-answer book with inventive collage illustrations that incorporate recycled materials poses questions that can be answered in dog speak. For example, the question, "What's on that tree?" is answered with "Bark."

Faller, Regis. 2006. *The Adventures of Polo*. New York: Roaring Brook. **(P, K, 1st, 2nd, 3rd)**

This is the first in a series of wordless books about Polo, an adventure-loving dog. The pictures are large and clear, so even younger readers can follow along easily as Polo travels by boat, by cloud, by bubble, and by spaceship.

Gal, Susan. 2010. *Please Take Me for a Walk*. New York: Knopf. **(T, P, K, 1st)**

An active pup begs to be walked in this simple story by giving lots of good reasons. Use the book to talk about an animal's requirements for being healthy and happy.

Going, K.L. 2012. *Dog in Charge*. New York: Dial. **(P, K, 1st, 2nd)**

Many families consider their pets to be members of their family. This silly story reverses the rules, and a dog is left in charge. Children can dictate or write stories about what might happen if various creatures were left in charge.

Hubbell, Patricia. 2011. *Shaggy Dogs, Waggy Dogs*. Tarrytown, NY: Marshall Cavendish. **(P, K, 1st, 2nd)**

A poem and charming illustrations give young children a sense of the vast differences among the animals that have earned the title of best friend for humans.

Katz, Jon. 2011. *Meet the Dogs of Bedlam Farm*. New York: Holt. **(K, 1st, 2nd 3rd)**

The well-known writer introduces young children to his four dogs. Photographs reinforce the idea that different dogs have different strengths and jobs, whether it is herding sheep, visiting at a hospital, or just being a best friend.

McDonnell, Patrick. 2009. *Wag!* New York: Little, Brown. **(P, K, 1st)**.

The secret to what makes Earl's tail wag is love. Young readers could not only practice reading the story with their companion animal but discuss what makes their pets happy.

Singer, Marilyn. 2012. *Every Day's a Dog's Day: A Year in Poems*. New York: Dial. **(K, 1st, 2nd, 3rd)**

A dog-themed collection of poems suitable for reading aloud.

Wahman, Wendy. 2009. *Don't Lick the Dog: Making Friends with Dogs*. New York: Henry Holt. **(K, 1st, 2nd)**

Sound advice with a sense of humor about interacting safely with dogs.

Yolen, Jane. 2010. *How Do Dinosaurs Love Their Dogs?* New York: Blue Sky. **(P, K, 1st)**

Children will enjoy the humor in this book about dinosaurs becoming pet owners. Use it to orient children to interacting with dogs in gentle ways.

T = **Toddlers** (ages 1–2)

P = **Preschool** (ages 3–5)

K = **Kindergarten** (ages 5–6)

1st = **First grade** (ages 6–7)

2nd = **Second grade** (ages 7–8)

3rd = **Third grade** (ages 8–9)

Graphic Organizers to Teach Story Elements

What Is It?

A graphic organizer is a chart or diagram that helps make thinking more visible. Also referred to as concept maps, webs, or mind maps, these visual displays structure information and arrange important aspects of a concept or topic into a labeled visual pattern. The most common graphic organizers are concept maps, with a main vocabulary word or idea and details radiating out from the center; sequence charts that show a process step by step; comparison and contrast diagrams, such as the Venn diagram; and cause-and-effect diagrams.

Why Is It Important?

There is a large body of research that supports using graphic organizers to support comprehension and to integrate subject areas. Representing ideas through a combination of diagrams, sketches, pictures, and words is a way for children to demonstrate their understanding of ideas and to give all children an opportunity to participate. Graphic organizers also enhance students' retention of new information. Use these tools before, during, and after sharing a story book or information book.

How Does It Work?

Researchers Donna Merkley and Debra Jefferies offer the following tips for using graphic organizers:

- Activate prior knowledge, and set a purpose for listening.
- Identify the words and concepts that students need to understand to get the gist of the material from the book.
- Arrange the images, words, and concepts clearly, simply, and in an organized way.
- Give children an opportunity to return to the graphic organizer after listening so they can add details.

For example, if you are sharing a book about guinea pigs to learn more about your classroom pet, a simple graphic organizer might include different types of guinea pigs, things that every guinea pig needs, and tips on how to handle a guinea pig.

Graphic organizers are most effective when they are:

- consistent—select a few models and use them often, such as at the beginning, middle, and end of a lesson and for homework or review;
- coherent—deal with a limited number of concepts and clearly label the relationships among them;
- creative—pair pictures with words; use them across subject areas; and incorporate them into partner or cooperative group work.

Connections with the Common Core State Standards

Age	Category	Standard
Kindergarten	Comprehension and Collaboration	SL.K.1. Participate in collaborative conversations with diverse partners about kindergarten topics and texts with peers and adults in small and larger groups.
First Grade	Comprehension and Collaboration	SL.1.1. Participate in collaborative conversations with diverse partners about first-grade topics and texts with peers and adults in small and larger groups.
Second Grade	Comprehension and Collaboration	SL.2.1. Participate in collaborative conversations with diverse partners about second-grade topics and texts with peers and adults in small and larger groups.
Third Grade	Comprehension and Collaboration	SL.3.1. Engage effectively in a range of collaborative discussions (one-on-one, in groups, and teacher-led) with diverse partners on third-grade topics and texts, building on others' ideas and expressing their own clearly.

Leveled Adaptations

Level I: Relying on Actions and Oral Language

1. Sing the song "Head, Shoulders, Knees, and Toes" and read the book by Annie Kubler. Find the song in Spanish on YouTube.com by searching for "Head Shoulders Knees and Toes in Spanish." Another video on YouTube.com of "Head, Shoulders, Knees, and Toes" by Muffin Songs leaves words out for the children to supply (search "Muffin Songs Head Shoulders Knees and Toes").

2. Make a cutout of a person and use it as the basis for a graphic organizer. Label the body parts: *head*, *shoulders*, *knees*, and *toes*; in Spanish, *cabeza*, *hombros*, *rodillas*, and *pies* (feet).

3. Have the children take turns being the director and pointing to the correct word as the other children sing and perform the motions.

Level II: Relying on Visual Images

1. Create a rebus-type of graphic organizer that represents a routine familiar to the children, such as the care of a classroom pet. Put a picture of the pet in the center with its name.

2. Create lines radiating out with the following questions:
   - What does it eat?
   - Where does it sleep?
   - What does it like to do?

3. Take dictation from the children and fill in the chart with words and sketches.

4. Supply them with a similar graphic organizer about another animal, and fill it in together after viewing a short film or reading a book about that animal.

Level III: Beginning to Use Symbols

1. For children who are reading independently, have them choose a graphic organizer after looking at several different types. The SmartArt feature of Microsoft Word has many different graphic organizers categorized by purpose.

2. Give the children a blank graphic organizer to complete as they listen to and discuss a story book or an information book that you read aloud. Encourage them to add drawings and use their invented spelling.

Extensions

1. Have children read a fiction text and a nonfiction text on the same topic.

2. Let them compare and contrast the two with a chart that has two columns: "Real" and "Pretend." For more ideas on using information books, see *35 Strategies for Guiding Readers through Informational Texts* by Barbara Moss and Virginia Loh.

Picture Book Recommendations

T = Toddlers (ages 1–2)
P = Preschool (ages 3–5)
K = Kindergarten (ages 5–6)
1st = First grade (ages 6–7)
2nd = Second grade (ages 7–8)
3rd = Third grade (ages 8–9)

Bell, Cece. 2012. *Rabbit and Robot: The Sleepover.* Somerville, MA: Candlewick. **(1st, 2nd)** Two friends with very different ideas about what a good time is work their way through a sleepover in this easy reader. Create a Venn diagram to identify where their interests overlap.

Leedy, Loreen. 2003. *Mapping Penny's World.* New York: Square Fish. **(K, 1st, 2nd, 3rd)** Lisa's agreeable dog, Penny, helps her to practice her map-making skills. As you read the story, make a word web with the word *map* in the center. Make a list of what children learn about maps, and then categorize their ideas, such as parts of a map, purposes for a map, and how to draw a map.

Llewellyn, Claire. 2005. *The Best Book of Bugs.* London, UK: Kingfisher. **(K, 1st, 2nd, 3rd)** This nonfiction book describes the characteristics, habits, and differences among insects and spiders. After reading it, children can fill in a comparison-contrast chart describing insects and arachnids (spiders).

Yoon, Salina. 2012. *Space Walk.* New York: Sterling Children's Books. **(T, P, K, 1st)** This lift-the-flap book introduces children to the planets. After listening to the book, children can create concept webs about the planet of their choice by dictating the text for the concept map.

What Is It?

Storytelling Drama to Link Actions with Words

Storytelling drama refers to the practice of using children's original stories—dictated or written—and dramatizing them for the class with the teacher's guidance. Other children in the class get the opportunity to play various roles in the child's story. Unlike traditional plays, storytelling drama does not use scripts, costumes, sets, or rehearsals.

When children dramatize their own stories, the activity matches their developmental level. For example, a three-year-old might tell a story with a single phrase, such as "baby crying," and demonstrate using a toy doll. For children who are just learning to use language, a story might consist of one sentence, such as, "Me and my cousins played outside," and other children could act out playing. With additional practice and advances in their development, children can dictate stories with greater detail to the teacher, an adult volunteer, or an older child capable of writing the child's words verbatim.

Why Is It Important?

Researchers have found that encouraging children to dramatize their own stories offers many benefits:

- Builds the children's confidence as speakers
- Extends their vocabulary
- Teaches self-regulation
- Builds a sense of community in the classroom
- Motivates children to invent new and exciting stories

How Does It Work?

Write down the child's story word for word. Read the dictated story back to the child, and underline or highlight all of the actors' names that are necessary to act out the story. Children can begin thinking about who might play the various roles. Later the same day, dramatize these stories (without props) for the entire class.

Designate an area as the stage. (This can be accomplished with some masking tape on the floor.) When it is a child's turn to have his story dramatized, position the child next to you. Remind the children about their roles as audience members and as performers:

- No one should be on the stage unless invited.
- No touching of the other people on the stage.
- Any fighting or other types of actions must be controlled and pretend.
- Audience members are expected to pay attention.
- Authors of the story can choose to play themselves in a story, to play another character, or to remain in a coaching role only.

As you read the story aloud, children can volunteer or be invited to play the various characters. At first, you may need to model how to do this. Some disagreements are to be expected as children negotiate who will play the various roles. Intervene if some children are not included in the dramatizations.

Connections with the Common Core State Standards

Age	Category	Standard
Kindergarten	Key Ideas and Details Comprehension and Collaboration	RL.K.3. With prompting and support, identify characters, settings, and major events in a story. SL.K.6. Speak audibly and express thoughts, feelings, and ideas clearly.
First Grade	Key Ideas and Details Craft and Structure	RL.1.2. Retell stories, including key details, and demonstrate understanding of their central message or lesson. RL.1.6. Identify who is telling the story at various points in a text.
Second Grade	Integration of Knowledge and Ideas	RL.2.7. Use information gained from the illustrations and words in a print or digital text to demonstrate understanding of its characters, setting, or plot.
Third Grade	Craft and Structure	RL.3.5. Refer to parts of stories, dramas, and poems when writing or speaking about a text, using terms such as chapter, scene, and stanza; describe how each successive part builds on earlier sections.

Leveled Adaptations

Level I: Relying on Actions and Oral Language

1. Children's first attempts at dictating a story may be very simple—for example: "Grandma took me to Walmart. I got new flip-flops." Write down what they say.
2. Read the story out loud and then decide, with the child, how to portray this. Questions such as, "Did you walk there, go in a car, or ride the bus?" "Did you try on different shoes?" and "Did you pay and check out at the register?" will get the child thinking about the gestures she will make and the number of roles required to act out the story.
3. Assign roles and let the children act out the story.

Level II: Relying on Visual Images

To get children started with the concept of mapping out a story, begin with a book that they know. Create pictures to show the sequence of events in the plot. Go to http://www.bing.com and type in "storyboard for young children" to see many different examples.

Level III: Beginning to Use Symbols

1. As children begin to draw representationally, they can produce a series of drawings. Let the child dictate the story at first and then gradually begin to use the child's invented spelling. Often, these stories are one adventure after another rather than a story with a clear beginning, middle, and end.

2. Have the child draw pictures to represent what happens in the story (to go along with the words).

3. Have the child share her drawings with the class so that they get a preview of the entire story.

4. Let the child author decide about the actions and roles needed.

5. Let the children act out the story.

Extensions:

Storyboards are used by film makers to depict each important scene. For children with gifts and talents in language, give them an opportunity to learn how to do this. They also can assist other children in the class in making storyboards to accompany their original stories. Learn more about storyboarding and see student work samples at http://www.scholastic.com/teachers/article/what-are-storyboards. Type the words "storyboard template" into your browser to locate forms that are suitable for young children. You will find examples of completed storyboards as well as blank, reproducible pages that children can fill in with their own drawings.

Picture Book Recommendations

Gallo, Tina. 2014. *Olivia: Star of the Show.* New York: Simon Spotlight. **(P, K, 1st)**
Olivia has her own television program on the Nickelodeon Channel, and many of the programs are on YouTube.com. In this book, Olivia wants to show how she can play the drums at her school talent show; however, her drums are damaged and she has to think quickly about what other talent she can share. Use this book to develop the idea of the "show must go on."

Morales, Yuyi. 2013. *Niño Wrestles the World.* New York: Roaring Brook. **(K, 1st)**
The wild imaginative play of a young boy transforms him into a wrestler in the style of Mexico (*lucha libre*). He defeats a series of opponents that the children will want to play. In a surprise conclusion, Niño allows his twin baby sisters to join in the play, and together they become *Los Tres Hermanos* (The Three Siblings). Use the book to demonstrate how play themes can inspire story drama.

Piercy, Helen. 2013. *Animation Studio.* Somerville, MA: Candlewick Press. **(1st, 2nd, 3rd)**
This boxed set includes a press-out monster puppet with movable parts, props, storyboard samples and sheets, and an animation handbook. Older children can use it to make a stop-motion movie on smartphone or digital camera.

Wells, Rosemary. 2003. *Max and Ruby Play School.* New York: Grosset and Dunlap. **(P, K, 1st)**
In this easy reader, big sister Ruby wants to play the role of teacher, but her little brother is an inattentive student. Use this book to talk about the need for cooperation during dramatizations.

T = Toddlers (ages 1–2)

P = Preschool (ages 3–5)

K = Kindergarten (ages 5–6)

1st = First grade (ages 6–7)

2nd = Second grade (ages 7–8)

3rd = Third grade (ages 8–9)

Repeated Oral Reading, Narrated Theater, and Readers' Theater

What Is It?

Although adults may grow tired of young children's requests to hear the same story again and again, there is ample research to suggest that revisiting a story until every word is familiar is a breakthrough in learning to read. Researchers have found that the *repeated interactive read-aloud*, a systematic method of reading aloud, allows teachers to scaffold children's understanding of the book, model strategies for making inferences and explanations, and teach vocabulary and concepts.

Why Is It Important?

Neuroscience suggests that each learning experience prepares the mind for future learning and that repeated exposure to a thought, idea, or experience enhances memory and recall of it. When a story is read over and over again, it increases the child's ability to remember and retell it. After children have heard a story many, many times, they often pretend to read it; eventually, they may memorize much of the text. Interactions between the adult reader and the child change with repeated readings; children actually learn how to talk about the story and initiate more talk over time. With repeated readings, children tend to move away from superficial comments and to ask more sophisticated questions about word or story meaning and cause-effect relationships.

How Does It Work?

Researchers Lea McGee and Judith Schickedanz describe the method as follows. Read a story book three times in slightly different ways to increase the amount and quality of children's analytical talk. During the first reading, introduce the story's problem, insert comments, ask a few key questions, elaborate on a few key vocabulary words, and finally ask a why question calling for extended explanation.

The second reading of the text capitalizes on children's growing comprehension of the story by providing enriched vocabulary explanations and asking additional inference and explanation questions. During the third reading, guide the children, requiring them to recount information as well as provide explanations and commentary. Repeated reading also can make children's silent reading practice more focused and effective.

Connections with the Common Core State Standards

Age	Category	Standard
Kindergarten	Range of Reading and Level of Text Complexity	RL.K.10. Actively engage in group reading activities with purpose and understanding.
First Grade	Range of Reading and Level of Text Complexity	RL.1.10. With prompting and support, read informational texts appropriately complex for first grade.
Second Grade	Integration of Knowledge and Ideas	RL.2.7. Use information gained from the illustrations and words in a print or digital text to demonstrate understanding of its characters, setting, or plot.
Third Grade	Integration of Knowledge and Ideas	RL.3.7. Use information gained from the illustrations and words in a print or digital text to demonstrate understanding of its characters, setting, or plot.

Leveled Adaptations

Level I: Relying on Actions and Oral Language

1. Read *Owl Babies* by Martin Waddell or watch the animated video on YouTube.com. (Type "Owl Babies picture book animation" into the search bar.)
2. Have three children line up in order of the characters' ages in the story: older sister Sarah, then middle sibling Percy, and finally baby owl Bill. Select a child to be the Mother Owl.
3. The children can mime the actions to go along with the owls' words as you read the text or listen to the video.

Level II: Relying on Visual Images

1. *Wow! Said the Owl* by Tim Hopgood is the story of a little owl who decides to stay awake all day to see what she is missing by being nocturnal. The book teaches the names of colors through what the owl sees (pink sky, yellow sun, white clouds, blue sky, green leaves, red butterflies, orange flowers, gray clouds, and a rainbow). Make clip art images of each of these things that the little owl sees, and make them the colors as described.
2. Share the book with the children.
3. After you share the book, post the images in order, so that they serve as a reminder of the story sequence. Have the children chime in on the refrain as you read the text again.
4. Afterward, the children can use the images to dramatize or retell the story.

Level III: Beginning to Use Symbols

1. Search book talks on the Scholastic website http://teacher.scholastic.com/products/trade-books/booktalks.htm or on Reading Rainbow http://www.tv.com/shows/reading-rainbow.
2. Have the children create a book talk that is a one-minute "commercial" for a favorite book. Many additional examples are available at Nancy Keane's site http://nancykeane.com/booktalks/student.htm.

Extensions

1. Share examples of readers' theater scripts with advanced students. Websites such as Dr. Young's Reading Room (http://www.thebestclass.org/rtscripts.html), Teaching Heart (http://www.teachingheart.net/readerstheater.htm), and Mandy's Tips for Teachers (http://tips-for-teachers.com/readers_theater.htm) give examples and suggestions.
2. Give advanced students the challenge of converting a brand new book into a readers' theater script.

Picture Book Recommendations

| T = Toddlers (ages 1–2) |
| P = Preschool (ages 3–5) |
| K = Kindergarten (ages 5–6) |
| 1st = First grade (ages 6–7) |
| 2nd = Second grade (ages 7–8) |
| 3rd = Third grade (ages 8–9) |

Brown, Peter. 2013. *Mr. Tiger Goes Wild.* Boston, MA: Little, Brown. **(P, K, 1st, 2nd)**

A tiger gets tired of city life and decides to go back into the jungle where he can roar, rampage, and get back to nature. Read the book aloud while children dramatize Mr. Tiger's behaviors.

DeFelice, Cynthia. 2006. *One Potato, Two Potato.* New York: Farrar, Straus, and Giroux. **(K, 1st, 2nd, 3rd)**

A couple with very few material things locates a magic pot that replicates whatever is put into it. They begin with a potato but soon decide to try it with more interesting items. Children will want to hear this story again and talk about what they would put in the pot to duplicate.

Fleming, Candace. 2002. *Muncha! Muncha! Muncha!* New York: Atheneum. **(P, K, 1st)**

A farmer is desperate to keep rabbits out of the garden, but these bunnies are beyond persistent. Children will enjoy chiming in on the refrain as the book is read aloud.

Hall, Michael. 2013. *It's an Orange Aardvark!* New York: Greenwillow.

Some ants inside a log hear a noise and fear it is an aardvark, in this dramatic story that is well-suited to narrated theater.

Hopgood, Tim. 2009. *Wow! Said the Owl.* New York: Farrar, Straus, and Giroux. **(T, P)**

What is life like during the day when owls are asleep? A curious young owl decides to stay up all day to find out and discovers an explosion of bright colors.

Vamos, Samantha. 2011. *The Cazuela That the Farm Maiden Stirred.* Watertown, MA: Charlesbridge. **(T, P, K, 1st, 2nd)**

This cumulative tale follows a woman making *arroz con leche* (a pudding of rice with milk) in a simmering pot (*cazuela*). Each animal plays a role—the cow gives milk, the hen lays the eggs, the goat gives butter, the donkey picks the lime, and so forth—while the name of each ingredient is given in Spanish and in English. After all is prepared, the happy group dances until the dish is ready to eat. Reminiscent of "This is the House that Jack Built," this bilingual tale really lends itself to repeated oral reading, narrated theater, or readers' theater.

Wild, Margaret. 2003. *Kiss Kiss!* New York: Simon and Schuster. **(T, P)**

A baby hippo rushes outside to play and forgets to kiss his mom goodbye. Seeing other animal babies and parents along the way—including a rhino, lion, zebra, and chimpanzee—reminds him that he neglected something very important! Read the story as children dramatize the parts, and get the rest of the class to repeat the refrain of "kiss, kiss" after each animal is introduced.

What Is It?

Books for dual-language learners include books originally published in a language other than English that are available in the United States; those with the complete text in both languages, side-by-side in the same book; popular U.S. picture books translated into other languages; and books written mainly in English with some interspersed words or phrases in another language.

Why Is It Important?

As researchers Gisela Ernst-Slavit and Margaret Mulhern have pointed out, bilingual books have many uses:

- Previewing or introducing a new topic or reviewing a topic
- Supporting transfer of reading skills from the first language to the second
- Encouraging independent reading
- Comparing and contrasting two languages
- Supporting family literacy
- Teaching teachers and peers words in students' native languages
- Promoting reading enjoyment
- Communicating respect for children's home languages

Using (and Making) Bilingual Children's Literature

How Does It Work?

Bilingual books give children a chance to use their first language as a way to develop skills in the second language. Sending home materials in both languages gives families age-appropriate reading material for their child and improves communication between home and school. The Technology Supports for Strategy 32, available online, lists sites where you can download many children's stories in different languages. Many search engines, such as Bing and Google, offer free online translation tools for texts that you already have; however, you probably will need to have a native speaker check the results, because these programs are far from perfect.

Connections with the Common Core State Standards		
Age	**Category**	**Standard**
Kindergarten	Vocabulary Acquisition and Use	LK.4. Determine or clarify the meaning of unknown and multiple-meaning words and phrases based on kindergarten reading and content.
First Grade	Vocabulary Acquisition and Use	L.1.4. Determine or clarify the meaning of unknown and multiple-meaning words and phrases based on first-grade reading and content, choosing flexibly from an array of strategies.
Second Grade	Key Ideas and Details Integration of Knowledge and Ideas	RL.2.2. Recount stories, including fables and folktales from diverse cultures, and determine their central message, lesson, or moral. RL.2.9. Compare and contrast two or more versions of the same story, such as "Cinderella" stories, by different authors or from different cultures.
Third Grade	Integration of Knowledge and Ideas	RL.3.9. Compare and contrast the themes, settings, and plots of stories written by the same author about the same or similar characters, such as in books from a series.

Leveled Adaptations

Level I: Relying on Actions and Oral Language

1. Create a number line on the floor using masking tape.
2. Use a counting book in a child's first language and in English—see the recommended children's books for ideas.
3. Create images that represent the items counted in the book, such as puppies or seeds. Place the appropriate number of pictures next to each numeral on the number line so that children can count aloud as they hop across the line.
4. Afterward, let children choose ten favorite things to count and make images of each using clip art.
5. Have the class count together as the child hops to each numeral on the line.

Level II: Relying on Visual Images

1. View a video about the names of the colors in Spanish. (Type "Spanish colors for kids" in the search bar on YouTube.com.) Or, view a video about animals' names. (Search "animals in English and Spanish" on YouTube.com.)

2. Create books on familiar topics, such as days of the week, numbers 1–10, pets, and so forth. Label each page with the word in both languages.

Level III: Beginning to Use Symbols

1. Have children work in small groups to create pictionaries—dictionaries illustrated with pictures. Use one of the free translation tools online, such as Bing, Google, Babylon, FreeTranslation, or PROMT, to get the correct spelling of the word in the different languages represented by your students.

2. Try inventing a pictionary about the names of family members—*mother, father, sister, brother, grandmother, grandfather, aunt, uncle, cousin.* Make one of your own, and then encourage the children to create a bilingual version of their family members, illustrated with photos or drawings.

Extensions

1. Read the book *Spike, the Mixed-Up Monster* by Susan Hood with the children. Use it to illustrate how a story can use various words from another language (in this case, Spanish) and conclude with a glossary.

2. Have the children work in groups that include an English language learner so that they make their own stories that incorporate words from another language and contain a glossary at the end.

3. Place these books in the reading corner for children to share.

Picture Book Recommendations

Ada, Alma Flor. 2002. *I Love Saturdays y Domingos.* New York: Atheneum. **(K, 1st, 2nd)**
   A loving affirmation of two heritages, this is the story of a child's weekend visits with her European-American grandparents on Saturdays and her *abuelito* and *abuelita* on Sundays.

Ada, Alma Flor. 2011. *Ten Little Puppies/Diez perritos.* New York: Rayo/HarperCollins. **(T, P, K)**
   A brightly colored counting book about puppies.

Brown, Ruth. 2001. *Diez Semillas/Ten Seeds.* New York: Lectorum. **(P, K, 1st)**
   A young child plants and patiently waits for results in this counting book available in Spanish.

Elya, Susan. 2006. *Bebé Goes Shopping.* New York: Harcourt. **(T, P)**
   Retro illustrations and Spanish words interspersed throughout the text give this rhyming book about a shopping excursion its appeal.

Guy, Ginger. 2007. *My Grandma/Mi Abuelita.* New York: Rayo. **(T, P, K)**
   A celebration of time spent with Grandma.

Guy, Ginger. 2005. *Siesta.* New York: Greenwillow. **(T, P, K)**
   Brightly colored illustrations give naptime a fresh, bilingual treatment.

T = Toddlers (ages 1–2)
P = Preschool (ages 3–5)
K = Kindergarten (ages 5–6)
1st = First grade (ages 6–7)
2nd = Second grade (ages 7–8)
3rd = Third grade (ages 8–9)

MacDonald, Margaret, and Nadia Taibah. 2009. *How Many Donkeys? An Arabic Counting Tale*. Morton Grove, IL: Albert Whitman. **(K, 1st, 2nd, 3rd)**

In this tale, donkeys are taken to market but have to be counted and recounted—in Arabic.

Maze, Stephanie. 2011. *Healthy Foods from A to Z/Comida Sana de la A a la Z*. New York: Moonstone/HarperCollins. **(P, K, 1st, 2nd)**

A bilingual alphabet book that supplies information about healthful food choices. Connect with *How Did That Get In My Lunchbox? The Story of Food* by Chris Butterworth, which shows how food comes from farms to factories to homes. Or, connect with a book of poems about the food chain: *What's for Dinner? Quirky, Squirmy Poems from the Animal World* by Katherine Hauth will add different animals' perspectives of what makes a good meal.

Thong, Roseanne. 2004. *One Is a Drummer: A Book of Numbers*. San Francisco, CA: Chronicle. **(K, 1st, 2nd, 3rd)**

A Chinese-American girl enumerates her favorite things by counting in Chinese.

Walsh, Ellen Stoll. 2010. *Mouse Paint/Pintura de Ratón*. Boston, MA: HMH Books for Young Readers. **(T, P, K)**

This bilingual board book tells the story of three mice that discover three paint jars. Children can learn colors as well as beginning English and Spanish because the story is presented in both languages.

Zepeda, Gwendolyn. 2008. *Growing Up with Tamales/Los Tamales de Ana*. Houston, TX: Piñata Books. **(K, 1st, 2nd)**

This story follows sisters Ana and Lidia as they grow up learning how to make tamales during the holidays. A sweet story about family traditions—and sibling rivalry.

Zepeda, Gwendolyn. 2009. *Sunflowers/Girasoles*. Houston, TX: Piñata Books. **(K, 1st, 2nd)**

This text in English and Spanish tells the story of seven-year-old girl who helps her grandfather with the garden. After he gives her sunflower seeds, she plants them in various locations throughout her neighborhood.

What Is It?

Captioned Video and Voice-Recognition Software

DVDs and televisions now offer the option of viewing a film with or without captions. Captioned video provides a print version of oral language so that children viewing can follow along visually as they hear the words. English language learners can watch films in their first language as captions translate it into a second language (or vice versa). For children with hearing impairments, captions can make film more accessible after they learn to read. Voice recognition software, such as Dragon Naturally Speaking, can take the place of a teacher or volunteer taking dictation for the children as they compose a story using oral language.

Why Is It Important?

A large number of studies have concluded that children need to experience *print referencing*—pointing out text and the features of print—many, many times to be adequately prepared to learn to read. One way to do this is with captioned video in which the accompanying text appears as the words are heard. Many of the Weston Woods/Scholastic classic videos of high-quality literature use this approach; they also use a bouncing ball to indicate which word is being pronounced. With a modern television set, you can turn on closed captioning with just about any program.

How Does It Work?

You can find YouTube videos using "read-along books for children" as your search term. It is best to begin with a song that the children know well so that they can link the print lyrics to the words they hear. As children gain more experience and become emergent readers, use captioned video with predictable books that they have memorized. Prepare children for viewing the film by building background knowledge, generating interest, making predictions, and so forth.

Connections with the Common Core State Standards		
Age	**Category**	**Standard**
Kindergarten	Vocabulary Acquisition and Use	LK.4. Determine or clarify the meaning of unknown and multiple-meaning words and phrases based on kindergarten reading and content.
First Grade	Vocabulary Acquisition and Use	L.1.4. Determine or clarify the meaning of unknown and multiple-meaning words and phrases based on first-grade reading and content, choosing flexibly from an array of strategies.
Second Grade	Fluency	RF.2.4. Read with sufficient accuracy and fluency to support comprehension.
Third Grade	Fluency	RF.3.4. Read with sufficient accuracy and fluency to support comprehension.

Leveled Adaptations

Level I: Relying on Actions and Oral Language

1. Teach the children the humorous action song "Tooty Ta" by eFlashApps, posted on YouTube.com (search "Tooty Ta Eflashapps"). In this captioned video, the cartoon characters nod in time to the music, sing the refrain, and perform all of the actions.

2. The song is cumulative, so the children need to remember all of the previous actions. Try making a rebus type of chart to remind them of the actions. Use a pointer to go through them, as the leader of the song calls out the action.

Level II: Relying on Visual Images

1. Try using e-Touch English Learning Lite, a free app for iPad that children can use to hear a native English speaker pronouncing thirty-one categories of words—nouns, verbs, adjectives, and so on—just by touching the picture. They also can listen to sentences using the words.

2. Karaoke for children is another way to help them understand the connection between spoken and written language. Some machines are toys, such as the Hello Kitty or VTech machines, while others are for computer systems, such as the Wii. Be sure that the lyrics of the songs that you select are suitable for young children. You can also find children's songs with lyrics posted on YouTube.com.

Level III: Beginning to Use Symbols

The PBS television program *Super Why* is captioned throughout to give emergent readers practice. Episodes are available online free at http://pbskids.org/video. To turn on the closed captioning, click the CC button on the screen. PBS also offers *Peg and Cat, Arthur, Curious George, The Cat in The Hat, Martha, Clifford the Big Red Dog,* and *Buster.*

Extensions:

For children who are reading more independently, iPrompt is a free teleprompter app similar to what news broadcasters use. After text is entered, the speed can be adjusted to accommodate to different reading rates. For example, you can slow it down for the initial read of the text and gradually speed it up after the child has practiced it several times.

Picture Book Recommendations

Barefoot Books http://www.barefootbooks.com **(T, P, K, 1st, 2nd, 3rd)**

Has a wide selection of nicely illustrated song book and CD sets. The videos show a bouncing ball that highlights each word as it is sung.

Live Oak Media http://www.liveoakmedia.com **(T, P, K, 1st, 2nd, 3rd)**

Has high-quality read-along e-books. The cost is $30.00 for each book and a multiuse site license; however, it may be worth it to purchase a few favorites so that children can read along with the story. Check to see if your school or media center has any of these excellent productions.

Speakaboos http://www.speakaboos.com/stories/favorites **(T, P, K, 1st, 2nd, 3rd)**

Includes more than 150 stories with interactive text, animation, and music. Focusing on early childhood literacy, Speakaboos uses nursery rhymes, fables, fairy tales, and music along with read-along word highlighting.

Weston Woods Studios/Scholastic http://westonwoods.scholastic.com/products/westonwoods **(T, P, K, 1st, 2nd, 3rd)**

Offers award-winning books, audio recordings, and DVDs linked to standards. Some of them are in different languages, and some are captioned and in Spanish.

T = **Toddlers** (ages 1–2)
P = **Preschool** (ages 3–5)
K = **Kindergarten** (ages 5–6)
1st = **First grade** (ages 6–7)
2nd = **Second grade** (ages 7–8)
3rd = **Third grade** (ages 8–9)

Encouraging Families to Use the Library

What Is It?

One persistent concern among librarians is that children who have the least access to books and other literacy materials in the home may have families who do not use the resources of the public library. Deterrents to using the library include the following factors:

● Families may be unfamiliar with the concept of a free lending library.

● Families may assume that libraries are for books only and may be unaware of multimedia offerings and other services.

● Families may worry that they cannot afford to replace materials that their child might lose or damage.

● Families may be reluctant to share personal information due to their immigration status.

Why Is It Important?

Children's access to developmentally appropriate and engaging reading materials affects their motivation to read and how often they read. In a study of forty-two nations, researchers M. D. R. Evans, Jonathan Kelley, and Joanna Sikora found that the number of books in the home library was strongly correlated with children's academic achievement. And in their study of families with incomes below the poverty line, researcher Pamela High and colleagues found that only 40 percent of children less than five years of age owned ten or more books. Children and their families have a right to information, education, and literacy materials.

How Does It Work?

Work with parents and families to address these concerns, and help them get library cards so that children have access to resources. Arrange to have a librarian come to school to speak with families and children about the many different services that libraries provide.

Connections with the Common Core State Standards		
Age	**Category**	**Standard**
Kindergarten	Craft and Structure	RL.K.5. Recognize common types of texts, such as storybooks and poems.
	Craft and Structure	RI.K.5. Identify the front cover, back cover, and title page of a book.
	Range of Reading and Level of Text Complexity	RI.K.10. Actively engage in group reading activities with purpose and understanding.
First Grade	Craft and Structure	RL.1.5. Explain major differences between books that tell stories and books that give information, drawing on a wide reading of a range of text types.
	Craft and Structure	RI.1.5. Know and use various text features, such as headings, tables of contents, glossaries, electronic menus, icons, to locate key facts or information in a text.
	Range of Reading and Level of Text Complexity	RI.1.10. With prompting and support, read informational texts appropriately complex for first grade.
Second Grade	Range of Reading and Level of Text Complexity	RL.2.10. By the end of the year, read and comprehend literature, including stories and poetry, in the second- and third-grade text complexity band proficiently, with scaffolding as needed at the high end of the range.
Third Grade	Range of Reading and Level of Text Complexity	RL.3.10. By the end of the year, read and comprehend literature, including stories, dramas, and poetry, at the high end of the second- and third-grade text complexity band independently and proficiently.

Leveled Adaptations

Level I: Relying on Actions and Oral Language

1. The Treasure Basket activity, as suggested by Elinor Goldschmied and Sonia Jackson, is one that is suitable for babies and toddlers. Fill a container with interesting, everyday, durable, and inexpensive items that can be disinfected, such as a seashell or a plastic dinosaur.
2. Researcher Cathy Nutbrown suggests that teachers provide security for the children by being an attentive but not active presence, so that children can explore, make choices, develop eye-hand coordination, and interact with the items.

Level II: Relying on Visual Images

National programs such as Dolly Parton's My Imagination Library provide books, free of charge, to families. Find out if it or other national literacy programs are available to your students. If not, investigate resources in your local community.

Level III: Beginning to Use Symbols

See if your library offers a story time or if the librarian will come to your school or center to perform a puppet play or share a story-time program. Some communities also have toy libraries where children can borrow play materials suitable for their developmental levels; investigate what is available in your area. Some libraries have thematic collections of books, toys, and other materials that can be borrowed by teachers. Check into the services in your area and inform families about them.

Extensions:

Many public libraries offer a Summer Reading Club that young children can enroll in to keep them interested in reading throughout the summer months. Have the librarian visit your students and encourage them to use the library.

Picture Book Recommendations

T = Toddlers (ages 1–2)

P = Preschool (ages 3–5)

K = Kindergarten (ages 5–6)

1st = First grade (ages 6–7)

2nd = Second grade (ages 7–8)

3rd = Third grade (ages 8–9)

Bottner, Barbara. 2010. *Miss Brooks Loves Books (and I Don't).* New York: Knopf. **(P, K, 1st, 2nd)**
> A determined librarian works to find a book that a disaffected child will really love in this funny tale of diverse reading tastes.

Bruss, Deborah. 2001. *Book! Book! Book!* New York: Arthur A. Levine. **(K, 1st, 2nd)**
> A chicken decides to check out the library and, before long, the entire barnyard follows suit, eager to see what happens there.

Bunting, Eve. 2008. *Our Library.* New York: Clarion. **(P, K, 1st, 2nd, 3rd)**
> When Miss Goose's library faces financial issues, the animals rally to save it.

Child, Lauren. (2006). *But Excuse Me That Is My Book.* New York: Dial. **(P, K, 1st, 2nd, 3rd)**
> In this book from the Charlie and Lola series, Lola is dismayed when her favorite book is not on the shelf—and is being borrowed by someone else!

George, Kristine. 2001. *Book!* London, UK: Clarion. **(T, P, K)**
> Share this book, suitable for toddlers and threes, and talk together about what children see when they look at a library book—pages, front, back, pictures, and words. Ask an aide or volunteer to sit with a child and a board book to point out the parts and to teach book-handling behaviors.

Henson, Heather. 2008. *That Book Woman.* New York: Atheneum. **(P, K, 1st, 2nd, 3rd)**
> In this story about the packhorse librarians of rural Appalachia during the 1930s, a child who is not enthused about reading learns to appreciate books.

Kirk, Daniel. 2007. *Library Mouse.* New York: Harry N. Abrams. **(P, K, 1st, 2nd, 3rd)**
> A little mouse who lives at the library and loves books decides to become an author and leave his creations out for others to pick up and read.

Malaspina, Ann. 2010. *Yasmin's Hammer.* New York: Lee and Low. **(1st, 2nd, 3rd)**
> In this story about a child from Bangladesh, everyone in the family must work in order to survive. Yasmin yearns to attend school and learn to read, so her family comes up with a way to make her dream a reality.

McQuinn, Anna. 2006. *Lola at the Library.* Watertown, MA: Charlesbridge **(P, K, 1st)**
> The library and all the interesting activities that occur there give children an orientation to the library experience at their school or the public library.

Mora, Pat. 1997. *Tomás and the Library Lady.* New York: Knopf. **(P, K, 1st, 2nd)**
> The child of migrant farm workers finds a refuge and intellectual stimulation at the library in this true childhood story of Tomás Rivera, the famous writer.

What Is It?

Higher-Order Thinking Skills and Reciprocal Teaching

Based on Bloom's Taxonomy, the higher-order thinking skills are applying, analyzing, evaluating, and creating. They are higher-order because they require the learner to go beyond remembering or understanding; the learner has to actually do something with what was learned. Reciprocal teaching is a strategy that assigns different discussion roles to children so that they can gain more experience with higher-order thinking.

Why Is It Important?

Metacognition refers to a learner's ability to think about her own thinking. These insights into the most effective and efficient ways of learning are important for learners of all ages. The ability to monitor comprehension is particularly important in learning to read.

How Does It Work?

Before the text activities, activate the children's prior knowledge, build their background knowledge, and motivate them to listen. During the text activities, emphasize understanding the gist of the story. After the text activities, help children identify errors in their understanding.

Connections with the Common Core State Standards		
Age	**Category**	**Standard**
Kindergarten	Comprehension and Collaboration Comprehension and Collaboration	SL.K.1. Participate in collaborative conversations with diverse partners about kindergarten topics and texts with peers and adults in small and larger groups. SL.K.6. Speak audibly and express thoughts, feelings, and ideas clearly.
First Grade	Comprehension and Collaboration Presentation of Knowledge and Ideas	SL.1.1. Participate in collaborative conversations with diverse partners about second-grade topics and texts with peers and adults in small and larger groups. SL.1.4. Describe people, places, things, and events with relevant details, expressing ideas and feelings clearly.
Second Grade	Comprehension and Collaboration	SL.2.1. Participate in collaborative conversations with diverse partners about second-grade topics and texts with peers and adults in small and larger groups.
Third Grade	Comprehension and Collaboration	SL.3.1. Engage effectively in a range of collaborative discussions (one-on-one, in groups, and teacher-led) with diverse partners on third-grade topics and texts, building on others' ideas and expressing their own clearly.

Leveled Adaptations

Level I: Relying on Actions and Oral Language

1. Before-the-text activities are particularly valuable for young children because they model ways to activate prior knowledge. First, share the purpose of the lesson with the learners.

2. Activate prior knowledge through an activity such as making predictions about the story based on the title and cover.

3. Particularly if the subject is unfamiliar, build prior knowledge with activities such as watching a video related to the topic. For example, before sharing the book *This Moose Belongs to Me* by Oliver Jeffers, let children observe a video of twin moose babies playing in a backyard while their mom keeps watch: http://www.wimp.com/babymoose. Learn some facts about moose at the National Geographic site http://animals.nationalgeographic.com/animals/mammals/moose.

4. Read the book with the children.

5. After reading the book, talk about the concept of *belonging*.

Level II: Relying on Visual Images

1. Many children know the classic folktale of "The Little Red Hen." Stretch their thinking with a variation on this story, *The Little Red Hen (Makes a Pizza)* by Philemon Sturges. Revisit the original story, and then take a picture walk through the newer version.

2. Have the children make predictions about the newer version, based on the illustrations.

3. Read the newer version, inviting the children to join in with the refrain, and talk with them about whether or not their predictions were accurate.

4. Try the 3–2–1 strategy, developed by Vicky Zygouris-Coe, Matthew Wiggins, and Lourdes Smith, to help students summarize key ideas from a book:

5. Ask the students to draw and/or write about three things they discovered in the book.

6. Ask them to draw and/or write about two things they found interesting.

7. Ask them to write one question they still have.

8. In this way, writing becomes a tool for assessing listening or reading comprehension.

Level III: Beginning to Use Symbols

1. Before reading the two versions of the "The Little Red Hen," print out the refrains, and have the children read through them as you point to each word.

2. Provide the children with a Venn diagram. Have them suggest descriptive words for each little red hen that identify their differences, and in the shaded portion that overlaps, ask the children to suggest words that describe both little red hens.

3. Complete a plot diagram for each story with the children. Compare and contrast the plots in the two books.

Extensions:

1. Advanced students can use reciprocal teaching, developed for young children by Pamela Ann Myers, by fulfilling one of four roles.

   - The **reteller** recaps the story by saying who is in it, where the story takes place, what happens, and why it happens.

- The **summarizer** keeps the conversation going and describes what has been discussed thus far. This person takes some notes using sketches or writing and marks some of the comments with the group members' initials.
- The **questioner** asks questions about the story that support comprehension—primarily "Why" and "Do you think?" types of questions.
- The **predictor** encourages everyone to consider what might happen next with these characters, using questions that begin with *if you were*, *next time*, or *after*.

2. Give each child a card with the name of his role and a clip art image to remind him of what he is to do within the group

3. Read the stories and encourage the children to discuss them in their group.

Picture Book Recommendations

Jeffers, Oliver. 2012. *This Moose Belongs to Me*. New York: Philomel. **(P, K, 1st, 2nd, 3rd)**

Wilfrid has a pet moose and gives the animal many rules to follow; however, the moose does not comply because he does not understand that he belongs to Wilfrid.

Murphy, Mary. 2002. *How Kind!* Somerville, MA: Candlewick. **(T, P, K)**

A group of barnyard animals "pay it forward" after Hen gives Pig an egg—a chain reaction of kindnesses occurs. Before sharing the book, talk about what the word *kind* means.

Murphy, Mary. 2003. *I Kissed the Baby!* Somerville, MA: Candlewick. **(T, P)**

After a new duckling is born, the animals in the barnyard cannot resist putting all of their ideas about how to play with a baby to use.

Smith, Meggan. 2010. *Nico and Lola: Kindness Shared between a Boy and a Dog*. New York: HarperCollins. **(K, 1st, 2nd)**

When a young boy is asked to pet sit for his aunt's pug while she is away, he thinks about all of the ways that kindness can be expressed through actions. Watch the book trailer on YouTube.com. (Type "Nico and Lola book trailer" in the search bar.) Talk about what it means to be kind.

Stevens, April. 2011. *Edwin Speaks Up*. New York: Random House. **(P, K, 1st)**

A family of ferrets goes grocery shopping, and baby Edwin is overlooked as the mother tries to rein in his four boisterous older siblings. Pay attention! What appears to be babbling from Edwin actually are the solutions to the problems in this clever and funny book.

Urbanovic, Jackie. 2010. *Sitting Duck*. New York: HarperCollins. **(K, 1st, 2nd)**

What happens when a duck is put in charge of babysitting a boisterous pup? Duck assumes it will be easy until he sees just how much trouble a dog can get into. Other humorous books in the series are *Duck Soup*, *Duck and Cover*, and *Duck at the Door*.

Wilson, Karma. 2011. *Bear's Loose Tooth*. New York: Margaret McElderry. **(K, 1st, 2nd)**

Lots of slapstick humor as Bear's first adult tooth starts pushing out a baby tooth. Use the book to discuss how getting reliable information can help to defuse a concern or avert a problem.

Yoon, Salina. 2014. *Found*. New York: Walker. **(P, K, 1st, 2nd)**

A bear finds a toy rabbit in the forest and advertises to find its owner. But, as he waits, he becomes attached to the toy and really hopes that the owner does not come forward. Children will relate to the emotions of doing the right thing even when it is difficult and will enjoy the surprise ending.

T = Toddlers (ages 1–2)

P = Preschool (ages 3–5)

K = Kindergarten (ages 5–6)

1st = First grade (ages 6–7)

2nd = Second grade (ages 7–8)

3rd = Third grade (ages 8–9)

Recorded Books to Enhance the Motivation to Read

What Is It?

Recorded books that are audio only are known as "books on tape." They are professionally recorded, unabridged versions of fiction and nonfiction books. Usually, people listen to books on tape while they are doing other things, such as riding in the car or taking a walk. Increasingly, they are downloaded online. Several sources—Booksy, Storia, and Ruckus Reader—offer leveled e-book selections for children. Some resources for children's audiobooks include the Audio Publishers Association (http://www.audiopub.org), *AudioFile Magazine* (http://www.audiofilemagazine.com), Books on Tape (http://www.booksontape.com), and Recorded Books (http://www.recordedbooks.com).

Why Is It Important?

According to Sharon Grover and Lizette Hannegan, recorded books

- support listening comprehension;
- promote an interest in reading;
- give children independent access to literature;
- model expressive reading;
- provide many opportunities for practice; and
- include extras, such as an audible signal to turn the page, music and sound effects, and interviews with authors.

Recorded books also enable students with visual or physical disabilities to experience literature by listening alone. For emergent or beginning readers, audiobooks let children enjoy books that are above their independent reading levels.

How Does It Work?

Researchers have found that motivation is essential to engagement in reading, and engagement depends on the following elements:

- Children must see themselves as readers and be seen as readers by those around them.
- Children must regard reading as personally meaningful.
- Children must see reading as a low-risk, accomplishable activity.
- Children who are learning to read must have the opportunity to bond with other readers.
- Children need learning tasks at the right level of difficulty so that they can experience success.

Connections with the Common Core State Standards		
Age	**Category**	**Standard**
Kindergarten	Integration of Knowledge and Ideas	RI.K.10. Actively engage in group reading activities with purpose and understanding.
First Grade	Vocabulary Acquisition and Use	L.1.4. Determine or clarify the meaning of unknown and multiple-meaning words and phrases based on first-grade reading and content, choosing flexibly from an array of strategies.
Second Grade	Knowledge of Language	L.2.3. Use knowledge of language and its conventions when writing, speaking, reading, or listening.
Third Grade	Knowledge of Language	L.3.3. Use knowledge of language and its conventions when writing, speaking, reading, or listening.

Leveled Adaptations

Level I: Relying on Actions and Oral Language

1. Create a listening center using some equipment such as headphones, an mp3 player, or a cassette/CD player. Model for the children how to use the equipment.
2. Involve families in recording themselves reading children's books aloud. Include male as well as female voices reading aloud, both in English and in other languages. If parents do not have the time or are reluctant to do this, involve older students or other community volunteers who are native speakers of various languages.

Level II: Relying on Visual Images

1. Create a listening center.
2. Post step-by-step, illustrated instructions on how to access the recorded books that are matched to each child's interests and developmental level. These recordings can be borrowed from the public library and changed frequently; ask your librarian for advice on selections for your students' developmental levels.

Level III: Beginning to Use Symbols

1. Teach the children how to maintain a log of the audiobooks they have heard.

2. Have them rate each listening selection on a scale from a smiley face to a frown.

Extensions:

1. Have students record themselves reading a book aloud so that other children can revisit favorite books. Give younger children or not-yet-readers the opportunity to request to have specific books read aloud and recorded.

2. Teach the students to include embellishments such as an audible signal for when to turn the page, sound effects, or background music. The Technology Supports for Strategy 36, available online, suggest some ways to record audio books.

Picture Book Recommendations

T = Toddlers (ages 1–2)
P = Preschool (ages 3–5)
K = Kindergarten (ages 5–6)
1st = First grade (ages 6–7)
2nd = Second grade (ages 7–8)
3rd = Third grade (ages 8–9)

Classic Stories for Children in 5 Minutes/Cuentos infantiles en 5 minutos **(P, K, 1st, 2nd, 3rd)**
Offered by Cannonball Sound and available on Amazon.com, this downloadable audiobook offers forty-five minutes of classic children's stories in Spanish.

What Is It?

A family journal is a written record maintained by the family and children. Usually, it is a blank notebook sent home by the teacher with the child. The family can decide on an everyday event to report, write a journal entry, and return the journal to school to share with the class.

Why Is It Important?

Parents and families affect the child not only through heredity but also through the type of language environment they provide in the home. According to researcher Mariana Souto-Manning, their attitudes toward education and aspirations for their children, the language models and literacy materials they supply, and the activities they encourage all make a substantial contribution to children's language development.

How Does It Work?

When you send home a request that the family keep a journal, emphasize that it should be an everyday activity, such as a family gathering or preparing food, or a story about a family pet's humorous quirks. Make it clear that what is written will be shared with the class so that the child can comment on it.

Family Journals that Foster Home-School Communication

Connections with the Common Core State Standards

Age	Category	Standard
Kindergarten	Text Types and Purposes	W.K.1. Use a combination of drawing, dictating, and writing to compose opinion pieces in which they tell a reader the topic or the name of the book they are writing about and state an opinion or preference about the topic or book, such as "My favorite book is . . . ."
	Comprehension and Collaboration	SL.K.1. Participate in collaborative conversations with diverse partners about kindergarten topics and texts with peers and adults in small and larger groups.
First Grade	Comprehension and Collaboration	SL.1.1. Participate in collaborative conversations with diverse partners about first-grade topics and texts with peers and adults in small and larger groups.
Second Grade	Comprehension and Collaboration	SL.2.1. Participate in collaborative conversations with diverse partners about second-grade topics and texts with peers and adults in small and larger groups.
Third Grade	Text Types and Purposes	W.3.3. Write narratives to develop real or imagined experiences or events using effective technique, descriptive details, and clear event sequences.
	Production and Distribution of Writing	W.3.4. With guidance and support from adults, produce writing in which the development and organization are appropriate to task and purpose.

Leveled Adaptations

Level I: Relying on Actions and Oral Language

1. If parents and families do not feel comfortable sharing through writing, have the children collect free or inexpensive items, such as stones, shells, small plastic toys, and so forth.
2. Ask them to talk about why and how they collected the items and to share the collections with the class.
3. Display the children's collections in the room.
4. Read the book *Sort It Out!* by Barbara Mariconda, then talk about different ways that they could organize a collection.
5. Invite families and other community members to share some of their collections and have the children identify their favorites.

Level II: Relying on Visual Images

1. Highlight the children's achievements, such as "I can count to ten in English and Spanish," "I can say *please* and *thank you* in Farsi, Chinese, and Hmong," "I can write your name in Arabic," or "I can teach you some sign language" on a bulletin board.
2. Encourage the children to seek out these skills in their classmates so that they can contribute to the display.
3. Share the A. A. Milne poem, "Now We Are Six." (You can find it posted at http://www.familyfriendpoems.com/poem/now-we-are-six-by-a-a-milne.) It talks about growing up and learning to do things more independently.

4. Invite the children to work on a book at home called "I Used To . . . But Now . . . ." Each page of this book is a year of the child's life from age one to age six. Ask the children to think about what they used to do (or not yet know how to do) at each age. The parent can take dictation about what the child did as a baby, toddler, preschooler—and what she hopes to learn in the future.

Level III: Beginning to Use Symbols

1. There are a surprising number of names used to refer to mothers, fathers, siblings, and other family members. For example, in Spanish, the ending -*cita* is a way of showing affection, so *mamacita* means "dear, sweet little mother." Talk with the children about the different names, nicknames, and endearments they have heard or used. Have them make a family journal about their family members; their relationship to them, such as great aunt or brother; that person's name; and any nicknames.

2. Read the book *Little Treasures: Endearments from Around the World* by Jacqueline Ogburn. It will get children thinking about different possibilities. Another book that talks about the origins of children's names is *A Daisy Is a Daisy Is a Daisy (Except When It Is A Girl's Name)* by Linda Wolfsgruber.

3. As you talk about these endearments, emphasize that those differing from their own are not strange; rather, they are a reflection of that family's traditions, culture, and language.

Extensions:

1. Older students or children who have high verbal and linguistic intelligence can interview family members and collect proverbs, adages, or sayings. In Spanish, sayings such as, "Don't cry over spilt milk," are called *dichos*. For example, "*En boca cerrada no entran moscas*," means "A closed mouth doesn't allow flies to enter."

2. Ask the children to collect sayings, discuss them with their families, and make sure that they understand the meanings of the expressions.

3. Have the students illustrate each saying and make them into a big book or e-book to share with families at conference time.

Picture Book Recommendations

Ajmera, Maya. 2010. *Our Grandparents: A Global Album.* Watertown, MA: Charlesbridge.
(K, 1st, 2nd, 3rd)
Translates the words *grandma* and *grandpa* into nineteen different languages. The book also supplies reasons that children love their grandparents, such as "Our grandparents love us. They give the biggest hugs and hold our hands. Even when we speak softly, they listen. They encourage us." Have the children write their reasons for loving a particular family member and create picture books to give as gifts to them.

Fox, Mem. 2006. *Whoever You Are.* Boston, MA: HMH. **(P, K, 1st, 2nd, 3rd)**
In this celebration of diverse cultures, children are reminded that, although they are unique, they also have something in common with families throughout the world.

Lo, Ginnie. 2012. *Auntie Yang's Great Soybean Picnic.* New York: Lee and Low. **(2nd, 3rd)**
These childhood memories tell the story of two Chinese girls who were welcomed to the United States with a very special picnic. Use the book to inspire family stories.

T = Toddlers (ages 1–2)
P = Preschool (ages 3–5)
K = Kindergarten (ages 5–6)
1st = First grade (ages 6–7)
2nd = Second grade (ages 7–8)
3rd = Third grade (ages 8–9)

Ogburn, Jacqueline. 2012. *Little Treasures: Endearments from Around the World.* Boston, MA: Houghton Mifflin Harcourt. **(P, K, 1st, 2nd)**

In many cultures, families have special words that they use to express their affection, such as *honey* in the United States. In Russia, *dumpling* is a term of endearment, while in Finland it is *hug bunny*. Use this book to get children thinking about the endearments and nicknames that are part of their family's traditions.

Ritchie, Alison. 2007. *Me and My Dad!* Intercourse, PA: Good Books. **(T, P, K, 1st)**

This story about a bear and his father makes for a good partner-reading story at home. After reading about all of the things the father and child do together, the family can write in the journal about an activity that their family enjoys.

Wolfsgruber, Linda. 2011. *A Daisy Is a Daisy Is a Daisy (Except when It's a Girl's Name).* Toronto, Canada: Groundwood. **(1st, 2nd, 3rd)**

This book explores girls' names based on flowers, across cultures and languages.

What Is It?

Web 2.0 Translation Tools to Foster Communication

Web 2.0 is a term coined in 2004 that refers to the transition from a read-only environment to an interactive environment. This is an important transition because Web 2.0 allows fuller participation by people who do not have keyboarding skills or are not yet reading and writing independently, which frequently is the case for young children.

Why Is It Important?

It is important to have developmentally appropriate literacy materials in every child's first language and to be able to communicate with families who do not speak English. Online translation tools are important because they can be used to generate texts in the child's first language, demonstrate respect for the language, and improve communication with the family.

How Does It Work?

Most free translation sites enable the user to translate individual words as well as longer pieces of text. Although the translations that result are not perfect, these programs usually succeed in communicating the basic message. If you use Web 2.0 translation tools, it would be a good idea to get a native speaker to review the text and edit it before sharing it with others.

Connections with the Common Core State Standards		
Age	**Category**	**Standard**
Kindergarten	Knowledge of Language	L.K.5. With guidance and support from adults, explore word relationships and nuances in word meanings.
First Grade	Vocabulary Acquisition and Use	L.1.4. Determine or clarify the meaning of unknown and multiple-meaning words and phrases based on first-grade reading and content, choosing flexibly from an array of strategies.
Second Grade	Knowledge of Language	L.2.3. Use knowledge of language and its conventions when writing, speaking, reading, or listening.
Third Grade	Knowledge of Language	L.3.3. Use knowledge of language and its conventions when writing, speaking, reading, or listening.

Leveled Adaptations

Level I: Relying on Actions and Oral Language

1. Make a helper board that shows different tasks to be performed around the classroom, such as watering the plants, feeding the guinea pig, and distributing snacks.
2. Label the tasks in the languages spoken in your classroom. Type the word or phrase that you need into one of the free multilingual translators described in the Extensions below.
3. Point out the helper board to the children, and show them the different tasks.
4. Try reading the labels in the different languages. Most translators offer audible pronunciation, or families may be able to help you with the correct pronunciation.

Level II: Relying on Visual Images

1. Read the book *Healthy Kids* by Maya Ajmera, a book about health and safety practices around the world.
2. Talk with the children about ways to stay healthy and safe.
3. Encourage them to create a class book on how to stay healthy and safe. Then get the text translated into each child's first language.

Level III: Beginning to Use Symbols

1. Have the children work with a community volunteer or cross-age tutor to dictate a story in their first language to accompany a simple picture book.
2. Have them write and paste the English text on each page along with the first-language text.
3. Retain a copy for the classroom library, and send another copy home for the children to share with their families.

Extensions:

1. Have the children experiment with a free translation tool:
   - ImTranslator
   - Bing Translator
   - PROMPT
   - Babelfish
   - Reverso
   - SDL
   - Free Online Translation
   - ConveyThis
2. Have them translate a picture book for a classmate who speaks another language or translate a story that they have dictated or written.

Picture Book Recommendations

Ajmera, Maya, Victoria Dunning, and Cynthia Pon. 2013. *Healthy Kids*. Watertown, MA: Charlesbridge. **(T, P, K, 1st)**

A global perspective on what children can do to stay safe and healthy. Brilliant photographs from many different countries illustrate each recommended practice. Maya Ajmera has many different Global Fund books on various topics.

Choi, Yangsook. 2003. *The Name Jar*. New York: Dragonfly. **(P, K, 1st, 2nd)**

Unhei has a name that her classmates find difficult to pronounce, so she decides to select a new name for herself. After her real name is discovered, however, her new friends learn how to say it correctly. Have students talk to their families to learn how their names were chosen and discuss these findings with the class.

Crews, Nina. 2011. *The Neighborhood Sing-Along*. New York: HarperCollins. **(P, K, 1st, 2nd)**

This song collection, illustrated with multicultural images, is a great resource for songs to sing together.

Fox, Mem. 2006. *Whoever You Are*. Boston, MA: HMH Books for Young Readers. **(P, K, 1st, 2nd, 3rd)**

This book focuses on the similarities of children around the world despite different appearances and languages.

Katz, Karen. 2006. *Can You Say Peace?* New York: Henry Holt. **(K, 1st, 2nd, 3rd)**

A multicultural book that makes the abstract concept of peace more understandable to young children.

Kerley, Barbara. 2002. *A Cool Drink of Water*. Washington, DC: National Geographic Society. **(T, P, K, 1st, 2nd, 3rd)**

People throughout the world have their thirst quenched in this multicultural book.

Lyne, Alice. 2001. *A My Name Is—*. New York: Scholastic. **(P, K, 1st, 2nd)**

Uses rhymes and letters to introduce children to locations around the world. Have children use the first letter of their names to identify places in the world with the same beginning letter.

Morris, Ann. 2000. *Families*. New York: HarperCollins. **(P, K)**

Photographs from around the world develop the concept of family.

Prap, Lila. 2006. *Animals Speak*. New York: NorthSouth. **(P, K, 1st)**

This book gives the phonetic pronunciation of the sounds that animals make—in forty-one different languages. Young readers struggling to learn a new language may find enjoyment in seeing that even animals may speak in different languages.

| **T** = Toddlers (ages 1–2) |
| **P** = Preschool (ages 3–5) |
| **K** = Kindergarten (ages 5–6) |
| **1st** = First grade (ages 6–7) |
| **2nd** = Second grade (ages 7–8) |
| **3rd** = Third grade (ages 8–9) |

Word Families to Teach Spelling

What Is It?

One way that children can get the most from studying phonics and can improve their spelling is through understanding onsets and rimes, sometimes referred to as *word families*. An *onset* is the letter or letters at the beginning of the word; for example, a teacher might ask what letter would need to be added to *e* to make the word *me*. Then, she would guide the children in forming other words by changing the onset, such as *he, we,* or *she*. This sort of natural clustering helps children to get several instances of basic concepts in phonics.

A *rime* is the pattern at the end of the word—for example, *-in, -et, -op, -un, -oat, -ight, -all, -ope, -eal, -eed, -oice, -ide, -ike, -uck, -oil, -ook, -oon, -ink, -ish,* and so forth. The idea is that if phonics elements are taught directly, children will recognize them when they hear and see them.

Why Is It Important?

It takes a long time for children to learn to quickly match letters with the sounds that they make. Children often figure out new words by relating them to words they already know. Teaching them words that are alike except for the first letter, such as *make, take,* and *rake,* is an efficient way to support this.

How Does It Work?

In his article "Word Building: A Strategic Approach to the Teaching of Phonics" in *The Reading Teacher,* Thomas Gunning explains how to teach onsets and rimes in a five-step process. For example, to teach the *-at* pattern, a teacher would use the following strategy:

- **Build words by adding the onset.** Write *at* on the board, and have several students read it. Ask what letter should be added to *-at* to form the word *sat,* and then show how to form *hat* by adding *h* to *at.* Form the words *mat, fat, rat, cat,* and *that* in the same way. Have the students read all the *-at* words and tell what is the same about all of them. Have the students note that all the words end in the letters *a-t,* which make the sounds heard in *at.* Then have them tell which letter makes the /a/ sound and which letter makes the /t/ or ending sound in *at.*

- **Build words by adding the rime.** Write *s* on the board, and have students tell what sound it stands for. (Saying consonant sounds in isolation distorts them, but it helps students, especially those who are having difficulty detecting individual sounds in words.) Ask the students to tell you what you would add to /s/ to make the word *sat.* After adding *at* to *s,* say the word in parts (/s/ /at/) and then as a whole. Pointing to *s,* say /s/; pointing to *a* and *t,* say /at/. Running your hand under the whole word, say *sat.* Remind them that the *-at* part stays the same and does not need to be sounded out each time.

- **Select another model word.**
- **Provide guided practice.**
- **Apply the onset/rime strategy to a book that features a word family.**

Connections with the Common Core State Standards		
Age	**Category**	**Standard**
Kindergarten	Knowledge of Language	LK.5. With guidance and support from adults, explore word relationships and nuances in word meanings.
First Grade	Phonics and Word Recognition	RF.1.3. Know and apply grade-level phonics and word analysis skills in decoding words.
Second Grade	Phonics and Word Recognition	RF.2.3. Know and apply grade-level phonics and word analysis skills in decoding words.
Third Grade	Phonics and Word Recognition	RF.3.3. Know and apply grade-level phonics and word analysis skills in decoding words.

Leveled Adaptations

Level I: Relying on Actions and Oral Language

1. Read the book *Duck in a Truck* by Jez Alborough.
2. Choose a few volunteers to enact the story with simple props. The truck can be a large box with a chair inside. The four other characters—a duck, sheep, frog, and goat—can be represented with headbands, such as yellow for the duck, white for the sheep, green for the frog, and gray for the goat.
3. As you read the story again and the volunteers act it out, let the children listen for word families, such as -uck (*truck, stuck, yucky,* and *muck*). Help them as needed.

Level II: Relying on Visual Images

1. Give the children small boxes to decorate. Each of these boxes will become a "house" for a word family. The houses can be used as a small-group learning center activity by listing the correct words on the bottom of each box.
2. Begin with two word families that are very different, such as -ack (*back, crack, pack, tack, track, sack,* and *stack*) and -an (*can, fan, man, pan, ran,* and *van*). Create word/picture cards for each word.
3. Have the children listen and decide where each word/picture card should be placed.
4. Add more of these houses for other word families, and practice reading words and sorting them into the correct "house" as a group.

Level III: Beginning to Use Symbols

1. Introduce the concept of forming words using cut-out shapes of cartoon animals or characters.
2. Assign sounds that are the basis for a word family, such as -an, -op, -at, or -ig, to animals or characters. Write the ending on the character cutout.
3. To other characters or animals, assign a letter, such as *p*, that will create a complete word when combined with the word endings. Write the letter on the character cutout.

4. Have the children work with just one word family at a time. Let an animal or character with the first letter crash into a two-letter character, such as *p* crashing into *-ig*. Guide the children in pronouncing the combination: /p/, *-ig, pig*.

5. Continue practicing in this way until you have a word wall of word families.

Extensions:

1. Consonant blends, diagraphs, and endings make the word family activities more challenging. Have children who are more advanced in literacy work with word families that include different endings and beginnings; for example, *-ip* can include *flip, flipping, slipped, whipped,* and so forth.

2. Try a free app called Spell and Listen Cards. Children touch letters to form a word and, if it is spelled correctly, the app says the word and supplies a definition.

Picture Book Recommendations

| T = Toddlers (ages 1–2) |
| P = Preschool (ages 3–5) |
| K = Kindergarten (ages 5–6) |
| 1st = First grade (ages 6–7) |
| 2nd = Second grade (ages 7–8) |
| 3rd = Third grade (ages 8–9) |

Alborough, Jez. 2008. *Duck in the Truck.* La Jolla, CA: Kane/Miller. **(T, P, K, 1st, 2nd)**

This book uses several different word families to tell a humorous story about a duck that gets stuck and is assisted by a sheep, frog, and goat.

Chanke, Pamela. 2002. *The Clock Who Would Not Tock.* New York: Scholastic Teaching Resources. **(K, 1st, 2nd, 3rd)**

This funny story about a clock that cannot tock promotes the development of phonics skills and recognition of word families. Other books in this series include *Spring in the Kingdom of Ying, The Day Mr. Gump Helped Katie Krump,* and *To Sleep, Count Sheep.*

Cox, Phil. 2006. *Frog on a Log.* London, UK: Usborne Books. **(K)**

This book uses word families in the text so that children identify the patterns. When used with a word wall, students can acquire practice seeing and repeating word families.

Cox, Phil. 2006. *Mouse Moves House.* London, UK: Usborne. **(P, K, 1st, 2nd)**

The phonics-based text of this story helps children to assimilate new vocabulary words with familiar, similar-sounding words. Part of a series of ten books including other titles such as *Shark in the Park, Big Pig on a Dig,* and *Sam Sheep Can't Sleep,* these books help to build children's vocabulary through different word families.

Dodds, Dayle Ann. 2003. *Where's Pup?* New York: Dial. **(P, K, 1st)**

A clown searches for a pup throughout the circus in this colorful board book. Each section is a word family of rhyming words; for example, the magician responds, "Don't know./ Go ask Jo./ She's feeding Mo." On the last fold-out page, Pup is perched at the top of a human pyramid in the center of the big top.

Maslen, Bobby Lynn. 2006. *Bob Books: Set 3 Word Families.* New York: Scholastic. **(P, K, 1st, 2nd, 3rd)**

By using the same vowel sounds and adding different consonants, young readers can start to incorporate new words into their vocabulary. This set contains a series of ten books featuring many three-letter words with an introduction to related four- and five-letter words, some containing two syllables.

Open-Ended Questions that Expand Inferential Thinking

What Is It?

Open-ended questions typically begin with *who, what, when, where,* or *why.* There are three basic types of open-ended questions, ranging from literal to abstract:

- **Right-there questions** call on children to think literally and give short answers that could be found right in the story.
- **Inference questions** call on children to read between the lines and fill in information that is not directly stated.
- **Personal connection questions** invite children to relate books to their own lives and experiences.

Why Is It Important?

Open-ended questions expand children's thinking because these questions cannot be answered by a simple yes or no and require children to elaborate on ideas. When children respond to open-ended questions, they need to organize their thoughts, demonstrate understanding, and articulate their ideas. These types of questions are associated with improvements in children's vocabulary, knowledge of print, and narrative abilities.

How Does It Work?

To encourage children to think at the inferential and personal-connection levels, go beyond what is stated in the text of the book or shown in the pictures. As researchers Anne Van Kleeck, Judith Vander Woude, and Lisa Hammett have described, ask the children about such things as attitudes, points of view, feelings, mental states, or motives of characters; similarities and differences between people, objects, or events within the text or between the text and their world knowledge; causes of events that have occurred or predictions of events that might occur; meanings of words; and connections between information given within a text and their world knowledge.

Connections with the Common Core State Standards

Age	Category	Standard
Kindergarten	Key Ideas and Details	RL.K.1. With prompting and support, ask and answer questions about key details in a text.
First Grade	Integration of Knowledge and Ideas Presentation of Knowledge and Ideas	RI.1.7. Use the illustrations and details in a text to describe its key ideas. SL.1.4. Describe people, places, things, and events with relevant details, expressing ideas and feelings clearly.
Second Grade	Comprehension and Collaboration	SL.2.3. Ask and answer questions about what a speaker says in order to clarify comprehension, gather additional information, or deepen understanding of a topic or issue.
Third Grade	Key Ideas and Details	RI.3.2. Determine the main idea of a text; recount the key details and explain how they support the main idea. RI.3.3. Describe the relationship between a series of historical events, scientific ideas or concepts, or steps in technical procedures in a text, using language that pertains to time, sequence, and cause and effect.

Leveled Adaptations

Level I: Relying on Actions and Oral Language

Many children's books are guessing games in which the child has to observe closely and make a guess about what happens next. This gives them practice with making inferences. Try a book such as *What Do You Do with a Tail Like This?* by Steve Jenkins. Point to the images and ask the children to guess which animals have a nose, tail, or ears like that.

Level II: Relying on Visual Images

1. Model the thinking process for children through a think-aloud. A think-aloud is exactly what it sounds like—a person making her thought process accessible to others by giving a play-by-play account of the reasoning taking place. Share a book in which a character solves a problem, such as *The Doorbell Rang* by Pat Hutchins.

2. Ask questions such as, "Can you think of a time when you had a problem and figured out a way to solve it? What was the problem? What ideas did you have about solving it?" If the children seem unsure about how to respond, you might say, "If somebody asked me that question, I would tell them about . . ." Model thinking aloud.

3. Say, "Now you think about a problem that you had. It might help to get your thinking started if you begin with 'I had a problem when . . .' After you get an idea, turn and talk to your partner."

4. You could encourage children's thinking further by prodding, "Please tell me more about that," or "What happened then?"

Level III: Beginning to Use Symbols

1. Stories typically are about a character changing in pursuit of a goal. You can make children more aware of this characteristic of stories with a pattern such as: "Once there was a [insert main character's name] who wanted to [identify the goal], but [describe the problem], so he [explain the actions that were taken to solve the problem, in sequence], and what happened was [describe the story outcome]. The End."

2. Ask the children to think of a story they like and to describe what the character does in the story:
   - Once there was a [insert main character's name]
   - who wanted to [identify the goal],
   - but [describe the problem],
   - so he [explain the actions that were taken to solve the problem, in sequence],
   - and what happened was [describe the story outcome].
   - The End.

3. If a child gets stuck, prompt her with open-ended *who, what, when, where*, or *why* questions.

Extensions:

1. In their article "Using Higher Order Questioning to Accelerate Students' Growth in Reading" in *The Reading Teacher*, Debra Peterson and Barbara Taylor suggest first sharing a book about a person who follows her dreams.

2. Then say, "Describe a time in your life when someone told you that you couldn't do something you really wanted to do. How did you respond? Did you keep working to follow your dream or did you change your goals? Why?"

3. Have the children answer these questions then create original picture books to depict their stories.

Picture Book Recommendations

T = Toddlers (ages 1–2)	
P = Preschool (ages 3–5)	
K = Kindergarten (ages 5–6)	
1st = First grade (ages 6–7)	
2nd = Second grade (ages 7–8)	
3rd = Third grade (ages 8–9)	

Catchpool, Michael. 2012. *The Cloud Spinner*. New York: Knopf. **(K, 1st, 2nd, 3rd)**

> The boy in this story has a unique talent—he can weave cloth from clouds. After the greedy king insists that the boy weave more and more, the sun beats down unrelentingly and causes a drought. It is not until the princess intervenes that the land is saved.

Frazee, Marla. 2012. *Boot and Shoe*. New York: Beach Lane. **(P, K, 1st, 2nd)**

> What do dogs think about? This interesting book shows the inner workings of the brains of two dogs—and their run-in with a squirrel. It is a good choice for talking about motives.

Garton, Sam. 2013. *I Am Otter*. New York: Balzer and Bray. **(P, K, 1st)**

> Some ants inside a log hear a noise and think it must be an anteater. Have children make predictions as you go through the story and provide a rationale for their predictions.

Jenkins, Steve. 2003. *What Do You Do with a Tail Like This?* Boston, MA: Houghton Mifflin Company. **(P, K, 1st)**

> This book has been selected as a Common Core Text Exemplar. Children make predictions as they learn fun facts about animals.

Politi, Leo. 2009. *Song of the Swallows*. Los Angeles, CA: J. Paul Getty Museum. **(2nd, 3rd)**

> This book uses lyrics and music to "La Golondrina," a song about swallows. What makes the book unique is that it takes a child's perspective. Encourage families to talk with older children about the way they see something in comparison to someone else's viewpoint.

Tafuri, Nancy. 2001. *Silly Little Goose!* New York: Scholastic. **(T, P, K)**

> A goose experiments with different possibilities for the placement of her nest. Use this book to get young children thinking about why some of these places would not work well at all.

Tidholm, Anna-Clara. 2009. *Knock! Knock!* San Francisco, CA: Mackenzie Studios. **(T, P, K)**

> What's behind that big door? This book is full of surprises, such as four silly monkeys having a pillow fight. Children will be eager to turn the page and join in after the first time through.

What Is It?

Shared Reading with Predictable Big Books

Predictable books use everyday language, are relevant to children's experiences, and support readers in anticipating what comes next in the text of the book. When used for shared reading with beginning readers, the books have pictures, repetition, rhythm, rhyme, or patterns to support the beginning reader's efforts to make sense out of the text. Shared reading typically relies on using poster-sized "big books" or on images projected on a large screen so that children in a group can see both the text and the illustrations.

Why Is It Important?

Fluent readers have learned to apply their background knowledge of the subject matter and familiarity with different types of texts, such as a friendly letter or an information book, and have learned to make good guesses about what is coming up next in the text. Predictable books have patterned text and controlled vocabulary to make those guesses by less fluent readers more accurate. Predictable books are especially important for children who are learning English.

How Does It Work?

In their book *Perspectives on Shared Reading*, Bobbi Fisher and Emily Medvic offer strategies for using predictable books. Shared reading usually follows a procedure such as the following, which can be accomplished over more than one day:

- Read the book aloud first.
- Read the book again while pointing to each word.
- Have children join in while you read the book.
- Have the children dramatize the story or parts of the story.
- At the next reading, read all but the last word on each page, and have the children supply the word. This helps teach the concept of what a word is.
- At the next reading, arbitrarily leave out certain words and have the students tell you the words.
- Write the story on an overhead, blackboard, or handout so that the children can read it from a different source.
- Point out the concept of letters, words, and phrases as you reread the text with the children. For example, ask, "What is the third letter on this page?" "What is the fourth word on this page?"
- Record the story for use at the listening center.
- Give small groups of children a copy of one page of text from the book and have them create their own illustration for it.
- Guide the children in creating an original group story that follows the same basic pattern as the big book.

Connections with the Common Core State Standards

Age	Category	Standard
Kindergarten	Knowledge of Language	L.K.6. Use words and phrases acquired through conversations, reading and being read to, and responding to texts.
First Grade	Vocabulary Acquisition and Use	L.1.6. Use words and phrases acquired through conversations, reading and being read to, and responding to texts, including using frequently occurring conjunctions to signal simple relationships.
Second Grade	Vocabulary Acquisition and Use Phonics and Word Recognition Fluency	L.2.6. Use words and phrases acquired through conversations, reading and being read to, and responding to texts, including using frequently occurring conjunctions to signal simple relationships. RF.2.3. Know and apply grade-level phonics and word analysis skills in decoding words. RF.2.4. Read with sufficient accuracy and fluency to support comprehension.
Third Grade	Vocabulary Acquisition and Use	L.3.6. Acquire and use accurately grade-appropriate conversational, general academic, and domain-specific words and phrases, including those that signal spatial and temporal relationships.

Leveled Adaptations

Level I: Relying on Actions and Oral Language

1. Begin with a simple, cumulative folksong such as "I Bought Me a Cat." (If you do not know this song, you can find it on YouTube.com. Just type "I Bought Me a Cat musick8" into the search bar.) In this song, each animal makes a silly sound. Sing or listen to the song with a small group of children.
2. Give each child a stick puppet, hand puppet, or toy to represent each animal in the cumulative song. Line them up in the same sequence as the verses of the song.
3. Sing the song again. When each animal is named, have the child holding that animal take one giant step forward and lead the class in making that animal's characteristic sound.

Level II: Relying on Visual Images

1. Teach the children the song "The Green Grass Grows All Around." Find it on YouTube.com by typing the song title into the search bar. Several versions show images for each verse to get across the concept of a cumulative story.
2. *The Napping House* by Audrey Wood uses a similar cumulative approach. You will need a large outline of a house and images that you can pile up on a "cozy bed" as you read the book: a snoring granny, a dreaming child, a dozing dog, a snoozing cat, a slumbering mouse, and a wakeful flea. After the wakeful flea bites, all of the characters wake up, so remove them one at a time.

Level III: Beginning to Use Symbols

1. Joy Cowley has many different predictable books for children, including a series about Mrs. Wishy-Washy. *Mrs. Wishy-Washy's Farm* features a cow, pig, and duck that get dirty and need baths. Practice shared reading of the text.

2. Later, to extend the story and their practice, the children can suggest other animals that get dirty and have to be washed.

3. Use clip art of the animals or have the children create their own versions of the book. Send their books home so that the children can demonstrate progress in learning to read.

Extensions:

1. Read a fun predictable book with the children. A good choice is a version of the song "If You're Happy and You Know It" called *If You're a Monster and You Know It* by Ed Emberley and Rebecca Emberley.

2. Have the children invent their own predictable book to share with other students.

Picture Book Recommendations

Aylesworth, Jim. 2010. *The Mitten.* New York: Scholastic. **(P, K)**

This cumulative folktale in which a series of animals crawls into a lost mitten to find some warmth is reinterpreted through Barbara McClintock's beautiful illustrations.

Beaumont, Karen. 2011. *No Sleep for the Sheep!* Chicago, IL: Harcourt. **(P, K, 1st, 2nd)**

Children's familiarity with the sounds made by farm animals—plus the rhyme and the refrain—will support children's reading of this humorous text.

Church, Caroline. 2002. *Do Your Ears Hang Low?* Somerset, UK: Chicken House. **(T, P, K, 1st)**

The illustrations in this book bring the story of the song to life. Young readers can sing along with the easy-to-learn song and can make connections between the song and the words on the page. The book contains instructions for hand gestures to get readers further involved in the song and story.

Cowley, Joy. 2003. *Mrs. Wishy-Washy's Farm.* New York: Philomel. **(T, P, K)**

Another engaging predictable book about Mrs. Wishy-Washy, who has a New Zealand farm. The main character is obsessed with cleanliness, so the cow, duck, and pig try go to the city to escape her constant scrubbing.

Emberley, Rebecca, and Ed Emberley. 2012. *If You're a Monster and You Know It.* New York: Orchard. **(P, K)**

Children can build on their familiarity with the song "If You're Happy and You Know It" to master this version in which the monsters snort, growl, smack, stomp, twitch, wiggle, and roar.

Fox, Mem. 2012. *Two Little Monkeys.* San Diego, CA: Beach Lane. **(P, K, 1st)**

This suspenseful story about monkeys being pursued by a jaguar uses repetition and rhyme to support emergent readers.

Katz, Karen. 2008. *Ten Tiny Babies.* New York: Simon and Schuster. **(T)**

In this predictable book with rhyming text, one baby takes off running, gathering other babies and doing different activities along the way. Ultimately, all of them settle down for bed.

T = Toddlers (ages 1–2)
P = Preschool (ages 3–5)
K = Kindergarten (ages 5–6)
1st = First grade (ages 6–7)
2nd = Second grade (ages 7–8)
3rd = Third grade (ages 8–9)

Lewison, Wendy. 2004. *Raindrop, Plop!* New York: Viking. **(T, P, K)**

Up to ten and down again, this predictable, rhyming text encourages emergent readers to revisit the text and try to read it.

Litwin, Eric. 2012. *Pete the Cat: Rocking in My School Shoes.* New York: HarperCollins. **(K, 1st, 2nd)**

Part story, part song, this book about a cool cat declares, "It's all good." Teach the children the song before sharing the book so that they can join in. The series includes *Pete the Cat: I Love My White Shoes* and *Pete the Cat and His Four Groovy Buttons.*

Nichols, Grace. 2011. *Whoa, Baby, Whoa!* New York: Bloomsbury USA Children's. **(T)**

A curious and active baby gets into all sorts of mischief until he puts his energy to a better use by learning to walk.

Wood, Audrey. 2009. *The Napping House.* San Diego, CA: Harcourt Children's. **(P, K, 1st, 2nd)**

On a rainy afternoon, people and animals—arranged from largest to smallest—take a snooze. They pile up on the bed, each one resting on the previous napper, until a wakeful flea gets everyone moving again and outside into what is now a sunny day. Children can use clip art to add to the group of nappers, numbered in the correct sequence, and use it to retell the story later.

> **Not all books are available in poster-size formats, and even if they are, they can be expensive. Using technology, such as a document camera or LCD projector, to enlarge the images from a smaller picture book may be the most affordable alternative for generating big books.**

What Is It?

Gestures and Pantomime as Tools for Communication

Gestures and pantomime are nonverbal ways of communicating. Pointing, nodding, and miming an action are highly effective ways of getting ideas, needs, and wants across to others. Using the Google toolbar, type in the words "children charades images," and many different ideas for pantomime will come up.

Why Is It Important?

Gesture plays a very important role in a young child's early communication. In a study of fourteen-month-olds, for example, researchers Meredith Rowe and Susan Goldin-Meadow found that the toddlers produced twenty-five meanings through gesture within a ninety-minute session. For English language learners, pantomimed actions may take on particular importance when no one else in the classroom speaks their language.

How Does It Work?

Because young children are less experienced with words than adults, teachers of young children need to pay particular attention to nonverbal cues from students. When teachers incorporate gestures and pantomime into their talk with children, this more concrete way of communicating makes what they are saying more understandable to a wider group of students. Try the following suggestions:

● Teach the children the head movements associated with *yes* and *no*.

● When giving instructions about how to do something, pantomime some of the actions.

● Have the children demonstrate their understandings through actions; for example, have them stand up if they hear the correct answer or raise their hands when they are confused.

● Get the children involved in dramatizing various safety routines, such as what to do and what not to do on the school bus.

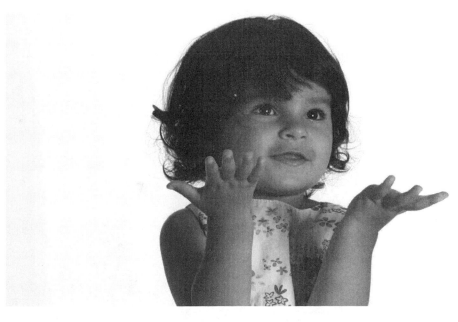

Connections with the Common Core State Standards

Age	Category	Standard
Kindergarten	Range of Reading and Level of Text Complexity	RL.K.10. Actively engage in group reading activities with purpose and understanding.
First Grade	Presentation of Knowledge and Ideas	SL.1.5. Add drawings or other visual displays to descriptions when appropriate to clarify ideas, thoughts, and feelings.
Second Grade	Presentation of Knowledge and Ideas	SL.2.5. Create audio recordings of stories or poems; add drawings or other visual displays to stories or recounts of experiences when appropriate to clarify ideas, thoughts, and feelings.
Third Grade	Integration of Knowledge and Ideas Comprehension and Collaboration	RI.3.7. Use information gained from illustrations, such as maps and photographs, and the words in a text to demonstrate understanding of the text—where, when, why, and how key events occur. SL.3.2. Determine the main ideas and supporting details of a text read aloud or information presented in diverse media and formats, including visually, quantitatively, and orally.

Leveled Adaptations

Level I: Relying on Actions and Oral Language

Use the following pantomime to teach the correct procedure for hand washing:

Washing Hands

by Mary Renck Jalongo

Turn on the water. (Mime turning on the faucet.)

Watch it pour. (Mime peering into the sink.)

Soap and rinse. (Pretend to scrub, then mime turning off faucet.)

Cross the floor. (Walk the fingers of one hand over the palm of the other.)

Get a towel. (Make the gesture of getting a paper towel.)

Dry and pat. (Make a hand-rubbing and patting motion.)

Nice and clean. (Display clean hands with palms forward and fingers outstretched.)

That is that! (Make the gesture of sliding hands together back and forth to show that something is all finished.)

Level II: Relying on Visual Images

Share the following verse with the children, and have them decide what actions to perform to accompany the words.

Snow Day

by Mary Renck Jalongo

It's a snow day—YAY! No school!

Put on mittens made of wool.

Make an angel; lie down flat.

Oops! You dropped your winter hat.

Shape the snow into a ball.

Pile up more to build a wall.

Make a path and ride your sled.

Tie a scarf around your head.

Stack a snowman; make him smile.

Snow day's over; rest a while.

Level III: Beginning to Use Symbols

1. Use the following adaptation of the fingerplay "This is Jack O'Happy" along with pumpkins with different types of faces: happy, sad, silly, and mad. Use clip art to get colorful photographs that accompany each line, or make simple line drawings to illustrate the story. These images will prompt the children to mime the facial expressions on each pumpkin.

Pumpkins

by Mary Renck Jalongo

Pumpkins at the grocery store, on a bright fall day

Come and choose a nice one—carry it away.

Scoop out all the seeds and pulp. Think about Jack's face.

Where will Jack sit when he's done? What will be his place?

This is Jack all happy, and this is Jack all sad.

This is Jack so silly, and this is Jack all mad.

This Jack has a light but no stem or handle.

Here is Jack at night, glowing from his candle.

2. Let the children hold up the pumpkin faces at the appropriate times.

Extensions:

1. Type the words "charades for children" into your browser to view many different types of games and activities.

2. With the children, look through the possibilities and then let them develop a simple charades game for their classmates to play. The Technology Supports for Strategy 42, available online, include many different sources for picture cards and related activities.

Picture Book Recommendations

T = Toddlers (ages 1–2)

P = Preschool (ages 3–5)

K = Kindergarten (ages 5–6)

1st = First grade (ages 6–7)

2nd = Second grade (ages 7–8)

3rd = Third grade (ages 8–9)

Adler, Victoria. 2011. *Baby, Come Away.* New York: Dial. **(T)**

> Baby has an eventful day after resting in a nest with a bird, playing with yarn with a cat, playing catch with a dog, and taking a swim with a fish.

Lee, Suzy. 2010. *Shadow.* San Francisco, CA: Chronicle. **(P, K, 1st, 2nd, 3rd)**

> Shadows suggest different shapes and ideas in this book that separates the real and shadow worlds of a young girl.

London, Jonathan. 2002. *Snuggle Wuggle.* New York: Red Wagon. **(T, P)**

> Who doesn't like hugs? All of the animals in this book give different types of hugs with funny names that get children giggling. Ask preschoolers to invent actions that show each specific type of hug.

Meyers, Susan. 2005. *This Is the Way a Baby Rides.* New York: Abrams. **(T)**

> A baby's ways of moving are influenced by the various animals that he sees while enjoying a picnic with his parents. Combine the book with cue cards for the actions of bouncing, riding, running, jumping, and hiding so that toddlers can participate actively in the story.

Weeks, Sarah. 2006. *Overboard!* New York: Harcourt. **(T)**

> A baby rabbit who loves to drop things—including food off the highchair tray and toys out of the crib—contributes to the fast-paced action and appeal of this book for babies.

Wells, Rosemary. 2006. *Carry Me!* New York: Hyperion. **(T)**

> A baby rabbit eager for interaction with his parents asks to be carried, talked to, and sung to in this book that encourages active participation. Show children gestures they can use for each action in the story, and then have them perform those actions as you reread.

Wild, Margaret. 2009. *Itsy-Bitsy Babies.* Prahan, Australia: Wild Hare. **(T)**

> Although the babies like different things, such as clapping or banging on a drum, all of them like hugs. Toddlers can perform the actions to go along with the babies' different activities.

What Is It?

Comparing is the act of identifying similarities in two or more things; *contrasting* refers to identifying differences. When children apply comparing and contrasting to characters in books, they have both visual and verbal information upon which to base their ideas about the attributes of each character and how they are alike or different. The Picture Book Recommendations list includes lots of examples of picture books in which the two main characters are opposites in many ways.

Book Characters to Compare and Contrast

Why Is It Important?

Analysis is a higher-order thinking skill. When children identify likenesses and differences between two or more things, they are practicing analytical thinking.

How Does It Work?

Characters in children's books are a good way to introduce analysis of what is the same and what is different because they provide concrete, dramatic examples of these concepts. One way to illustrate it is with a Venn diagram. Begin with two large, overlapping circles. What is unique about each character goes in the part that does not overlap; what is similar about the two goes in the overlapping part. The BBC's Learning Zone website (http://www.bbc.co.uk/learningzone/clips) offers a two-minute film clip of a penguin sorting fish to teach a simple lesson on Venn diagrams. To find it, type "Venn diagram" in the search bar.

Connections with the Common Core State Standards

Age	Category	Standard
Kindergarten	Key Ideas and Details	RL.K.3. With prompting and support, identify characters, settings, and major events in a story.
	Key Ideas and Details	RI.K.3. With prompting and support, describe the connection between two individuals, events, ideas, or pieces of information in a text.
First Grade	Key Ideas and Details	RI.1.3. Describe the connection between two individuals, events, ideas, or pieces of information in a text.
	Key Ideas and Details	RL.1.3. Describe characters, settings, and major events in a story, using key details.
	Integration of Knowledge and Ideas	RL.1.9. Compare and contrast the adventures and experiences of characters in stories.
Second Grade	Integration of Knowledge and Ideas	RI.2.9. Compare and contrast the most important points presented by two texts on the same topic.
Third Grade	Integration of Knowledge and Ideas	RL.3.9. Compare and contrast the themes, settings, and plots of stories written by the same author about the same or similar characters, such as in books from a series.

Leveled Adaptations

Level I: Relying on Actions and Oral Language

1. Choose two picture-book versions of a familiar story or song. Good choices for this activity are *Señorita Gordita* by Helen Ketteman, a TexMex variant of *The Gingerbread Boy*, and *The Little Red Pen* by Janet Stevens and Susan Crummel, a version of *The Little Red Hen* in which the main character is a teacher with tons of papers to grade. Read the stories to the children.
2. Guide the children in making a list of what is alike and different between the two.
3. Introduce the Venn diagram. Share the familiar folktale first and then the variant. Lead children in comparing and contrasting by filling in a blank Venn diagram together.

Level II: Relying on Visual Images

1. Read *The Duckling Gets a Cookie!?* by Mo Willems, or view a video of the story on YouTube.com (type the book title into the search bar). In this story, a sweet little duckling asks politely for a cookie and gets one, much to the crabby and constantly complaining Pigeon's consternation.
2. Have the children make a list of some of the duckling's characteristics and the pigeon's characteristics. How are they alike? How are they different? Try making a Venn diagram.

Level III: Beginning to Use Symbols

Make a three-column Plus Minus Equals chart for story characters in any of the books recommended below. In the "Plus" column, answer, "What are the strengths of each book character?" For the "Minus" column, answer, "What are their flaws?" For the "Equals" column, answer, "How does their friendship equal something good?"

Extensions:

1. Watch Pat Pavelka's writing ideas associated with the book *The Jolly Postman and Other People's Letters* by Janet Ahlberg and Allan Ahlberg on YouTube.com. (Type "writing activities by Pat Pavelka" in the search bar.)

2. Have the children compose different types of correspondence from one well-known story character to another. Include letters, email messages, text messages, invitations, greeting cards, and advertisements.

3. Compile their correspondence into a book.

Picture Book Recommendations

Ahlberg, Janet, and Allan Ahlberg. 2001. *The Jolly Postman or Other People's Letters.* Villas, NJ: JB Kids. **(K, 1st, 2nd, 3rd)**

This novelty book has many different examples of written communication, including a party invitation, a postcard, a greeting card, and so forth. The pages of the book are in the format of those types of correspondence—for example, the invitation is a card inside of a page that looks just like an envelope.

DiCamillo, Kate, and Alison McGhee. 2010. *Bink and Gollie.* Somerville, MA: Candlewick. **(1st, 2nd, 3rd)**

An easy reader chapter book about two funny—and very different friends.

Dotlich, Rebecca. 2009. *Bella and Bean.* New York: Atheneum. **(P, K, 1st, 2nd, 3rd)**

Bella is a bookworm type who wants to write poetry; her best friend Bean can't get enough physical activity. Hip-hop and rap poetry in this book with a companion CD show how Bean becomes the inspiration for Bella's poetry.

Kasza, Keiko. 2009. *Ready for Anything!* New York: G. P. Putnam. **(P, K, 1st, 2nd)**

Duck is adventurous and Raccoon is very cautious, but they plan a picnic together, achieve balance, and enjoy the day.

Ketteman, Helen. 2013. *Señorita Gordita.* New York: Albert Whitman. **(P, K, 1st, 2nd)**

In this retelling of *The Gingerbread Man*, Señorita Gordita—a fat little corn cake—escapes from the frying pan and runs through the desert with the refrain, "You'll never catch me!" She also evades other hungry creatures "with a flip, and a skip, and a zip-zoom-zip." Share a version of *The Gingerbread Man* first so that children can use their familiarity with this tale to compare and contrast the two.

Muir, Leslie. 2012. *C. R. Mudgeon.* New York: Atheneum. **(P, K, 1st, 2nd)**

A cranky hedgehog that is very set in his ways meets a free-spirited squirrel in this charming story about how opposites can attract when it comes to friendships. Children will enjoy miming the actions as this book is read aloud.

Stevens, Janet, and Susan Crummel. 2012. *The Little Red Pen.* Chicago, IL: Harcourt. **(P, K, 1st, 2nd)**

Children can use their familiarity with the theme of "The Little Red Hen" to interpret the meaning of this story in which no one wants to pitch in to help a teacher correct piles of homework.

Willems, Mo. 2009. *Elephants Cannot Dance!* New York: Hyperion. **(P, K, 1st, 2nd, 3rd)**

Best friends Gerald and Piggie are opposites, but that does not prevent them from enjoying one another's company.

Yee, Wong Herbert. 2007. *Upstairs Mouse, Downstairs Mole.* HMH Books. **(P, K, 1st)**

Two very different personalities work out their differences in this series about a mouse and a mole that includes many different adventures related to holidays such as Halloween, Valentine's Day, and so forth.

T = Toddlers (ages 1–2)

P = Preschool (ages 3–5)

K = Kindergarten (ages 5–6)

1st = First grade (ages 6–7)

2nd = Second grade (ages 7–8)

3rd = Third grade (ages 8–9)

STRATEGY 44

The Seven Traits of Writing and Multimedia Composing

What Is It?

An approach to writing instruction that has gained momentum in recent years is called "The Seven Traits of Writing" (sometimes called "six traits plus one"). These traits are the universal attributes of highly effective writing that cut across the different genres.

- **Ideas:** the content of the pieces of writing, the heart of the message
- **Organization:** the structure of the piece of writing, how it is put together
- **Voice:** the soul of the piece, the characteristics that make the writer's style individual and that convey thoughts and feelings through words
- **Word Choice:** selecting just the right word, using language that moves and enlightens the reader
- **Sentence Fluency:** the flow of the language, the sound of word pattern, the way the writing plays to the ear not just the eye
- **Conventions:** precision and correctness, the extent to which the writer uses grammar and mechanics appropriately
- **Presentation:** the overall impression created by the work, the ways in which the whole is more than the sum of its parts

Why Is It Important?

Although children in the middle grades are expected to produce writing that reflects the seven traits, younger children can learn to recognize the traits in other people's writing. When children learn something in different modalities, they tend to understand it better.

How Does It Work?

High-quality picture books offer excellent examples of the seven traits of writing. As you share the books that illustrate each trait, discuss that trait with children so that they will incorporate it into their oral and written compositions.

In multimedia composing, children combine writing with visual and aural multimedia in their school projects by using various software programs. The advantage of multimedia is that it results in complex, multilayered compositions that simultaneously support children's growth in drawing and writing. Children can combine widely available technologies and software, such as digital photography or PowerPoint, to construct digital stories and improve their literacy with print.

Connections with the Common Core State Standards

Age	Category	Standard
Kindergarten	Production and Distribution of Writing	W.K.5. With guidance and support from adults, respond to questions and suggestions from peers and add details to strengthen writing as needed.
First Grade	Production and Distribution of Writing	W.1.5. With guidance and support from adults, focus on a topic, respond to questions and suggestions from peers, and add details to strengthen writing as needed.
Second Grade	Production and Distribution of Writing	W.2.5. With guidance and support from adults and peers, focus on a topic and strengthen writing as needed by revising and editing.
Third Grade	Production and Distribution of Writing Range of Writing Knowledge of Language	W.3.5. With guidance and support from peers and adults, develop and strengthen writing as needed by planning, revising, and editing. W.3.10. Write routinely over extended time frames (time for research, reflection, and revision) and shorter time frames (a single sitting or a day or two) for a range of discipline-specific tasks, purposes, and audiences. L.3.3. Use knowledge of language and its conventions when writing, speaking, reading, or listening.

Leveled Adaptations

Level I: Relying on Actions and Oral Language

1. Choose a book that is pleasing to the ear, and read it aloud. Some good classic choices are *17 Kings and 42 Elephants* by Margaret Mahy, *Hairy Maclary from Donaldson's Dairy* by Lynley Dodd, and *Silly Sally* by Audrey Wood.
2. Talk with the children about how and why these books "sound good"—the trait of sentence fluency.

Level II: Relying on Visual Images

1. Use a book that shows how ideas—the heart of the message—are essential in effective writing. A good choice is the Caldecott Honor Book *Extra Yarn* by Mac Barnett. Before you begin, teach children the meaning of several key words in the book, including *extra, yarn, knitting, greedy,* and *curse*.
2. In this story, a young girl who lives in a black-and-white world discovers an endless box of yarn and begins knitting sweaters for everyone and everything. When a greedy archduke travels to buy the box of yarn for himself, Annabelle refuses, so he sends robbers to steal it for him. However, back at his castle, the magic will not work for him, and the box appears to be empty. When he tosses it into the sea (along with a curse that she will never be happy), the box finds its way back to the girl, and she lives happily ever after.
3. Help the children get the gist of this story by paying particular attention to the pictures, because the images show Annabelle pulling the extra yarn box out of the water.
4. Make a chart with the seven traits of effective writing listed. Take dictation as children give examples of each from the book.

Level III: Beginning to Use Symbols

1. Choose a book that has a clear organizational structure. For example, *A Leaf Can Be . . .* by Laura Salas describes in couplets what a leaf can be.

   A leaf can be a . . .

   Shade spiller Mouth filler Tree topper Rain stopper.

2. To share with the children, create a page that follows this structure in couplets. For example:

   A dog can be a . . .

   Ball player Bark sayer Tail wagger Leash dragger.

3. Let the children create couplets of their own.

4. Put all of the pages into a book for the class to read.

Extensions

1. A book that illustrates effective word choice is *The Boss Baby* by Marla Frazee. Before you read the book, introduce some of the key vocabulary and phrases, such as *boss, obvious, immediate, round-the-clock schedule, no time off, conducted meetings, asap, smack dab in the middle, all activity ground to a halt,* and *perqs.*

2. Read the book with the children. They will get the humor of a baby who becomes the focal point of the family. Sophisticated, humorous text shows children the value of choosing just the right word.

Picture Book Recommendations

T = Toddlers (ages 1–2)
P = Preschool (ages 3–5)
K = Kindergarten (ages 5–6)
1st = First grade (ages 6–7)
2nd = Second grade (ages 7–8)
3rd = Third grade (ages 8–9)

Barnett, Mac. 2012. *Extra Yarn.* New York: Balzer and Bray. **(K, 1st, 2nd)**

Annabelle's world is black and white, literally, until she discovers a box of colorful yarn and uses her knitting talent to bring color to everything. All is well until a greedy archduke covets her talents and wants the yarn for himself.

Cooper, Elisha. 2012. *Homer.* New York: Greenwillow. **(P, K, 1st, 2nd)**

Homer, a faithful old dog, watches his humans from a comfortable place on the porch. Use the book to illustrate the writing trait of presentation.

Dodd, Lynley. 1983. *Hairy Maclary from Donaldson's Dairy.* New York: Tricycle Press. **(P, K, 1st)**

A dog and all of his canine pals have a run-in with a grouchy cat in this cumulative, rhyming tale that is great for reading aloud. There are several more books in the series.

Frazee, Marla. 2010. *The Boss Baby.* New York: Simon and Schuster. **(1st, 2nd, 3rd)**

Older children will enjoy the humor of a demanding baby who runs the entire household. This book illustrates effective word choice.

Rotner, Shelley. 2009. *Senses on the Farm.* Millbrook Press. **(T, P, K)**

Stunning photographs describe the farm from the perspective of sensory impressions. Use this book to exemplify the trait of ideas—the heart of the message.

Salas, Laura. 2012. *A Leaf Can Be. . .* New York: Lerner. **(K, 1st, 2nd, 3rd)**

This book about leaves demonstrates effective word choices and writing that is pleasing to the ear.

Seeger, Laura. 2012. *Green.* New York: Roaring Brook. **(P, K, 1st)**

Seeger's celebration of the color green shows many examples in the natural world. Use it to illustrate the trait of organization—the structure of a piece of writing.

Wood, Audrey. 1999. *Silly Sally.* Boston, MA: HMH Books. **(T, P, K, 1st)**

This rollicking rhyme illustrates sentence fluency—how the sounds of language are pleasing to the ear.

What Is It?

Fingerplays and action rhymes are brief stories or songs that are accompanied with hand gestures, such as "The Eency Weency Spider." Today this idea from the past continues to delight and fascinate young children and provide optimum learning opportunities.

Why Is It Important?

Teaching children fingerplays has a long history and, in fact, was part of Friedrich Froebel's first kindergarten. In the book *Fingerplays for Nursery and Kindergarten,* published in 1893, Emilie Poulsson quotes Froebel as saying, "What the child imitates, he begins to understand."

STRATEGY 45

Linking Actions with Words: Fingerplays and Action Rhymes

How Does It Work?

Fingerplays are credited with helping children to develop language skills, follow directions, acquire basic math concepts, focus attention, coordinate with others, and memorize words accompanied by actions. Teachers often use fingerplays to smooth transitions, introduce a theme or unit, teach listening skills, and encourage participation. First, the children learn the fingerplay text or lyrics. Next, the teacher demonstrates the hand gestures that go along with parts of the fingerplay, and the children have a chance to practice. Finally, the children recite or sing the words and perform the actions.

Connections with the Common Core State Standards		
Age	Category	Standard
Kindergarten	Speaking and Listening	SL.K.6. Speak audibly and express thoughts, feelings, and ideas clearly.
First Grade	Range of Reading and Level of Text Complexity	RL.1.10. With prompting and support, read prose and poetry of appropriate complexity for grade.
Second Grade	Speaking and Listening	SL.2.1. Participate in collaborative conversations with diverse partners about second-grade topics and texts with peers and adults in small and larger groups.
Third Grade	Knowledge of Language	L.3.3. Use knowledge of language and its conventions when writing, speaking, reading, or listening.

Leveled Adaptations

Level I: Relying on Actions and Oral Language

Choose some fun fingerplays to teach the children. The Technology Supports for Strategy 45, available online, include many different free videos that demonstrate how to perform various fingerplays. In addition, there are several books that include diagrams of how to do the hand gestures, such as *The Wheels on the Bus and Other Action Rhymes* by Nicola Baxter, or are paired with video, such as *This Little Piggy and Other Rhymes to Sing and Play* by Jane Yolen and *1,000 Fingerplays and Action Rhymes: A Source-book and DVD* by Barbara Scott.

Level II: Relying on Visual Images

1. Use one of the free sources in the Technology Supports for Strategy 45, available online, that has a video of fingerplays. Watch the fingerplay or action rhyme as it is performed.
2. Lead the children in following along.

Level III: Beginning to Use Symbols

1. Create a chart of the words to the fingerplay "Icky Sticky Ooey Gooey Bubble Gum."
2. Teach the children the chant. Hear it and see the hand gestures performed by The Learning Station on YouTube.com. (Type "Icky Sticky Ooey Gooey Bubble Gum Learning Station" into the search bar.) Use the chart and point to each word as it is said.
3. Teach the children the clapping chant "Bubble Gum, Bubble Gum in a Dish."
   Bubble gum, bubble gum, in a dish.
   How many pieces do you wish? (Ask one of the players.)
   Five. (The player can choose any number from one to ten.)
   One, two, three, four, five. (Count to the number chosen, pointing to a different child for each number.)
   And you must go out. (The person you land on is out.)
4. After they know the chant, take them through the text on a chart-sized copy.
5. Combine the chants with the story *Bubble Gum, Bubble Gum* by Lisa Wheeler to carry on with the bubble-gum theme.

Extensions

1. Introduce a chant with a book such as *Rah, Rah, Radishes! A Vegetable Chant* by April Pulley Sayre. Hear it converted into a song on YouTube.com. (Type "Rah Rah Radishes 6" into the search bar.)
2. Older students can invent a cheer for younger children that has hand and body gestures to accompany it.

Picture Book Recommendations

Baxter, Nicola. 2013. *The Wheels on the Bus and Other Action Rhymes*. San Francisco, CA: Armadillo. **(P, K, 1st, 2nd, 3rd)**

This board book has three traditional action rhymes: "The Wheels on the Bus," "'Round and 'Round the Garden," and "Peter Hammers with One Hammer."

Beaton, Clare. 2010. *Clare Beaton's Action Rhymes*. Cambridge, MA: Barefoot. **(T, P, K)**

Illustrations made of stitched fabric collages give a fresh look to familiar rhymes shared with the very young.

McQuinn, Anna. 2009. *If You're Happy and You Know It!* Cambridge, MA: Barefoot Books. **(T, P, K)**

This book suggests lots of new actions to go along with the familiar song.

Orozco, José-Luis, ed. 2002. *Diez Deditos/Ten Little Fingers and Other Play Rhymes and Action Songs from Latin America*. New York: Dutton. **(T, P, K)**

Traditional action rhymes and songs in Spanish are the focus of this book.

Sayre, April Pulley. 2011. *Rah, Rah, Radishes! A Vegetable Chant*. New York: Simon and Schuster. **(P, K, 1st, 2nd)**

The rhythm of this chant encourages children to chime in. Great for converting into a rebus with images of each vegetable—both familiar and less well known—to draw children's attention to print and encourage them to join in the cheerleading.

Scott, Barbara. 2010. *1,000 Fingerplays and Action Rhymes: A Source-book and DVD*. New York: Neal-Schuman. **(T, P, K, 1st, 2nd, 3rd)**

Organized by theme from *apples* to *zoo*, this compendium includes the texts as well as demonstrations of the actions on the DVD.

Stetson, Emily, and Vicky Congdon. 2007. *Little Hands Fingerplays and Action Songs*. Charlotte, VT: Williamson. **(T, P, K)**

This collection includes fingerplays and action songs as well as related art and craft activities.

Wheeler, Lisa. 2004. *Bubble Gum, Bubble Gum*. Boston, MA: Little, Brown. **(T, P, K, 1st)**

A glop of bubble gum on the road gets a sequence of animals—toad, shrew, goose, bee, and crow—stuck. Just in time, they chew their way out of trouble, and a new set of animals is captured by the sticky mess.

Yolen, Jane. 2006. *This Little Piggy and Other Rhymes to Sing and Play*. Somerville, MA: Candlewick. **(T, P, K)**

Lovely illustrations present a large assortment of fingerplays and action songs for the very young. CD included.

T = Toddlers (ages 1–2)
P = Preschool (ages 3–5)
K = Kindergarten (ages 5–6)
1st = First grade (ages 6–7)
2nd = Second grade (ages 7–8)
3rd = Third grade (ages 8–9)

Total Physical Response (TPR) to Assess Understanding

What Is It?

The premise of TPR, as described by James Asher, is that the best way to acquire a second language is to use the same process that was used to acquire the first language. Rather than memorizing lists of words and definitions or conjugating verbs, children first learn words by listening, observing, and imitating.

Why Is It Important?

A combination of visual, auditory, and kinesthetic modes is the best way to reach the largest number of students, including English language learners. To understand the philosophy behind TPR, watch the video from Appleton Bilingual School posted on YouTube.com. (Type "Appleton Bilingual School TPR" into the search bar.)

How Does It Work?

In general, there are seven steps to the process:

1. Introduce the situation in which students will follow a set of instructions, supported by props.
2. Demonstrate the series of actions for the students.
3. Practice the sequence of commands with the whole group.
4. Write the sequence of steps.
5. Do choral reading of the procedure
6. Give the students opportunities to lead the activity.
7. Have small-group practice in which some children are the leaders and some are the followers.

To see a model of how this is done, watch some of the TPR training videos posted on YouTube.com. For example, type "total physical response helbling" into the search bar. It is easy to invent your own picture-action pairs or to compose a simple story from them. Note that the sequence of commands given can be for something that the children are pretending to do, such as assembling a pretend taco, or are really doing, such as learning how to tie a shoe.

Connections with the Common Core State Standards

Age	Category	Standard
Kindergarten	Comprehension and Collaboration	SL.K.2. Confirm understanding of a text read aloud or information presented orally or through other media by asking and answering questions about key details and requesting clarification if something is not understood.
First Grade	Comprehension and Collaboration Key Ideas and Details	SL.1.2. Recount or describe key ideas or details from a text read aloud or information presented orally or through other media. RL.1.1. Ask and answer questions about key details in a text.
Second Grade	Comprehension and Collaboration Comprehension and Collaboration	SL.2.1. Participate in collaborative conversations with diverse partners about second-grade topics and texts with peers and adults in small and larger groups. SL.2.3. Ask and answer questions about what a speaker says in order to clarify comprehension, gather additional information, or deepen understanding of a topic or issue.
Third Grade	Comprehension and Collaboration	SL.3.3. Ask and answer questions about information from a speaker, offering appropriate elaboration and detail.

Leveled Adaptations

Level I: Relying on Actions and Oral Language

1. Play a follow-the-leader type of game. For example, in the game called Clap! Clap! Clap! Nose! children clap three times and then quickly point to the part of their body that is said by the leader.
2. Try a new version of the children's game of Simon Says—the child is not eliminated from the game after making a mistake. To see an explanation, type "Simon Says camp tv" in the search bar on YouTube.com.

Level II: Relying on Visual Images

1. Read *The Fat Cat: A Danish Folktale* by Jack Kent or *Fat Cat: A Danish Folktale* by Margaret MacDonald, which are versions of a story in which a cat devours everyone he meets on the road until a woodcutter's axe helps them to escape.
2. One interesting way of telling the story is to make a large cardboard face for the cat and attach it to a paint stirrer or ruler. Then, pull the stick through a hole cut in the center of an old sheet, and have a child stand underneath it.
3. As you tell the story, other children playing the characters eaten by the cat crawl underneath the sheet, causing the Fat Cat to expand rapidly.
4. When the Woodsman intervenes, the other characters can emerge in reverse order until the Fat Cat is reduced to his original size.
5. As a grand finale, the children can wrap a strip of sheet to represent the bandage around the Fat Cat's "incision."

Level III: Beginning to Use Symbols

1. Show the children the wordless alphabet book *A Long Piece of String,* in which a simple piece of string is rearranged to depict items that correspond to each letter, *A* to *Z.*

2. You can plan a TPR activity that teaches the children names of common shapes such as *circle, triangle, rectangle, oval,* and *diamond.* Provide the children with a length of string, yarn, or ribbon, and have them use it to make the different shapes as you call them out.

Extensions

1. Share a website with sample Total Physical Response stories with the students. A good one to try is http://www.tprstories.com/what-is-tprs.

2. Have them invent a TPR activity for the class or for younger students.

Picture Book Recommendations

T = Toddlers (ages 1–2)

P = Preschool (ages 3–5)

K = Kindergarten (ages 5–6)

1st = First grade (ages 6–7)

2nd = Second grade (ages 7–8)

3rd = Third grade (ages 8–9)

Allen, Kathryn. 2012. *A Kiss Means I Love You.* New York: Whitman. **(T, P, K)**

This book, illustrated with multicultural photographs, matches emotions with their physical expressions, such as hugging, sharing, and so forth. Children can mime the actions as the book is read aloud.

Manning, Maurie. 2012. *Laundry Day.* Boston, MA: Clarion. **(K, 1st, 2nd)**

The main character in this book is a shoeshine boy from the early twentieth century. He locates a piece of red cloth and goes through his multicultural neighborhood trying to find the owner. Lots of physical actions—such as jumping, climbing, and swinging on a clothesline—can be demonstrated as the book is read aloud.

Nelson, Robin. 2014. *How I Clean My Room.* Minneapolis, MN: Twenty-First Century. **(P, K, 1st)**

Children can pretend to do the cleaning around their homes after reading about cleaning their own rooms. Props such as sweepers, buckets, and dust cloths can add to the fun.

Polacco, Patricia. 2005. *Mommies Say Shhh!* New York: Philomel. **(P, K, 1st)**

In this story, the sounds that farm animals make are described in sometimes surprising ways: "Dogs say buff, buff, buff. Sheep say baa, baa, baa. Geese say honk, honk, honk. Bunnies say nothing at all." When all the animals decide to talk at once, a mom who wants her baby to sleep says, "Shhh, shhh, shhh." Have children chime in on the sounds.

Thomas, Jan. 2009. *Can You Make a Scary Face?* San Diego, CA: Beach Lane. **(P, K, 1st, 2nd, 3rd)**

In this interactive book about a ladybug and a frog, children are asked to make facial expressions that show different emotions.

Wondriska, William. 1963. *A Long Piece of String.* San Francisco, CA: Chronicle. **(P, K, 1st, 2nd)**

This wordless book illustrates how a simple piece of string can depict an item that corresponds to each letter of the alphabet.

What Is It?

Picture Books to Teach Words for Daily Routines

Some picture books for young children depict familiar routines. Many of these books are board books with cardboard pages that are easy to turn and have the durability to withstand rough handling by children. These books are matched to the interests of the very young and frequently focus on daily routines; bonds with families, friends, and pets; and all types of mothers and babies and contain bold, distinct pictures with uncluttered backgrounds.

Why Is It Important?

Reading with children is a highly social event, providing an experience that helps to develop children's conversational skills and prepares them for formal reading instruction. According to Maryann Manning, books that describe daily routines build on familiarity to extend children's book awareness, print awareness, vocabulary development, fluency, and comprehension.

How Does It Work?

Books build very young children's sensory awareness as they focus, track, and recognize objects; listen and enjoy the sounds of language; and point to objects and feel the textures. While these books often include the familiar, they also extend children's experiences and imagination, introduce new vocabulary, teach book-handling behaviors and book terminology, demonstrate how books are read and discussed, and show children that enjoyment is part of book sharing.

Connections with the Common Core State Standards

Age	Category	Standard
Kindergarten	Integration of Knowledge and Ideas	RI.K.7. With prompting and support, describe the relationship between illustrations and the text in which they appear, such as what person, place, thing, or idea in the text an illustration depicts.
First Grade	Integration of Knowledge and Ideas Vocabulary Acquisition and Use	RL.1.7. Use illustrations and details in a story to describe its characters, setting, or events. L.1.5. With guidance and support from adults, demonstrate understanding of figurative language, word relationships and nuances in word meanings.
Second Grade	Craft and Structure	RI.2.6. Identify the main purpose of a text, including what the author wants to answer, explain, or describe.
Third Grade	Craft and Structure	RI.3.4. Determine the meaning of general academic and domain-specific words and phrases in a text relevant to a third-grade topic or subject area.

Leveled Adaptations

Level I: Relying on Actions and Oral Language

1. Choose a book that features a child's daily routine, such as *Ollie's School Day: A Yes-and-No Book* by Stephanie Calmenson, which follows a young boy as he gets ready to go to school. Before reading the book, have the children practice saying *yes* and *no* in unison in response to several simple questions.

2. Read the book with the children. The text invites children to participate by asking a series of questions on each page—for example, "What will Ollie wear to school? a bathing suit? a space suit? a police officer's uniform? Will Ollie wear pants, a shirt, socks, and shoes?"

Level II: Relying on Visual Images

1. How does a train spend its time? *Train* by Elisha Cooper shows several different trains as they travel through their daily routines. Read the book with the children.

2. Have the children make simple books with three pages: morning, afternoon, and evening. Then, have them draw pictures of a day in the life of a person, place, or thing.

Level III: Beginning to Use Symbols

1. Watch Neil Sedaka's version of his pop song "Breaking Up Is Hard to Do" for children, "Waking Up Is Hard to Do," on YouTube.com. (Type "Waking Up Is Hard to Do Neil Sedaka" into the search bar.)

2. Create a poster with the lyrics printed on it. You can find them at http://www.metrolyrics.com/waking-up-is-hard-to-do-lyrics-neil-sedaka.html.

3. Have the children make a big book version of the song by illustrating each line.

Extensions

1. If the children are already familiar with their own daily routines, have them investigate the routines of other living things, such as classroom pets or animal companions at home.

2. Let each child choose a pet (real or wished for) and draw and write about what she thinks that animal would need to be safe, healthy, and happy.

3. Work with the librarian to have books about each type of animal and its requirements. Let the children read to learn more about the needs of their chosen pets.

4. After reading the books and locating additional information online, have the children compare what they drew and what the animal actually needs.

5. Have the children generate a calendar of daily, weekly, and annual tasks to make the responsibility for the pet clear.

Picture Book Recommendations

Aliki. 2003. *All by Myself*. New York: HarperCollins. **(P, K)**

What can young children do all by themselves? Ordinary tasks such as buttoning clothes, scrubbing clean, and painting and writing at school are celebrated in this book.

Calmenson, Stephanie. 2012. *Ollie's School Day: A Yes-and-No Book*. New York: Holiday House. **(P, K)**

In this humorous book, children are asked a series of questions as the main character gets ready for school.

Cooke, Trish. 2003. *Full, Full, Full of Love*. Somerville, MA: Candlewick. **(T, K, P)**

What does one African American toddler do all day? He spends time with his loving family!

Cooper, Elisha. 2013. *Train*. New York: Orchard. **(K, 1st, 2nd, 3rd)**

Cooper follows several trains through their daily routines in this exhilarating glimpse of life on the rails. The languid, rolling language works well with the looseness of the watercolors, which offer spectacular views of trains, faraway and close up.

Gal, Susan. 2010. *Night Lights*. New York: Knopf. **(T, P, K)**

A simple text recounts all the different types of lights that a young child encounters while going through the family rituals of getting ready for bed. A lovely, gentle story to reassure children that the dark is not so frightening after all.

Jenkins, Emily. 2013. *Water in the Park: A Book about Water and the Times of the Day*. New York: Schwartz and Wade. **(K, 1st, 2nd)**

A hot day at a city park is brought to life in this appealing picture book. The quiet text creates a satisfying, structured narrative, while the intriguing illustrations offer different views of park places throughout the day.

Lamb, Albert. 2011. *Tell Me the Day Backwards*. Somerville, MA: Candlewick. **(P, K, 1st, 2nd)**

Instead of counting sheep, a little bear and his mom recount everything that he did during the day, in reverse order. Use this idea to revisit the school day backwards by reviewing the schedule from the most recent event back to the start of the school day.

Martin, Bill, Jr., and Michael Sampson. 2012. *Chicka Chicka 1, 2, 3: Lap Edition*. New York: Simon and Schuster. **(T, P)**

This board-book edition of one of Martin's lilting rhyming books is ideal for toddlers just learning to count.

T =	**Toddlers (ages 1–2)**
P =	**Preschool (ages 3–5)**
K =	**Kindergarten (ages 5–6)**
1st =	**First grade (ages 6–7)**
2nd =	**Second grade (ages 7–8)**
3rd =	**Third grade (ages 8–9)**

McPhail, David. 2013. *Ben Loves Bear*. New York: Harry N. Abrams. **(T, P, K)**

    This book follows a child and his teddy bear as they play together from early morning until bedtime, when Ben and Bear get tucked in together and fall asleep.

Sedaka, Neil. 2010. *Waking Up Is Hard to Do*. Watertown, MA: Charlesbridge. **(K, 1st, 2nd)**

    The pop musician's humorous version of his hit song "Breaking Up Is Hard to Do" puts a getting-ready-for-school spin on the tune through this lively book and accompanying CD.

Schwartz, Amy. 2010. *A Glorious Day*. New York: Atheneum. **(P, K)**

    A child's day, from breakfast to bedtime, is depicted in this book. Ordinary things—such as playing with friends, seeing the garbage truck, and counting the steps to the door of his brick building—remind children about their customary behavior.

Watson, Wendy. 2010. *Bedtime Bunnies*. New York: Clarion. **(T, P, K)**

    Even rabbits get ready for bed by brushing their teeth, bathing, listening to a story, and settling down for the night after a bit of romping around. With just four words per page, this book encourages children to identify with the rabbits' nightly ritual.

Yolen, Jane. 2007. *Dimity Duck*. New York: HarperCollins. **(T, P, K)**

    This rhyming story follows a young duckling from the time she wakes up through the time she goes to bed.

What Is It?

Learning centers are areas of the classroom where children can work individually or in a small group to practice skills. Literacy learning centers focus on the four main areas of the language arts: listening, speaking, reading, and writing. They offer extension activities related to children's literature, such as drawing or dramatizing. In addition to providing practice with literacy skills, well-designed literacy centers support learners' independence and build skill in self-monitoring. For lots of learning-center ideas, see Rebecca Isbell's *The Complete Learning Center Book*, revised edition.

Literacy Learning Centers with Self-Correcting Materials

Why Is It Important?

Practice is an important element in acquiring skills; however, if children do not understand and perform a task incorrectly, practice can backfire by making these mistakes more ingrained. Maria Montessori is credited with inventing self-correcting activities for children. The advantage to self-correcting materials is that children can practice a skill correctly and do so individually or while working in small group. Therefore, self-correcting materials are a good choice for learning centers.

How Does It Work?

There are many different ways to construct activities that give children an opportunity to check their own work. To establish productive learning centers, consider these questions, adapted from *Reaching Every Reader* by Pat Miller.

- **Objectives:** What will students accomplish in the centers? How does this correlate with the curriculum, standards, and objectives?
- **Materials:** Will students be using technology? What resources and equipment will they need? When will the materials need to be replenished?
- **Activities:** Do the activities include a variety of media? Can they be done independently or with a partner? Are a variety of learning styles and intelligences included?
- **Differentiation:** How can children at different stages of literacy development succeed at the center? Can it be modified for students who are more advanced, have disabilities, or are learning English?
- **Physical space:** How many centers will there be? Where will the centers be located? How will they be stored when not in use?
- **Management:** How will the activities at each center be introduced to the children? What system will be used to determine which center students use, how many students at each center, and when will they move to a different center? What tracking system will be used to record each student's work at each center? How will students be supervised or get assistance?
- **Evaluation:** How will students know they have successfully completed the activity? Will they be provided self-check answer keys or a rubric? Who will do the evaluation?

Connections with the Common Core State Standards

Age	Category	Standard
Kindergarten	Key Ideas and Details	RL.K.1. With prompting and support, ask and answer questions about key details in a text.
	Key Ideas and Details	RL.K.3. With prompting and support, identify characters, settings, and major events in a story.
First Grade	Key Ideas and Details	RL.1.1. Ask and answer questions about key details in a text.
Second Grade	Comprehension and Collaboration	SL.2.2. Recount or describe key ideas or details from a text read aloud or information presented orally or through other media.
Third Grade	Comprehension and Collaboration	SL.3.1. Engage effectively in a range of collaborative discussions (one-on-one, in groups, and teacher-led) with diverse partners on third-grade topics and texts, building on others' ideas and expressing their own clearly.

Leveled Adaptations

Level I: Relying on Actions and Oral Language

1. Make learning centers on colors. In Center One, ask the children to match a cutout crayon shape in one of the basic colors to the printed word for that color. For ELLs, have the color name in their first language and in English. Matching stickers on the backs of the crayon shapes make the game self-correcting.

2. In Center Two, have the children listen to a story about blending primary colors into secondary colors, such as *Mouse Paint* by Ellen Stoll Walsh or *Color Dance* by Ann Jonas. After hearing the story, the children can fill out a worksheet using crayon colors to represent the words—for example, (red) + (yellow) = ? The child could then fill in the color orange.

3. In Center Three, have the children sort shades of the same basic color, such as royal blue, turquoise blue, pale baby blue, using paint color samples. Use empty plastic canisters and have children place the strip of different shades of paint into the correct container; draw a matching shape on the bottom of the canister and the strip of colors that belongs there so that children can check their answers.

4. The Center Four task is to play a game based on *Dog's Colorful Day* by Emma Dodd. Create pictures of the things that Dog does in the book, along with the colors, on index cards or card stock. Cut the ends of the cards in distinctive shapes to create an interlocking puzzle that, when done correctly, arranges the colors and images into the correct sequence. The pieces will not interlock unless the child has arranged them in the right order.

Level II: Relying on Visual Images

1. Make learning centers that practice small motor skills in preparation for handwriting. In Center One, offer an assortment of puzzles from very simple ones with knobs to more challenging puzzles.

2. At Center Two, children can practice using a pincers grip to move small objects from one container to another. You can provide a commercially available game or let them use a small pair of plastic tongs and small toys.

3. In Center Three, provide lacing cards so that children can use their small motor skills to thread in and out around the outline of a picture or letter.

4. In Center Four, give the children practice tracing letters of the alphabet. They can follow the arrows in the numbered sequence to form some letters of the alphabet. See the Handwriting for Kids site for many printable examples: http://www.handwritingforkids.com/handwrite/manuscript/alphabets.

Level III: Beginning to Use Symbols

1. Make learning centers on different parts of speech. In Center One, provide a simple matching game for nouns using sets of cards with pictures. Print the word in English on one card and the word in Spanish (or the first languages of the children) on a second card. So, for example, if making English/Spanish cards, some noun pairs could be *rice/arroz* and *milk/leche*. Children can work individually, with a partner, or in a small group to spread out all of the cards and find the pairs.

2. Center Two teaches verbs ending in *-ing*, such as *painting, swimming, running*, and *playing*. Write the word in the child's first language and in English. Make another card that shows the action of the verb, using clip art or stick-figure drawings. Put the same sticker on the back of the word card and the matching image card so that the game is self-correcting.

3. Center Three is for adjectives that describe emotions, such as happy, sad, angry, and afraid. The children can read the word cards that have synonyms for each emotion and sort them into one of the four categories. So, for happy, the cards might read *glad, joyful*, and *pleased*. To check their answers, they can look at the emoticon on the back of each word card.

4. At Center Four, the children can match cards with similes to the cards that contain an image of the animal that each simile describes—for example, quiet as a _____ (mouse), as busy as a _____ (bee), as gentle as a _____ (lamb), as free as a _____ (bird), as brave as a _____ (lion), as slow as a _____ (turtle), as quick as a _____ (bunny), and as busy as a _____ (beaver). Using stickers, make the activity self-correcting; the children can look on the back of the card to see that the stickers match.

Extensions

1. Make learning centers on punctuation. In Center One, have the children watch a video on YouTube.com in which animated punctuation marks explain their roles. (Type "punctuation explained by punctuation" in the search bar.) After viewing the video, the children can fill in a task sheet about what each punctuation mark does.

2. In Center Two, offer a game with sentence strips in which the children decide which type of punctuation is required at the end of the sentence. Put the correct answers on the back of each sentence strip.

3. In Center Three, provide paragraphs without punctuation. Let the child decide where to place the commas, periods, exclamation points, and question marks. Provide an answer key.

4. In Center Four, offer grammar games to play on the computer. (See the Technology Supports for Strategy 48, available online, for ideas.)

Picture Book Recommendations

T = Toddlers
(ages 1–2)

P = Preschool
(ages 3–5)

K = Kindergarten
(ages 5–6)

1st = First grade
(ages 6–7)

2nd = Second grade
(ages 7–8)

3rd = Third grade
(ages 8–9)

Barretta, Gene. 2007. *Dear Deer: A Book of Homophones.* New York: Henry Holt. **(1st, 2nd, 3rd)**

This is a challenging book for children because they may recognize the sounds of a word but not realize two words that sound the same can have completely different spellings and meanings. Make a word wall of homophones to introduce the book, and refer to it afterward.

Bruno, Elsa. 2008. *Punctuation Celebration.* New York: Square Fish. **(2nd, 3rd)**

A collection of lively poems about punctuation.

Cleary, Brian. 2008. *A Lime, a Mime, a Pool of Slime: More about Nouns.* Minneapolis, MN: Millbrook. **(1st, 2nd, 3rd)**

Part of a series called Words Are CATegorical, this book defines what a noun is, with many humorous examples, and explains that the first letter of a proper noun is capitalized.

Piven, Hanoch. 2012. *My Dog Is as Smelly as Dirty Socks.* New York: Dragonfly. **(P, K, 1st, 2nd, 3rd)**

This book of similes encourages children to think about comparisons that use *like* or *as* and to invent some of their own.

Pulver, Robin. 2004. *Punctuation Takes a Vacation.* New York: Holiday House. **(K, 1st, 2nd, 3rd)**

The underappreciated punctuation marks go on hiatus, leaving everyone confused about the meaning of what is written.

Rosenthal, Amy. 2013. *Exclamation Mark!* New York: Scholastic. **(K, 1st, 2nd, 3rd)**

The exclamation point is excitable! This book follows him as he explores his purpose in life—and has an encounter with the persistent question mark.

Truss, Lynne. 2006. *Eats, Shoots, and Leaves: Why Commas Really Do Make a Difference!* New York: Putnam. **(2nd, 3rd)**

Part of a series about the importance of punctuation, these humorous books are suitable for older students with some knowledge of punctuation.

What Is It?

Free Voluntary Reading to Build Fluency

Free voluntary reading (FVR) refers to the independent practice children acquire by reading books during their free time. FVR is the foundation of language education as well as the best predictor of comprehension, vocabulary, and reading speed. In addition, FVR exerts a positive influence on writing style, spelling, and grammatical development.

Why Is It Important?

According to researcher Stephen Krashen, the chance of learning a word from a single exposure is between 5 and 20 percent, which means that children need to encounter words repeatedly in order to build a sight vocabulary and become fluent readers. They may actually need to encounter nearly one million words per year to make one thousand new words part of their active vocabularies.

How Does It Work?

To get children to engage in FVR, directly encourage them to read by recommending the right types of reading materials to them, offer opportunities for peers to talk about and recommend books to one another, provide book displays and model the appropriate use of materials, and increase children's access to books that are matched to their reading levels.

Connections with the Common Core State Standards		
Age	**Category**	**Standard**
Kindergarten	Vocabulary Acquisition and Use	L.K.6. Use words and phrases acquired through conversations, reading and being read to, and responding to texts.
First Grade	Vocabulary Acquisition and Use	L.1.6. Use words and phrases acquired through conversations, reading and being read to, and responding to texts, including using frequently occurring conjunctions to signal simple relationships, such as *because*.
Second Grade	Fluency	RF.2.4. Read with sufficient accuracy and fluency to support comprehension.
Third Grade	Fluency	RF.3.4. Read with sufficient accuracy and fluency to support comprehension.

Leveled Adaptations

Level I: Relying on Actions and Oral Language

1. Very young children and those who have few experiences with books need to acquire book-handling behaviors. The best way to teach this is with board books that have cardboard pages because they are easier to manipulate. If you have an aide or parent volunteer, ask them to sit with individual children to teach them the physical skills and basic terminology used when looking at books.
2. Equip each child with a book, and teach them some basic book-related vocabulary, such as *pages, front, back, pictures*, and *words*.
3. Demonstrate how to get the book oriented right-side up and how to move through the book from left to right.

Level II: Relying on Visual Images

To encourage children to look at books carefully, even before they are paying much attention to print, try a book with just a word or a phrase. This will build their confidence. For example, *Kitten for a Day* by Ezra Jack Keats follows a puppy who tries to do everything that some playful kittens do—with humorous results.

Level III: Beginning to Use Symbols

To facilitate free voluntary reading, give children the support of familiarity, such as *Old MacDonald Had a Farm* by Salina Yoon; the Spanish version *"La Granja del Viejo MacDonald,"* available on YouTube.com (type the Spanish title into the search bar); an African version, *Old Mikamba Had a Farm* by Rachel Isadora; or a woodworking spin on the song, *Old MacDonald Had a Woodshop* by Lisa Schulman. Children can rely on their knowledge of the original to help them read the new versions.

Extensions

1. Give older children and those with gifts and talents in language the challenge of writing a story about a school experience. The easy reader *Charlie and Lola: I Completely Know about Guinea Pigs* by Lauren Child is a good example to get them thinking about a story they might write.
2. Afterward, they can experiment with converting the files into digital versions with pages that flip and make a page-turning sound using free page-flipping software.

Picture Book Recommendations

Child, Lauren. 2008. *Charlie and Lola: I Completely Know about Guinea Pigs.* New York: Dial. **(K, 1st, 2nd, 3rd)**

In this easy reader, the duo care for a guinea pig that escapes and surprises them by having babies.

Dodd, Emma. 2010. *I Am Small.* New York: Scholastic. **(T, P, K)**

A little penguin is satisfied to be small and protected by his parents in this simple story that uses repetition.

Emberley, Rebecca. 2009. *There Was an Old Monster!* New York: Orchard. **(P, K, 1st)**

A humorous version of "There Was an Old Lady Who Swallowed a Fly."

Isadora, Rachel. 2013. *Old Mikamba Had a Farm.* New York: Penguin. **(P, K, 1st)**

The children's classic gets new life on the African plain. Children will love the handsome illustrations as they sing EIEIO with baboons and warthogs.

Keats, Ezra Jack. 1974. *Kitten for a Day.* New York: Four Winds. **(T, P, K, 1st)**

A puppy attempts to do everything that a group of kittens does, with humorous results, in this book with very few words and endearing pictures.

Lehrhaupt, Adam. 2013. *Warning: Do Not Open This Book!* New York: Simon and Schuster. **(K, 1st, 2nd)**

This inventive presentation shows the importance of heeding warnings, as mischievous monkeys, toucans, and alligators have fun breaking the rules.

Olson-Brown, Ellen. 2006. *Hush, Little Digger.* New York: Tricycle. **(P, K, 1st, 2nd, 3rd)**

A version of "Hush, Little Baby" with a vehicle theme. Young children can enjoy it as a lullaby while emergent readers can learn the lyrics and read it.

Pinkney, Brian. 2006. *Hush, Little Baby.* New York: Greenwillow. **(T, K, P, 1st, 2nd)**

Lovely illustrations bring this picture book to life. Younger children will enjoy it as a lullaby while older children can learn the lyrics and sing or read it.

Schulman, Lisa. 2002. *Old MacDonald Had a Woodshop.* New York: Putnam. **(P, K, 1st, 2nd)**

In this new twist to the song, Old MacDonald is a sheep who is working with a cat, a goat, a chicken, a pig, a cow, and a dog. They use various tools to construct a miniature toy farm for the baby animals.

Vetter, Jennifer. 2009. *Down by the Station.* New York: Tricycle. **(P, K, 1st)**

A fresh take on the old song about trains introduces different types of transportation.

Yoon, Salina. 2008. *Old MacDonald Had a Farm.* New York: Price Stern Sloan. **(T, P, K)**

Even the youngest readers will enjoy this board book depicting the popular children's song. Colorful images show each animal on the farm, and the accompanying text promotes both letter and word recognition. Young readers can sing along and identify the animals and, eventually, the words.

T = Toddlers (ages 1–2)

P = Preschool (ages 3–5)

K = Kindergarten (ages 5–6)

1st = First grade (ages 6–7)

2nd = Second grade (ages 7–8)

3rd = Third grade (ages 8–9)

Letter-Sound Correspondence to "Crack the Code"

What Is It?

The smallest units of sound in the English language are called phonemes. The ability to discriminate among sounds occurs very early in typically developing children; however, the ability to match phonemes to single letters and letter combinations, such as *-ar, fl-,* and *-ed,* develops more gradually.

Why Is It Important?

In 2005, the National Center for Education Statistics reported that one out of three kindergarten students knows the letter-sound relationships at the beginnings of words, and about one in five knows the letter-sound relationships at the ends of words. Very few kindergartners can read single words or words in sentences. Knowledge of letters and their corresponding sounds during kindergarten is a powerful predictor of later success in reading.

How Does It Work?

Teaching young children letter-sound correspondences follows a sequence. First, children learn the sounds of very distinctive letters, such as *S,* and its characteristic sound. Later, they learn the ending sounds and the vowel sounds in the middle. This can best be illustrated by children's invented spelling. At first, they might write only the letter *N* to mean *not;* later on, it might be *NT,* and later still, the conventional spelling, *not.*

You can lead children through word pronunciation by printing short words that have the most common sounds. For example, the word *me.* Tell the children to watch as you say the *m* sound, then the *e,* and merge them together. Do not draw out the sounds of the letters too much, as this can be confusing. Show how to combine them. As you demonstrate, touch under each letter, and then ask the children to do this with you. After children know the first word, you can teach other words with a similar structure, such as *see, we,* and *bee,* and show how they are pronounced.

Connections with the Common Core State Standards		
Age	**Category**	**Standard**
Kindergarten	Vocabulary Acquisition and Use

Vocabulary Acquisition and Use

Vocabulary Acquisition and Use | L.K.4. Determine or clarify the meaning of unknown and multiple-meaning words and phrases based on kindergarten reading and content.
Identify new meanings for familiar words and apply them accurately, such as knowing *duck* is a bird and learning the verb *to duck*.
Use the most frequently occurring inflections and affixes, such as *-ed, -s, re-, un-, pre-, -ful,* and *-less,* as a clue to the meaning of an unknown word. |
First Grade	Vocabulary Acquisition and Use	L.1.4. Determine or clarify the meaning of unknown and multiple-meaning words and phrases based on first-grade reading and content, choosing flexibly from an array of strategies.
Second Grade	Phonics and Word Recognition	RF.2.3. Know and apply grade-level phonics and word analysis skills in decoding words.
Third Grade	Phonics and Word Recognition	RF.3.3. Know and apply grade-level phonics and word analysis skills in decoding words.

Leveled Adaptations

Level I: Relying on Actions and Oral Language

One way to begin with letter sounds is using the characteristic sounds that animals make. The Raffi song "Down on Grandpa's Farm" includes attempts to make more realistic animal sounds. Teach the children the song, and have them try to match the sounds made by the animals as you hold up an image of each animal. Lyrics and a video are posted at http://www.lyricsnmusic.com/raffi/down-on-grandpa-s-farm-lyrics/3100431.

Level II: Relying on Visual Images

Type the words "images for initial consonants" into your browser to see many, many different activities that combine pictures of objects with the first letter in that word.

Level III: Beginning to Use Symbols

1. The free site Bembo's Zoo http://www.bemboszoo.com links letters of the alphabet to the name of an animal and then transforms the word into that animal.
2. Create a class alphabet book with factual information, such as *The Ocean Alphabet Book* or *The Yucky Reptile Alphabet Book* by Jerry Palotta.

Extensions

Older children and children who are advanced with language can learn consonant blends. The resources listed in the Technology Supports for Strategy 50, available online, have many games to develop these skills.

Picture Book Recommendations

T = Toddlers
(ages 1–2)

P = Preschool
(ages 3–5)

K = Kindergarten
(ages 5–6)

1st = First grade
(ages 6–7)

2nd = Second grade
(ages 7–8)

3rd = Third grade
(ages 8–9)

Dewdney, Anna. 2007. *Llama Llama Mad at Mama.* New York: Viking Juvenile. **(P, K, 1st)**

A shopping excursion results in some whining and a major tantrum from Baby Llama in this rhyming book.

Dodd, Emma. 2003. *Dog's Noisy Day.* New York: Dutton. **(P, K, 1st)**

A dog tries to imitate the characteristic sounds of the different animals that he meets—whether it is a songbird, bees, or a series of barnyard animals. The results are not quite right and will appeal to a preschooler's sense of humor. Finally, dog hears his favorite sound—a spoon touching his food bowl as dinner is prepared.

Franceschelli, Christopher. 2013. *Alphablock.* New York: Harry Abrams. **(T, P, K)**

This chunky board book has pages that are cut out in the shape of the letter. Hints at the animal or thing that begins with that letter invite children to guess at the hidden object.

Hines, Anna. 2001. *Whose Shoes?* New York: Harcourt Brace. **(T, P, K)**

A young girl mouse character tries on the shoes of various family members and asks readers to guess who they might belong to. For example, her mom's red high heels go, "clop, clip, clap" while Dad's work shoes go, "glump, glomp, clomp." Talk with children about words that are used to describe sounds.

Lichtenfeld, Tom, and Ezra Fields-Meyer. 2011. *E-mergency!* San Francisco, CA: Chronicle. **(1st, 2nd, 3rd)**

In this wildly imaginative alphabet book, all of the letters live together in one house. After E falls down the stairs and O replaces her, words get all mixed up. A good choice for older students who are learning the alphabet and letter sounds.

Marzollo, Jean. 2012. *I Spy Letters.* New York: Scholastic. **(P, K)**

This book takes children on an engaging hunt for letters of the alphabet and items that start with each letter located.

Zuckerman, Andrew. 2009. *Creature ABC.* San Francisco, CA: Chronicle. **(P, K, 1st)**

Striking photographs of animals illustrate each of the letter sounds in this book.

What Is It?

Joint Attention and Print Referencing to Support Reading

According to the What Works Clearinghouse report on dialogic reading, there is a particular style of sharing picture books that is the most effective in building literacy. Young children need adults to focus their attention on pictures and print, make story sharing interactive, make explicit references to print, and elaborate on words in the text. These practices are even more powerful for children who have fewer experiences with books.

Why Is It Important?

Reading aloud with young children is one of the most important predictors of success in reading. Reading to young children is linked with literacy development, later achievement in reading, and overall success in school. Reading aloud provides opportunities for children to learn about story schema or structure, ask and answer questions, retell stories, and participate in related activities.

How Does It Work?

Recent research indicates that both verbal and nonverbal means of drawing young children's attention to print exert a positive influence on children's emergent literacy skills. Before and during reading aloud, adults should ask children questions about the book, pose open-ended prompts about what is happening in the pictures, relate the pictures and words to the children's personal experience, and discuss key vocabulary, providing child-friendly definitions.

Patton Tabors advises the following when reading with young children:

- Keep it short.
- Consider small-group book reading.
- Choose books carefully.
- Talk and explain while reading.
- Revisit books.
- Encourage children to "read" to one another after they are familiar with a book.

Connections with the Common Core State Standards

Age	Category	Standard
Kindergarten	Range of Reading and Level of Text Complexity Craft and Structure Integration of Knowledge and Ideas	RL.K.1. Ask and answer questions about key details in a text. RL.K.4. Ask and answer questions about unknown words in a text. RI.K.8. With prompting and support, identify the reasons an author gives to support points in a text.
First Grade	Vocabulary Acquisition and Use	L.1.4. Determine or clarify the meaning of unknown and multiple-meaning words and phrases based on first-grade reading and content, choosing flexibly from an array of strategies.
Second Grade	Phonics and Word Recognition Key Ideas and Details	RF.2.3. Know and apply grade-level phonics and word analysis skills in decoding words. RI.2.1. Ask and answer such questions as who, what, where, when, why, and how to demonstrate understanding of key details in a text.
Third Grade	Phonics and Word Recognition	RF.3.3. Know and apply grade-level phonics and word analysis skills in decoding words.

Leveled Adaptations

Level I: Relying on Actions and Oral Language

Show the demo for the wordless, lift-the-flap book *Flora and the Flamingo* by Molly Idle. Find it on YouTube.com. (Type "Flora and the Flamingo book demo" into the search bar.)
The video will build the children's interest in this story about a bird and a chubby preschool dancer who learn how to dance together by imitating one another's best moves. Children will be fascinated by how the flaps are engineered to build suspense.

Level II: Relying on Visual Images

Use various items—a laser pointer; highlight tape; a "wild and crazy" pointer, such as a rubber glove stuffed with polyester fiber and attached to a stick; a plastic flyswatter with a "window" cut out; or a credit-card sized word magnifier—to point out letters and words to draw children's attention to specific words and features of print. For example, you might say, "This is a story about a bear. Look, his name begins with a *B*. Who else has a name that starts with the letter *B*?"

Level III: Beginning to Use Symbols

1. Ask children how they go about persuading someone else to do something—for example, if they want to get a particular food at the store, want another child to join in their play, or try to convince a caregiver to let them stay up later.
2. Talk about all the reasons that you could give to get a parent to let you have a pet.
3. Watch the video of *The Pigeon Wants a Puppy!* by Mo Willems on YouTube.com. (Type "The Pigeon Wants a Puppy" in the search bar.)

Extensions

1. Cut out three people shapes and draw a t-shirt on each. Write *to* on one t-shirt, *too* on the next, and *two* on the third. For *to*, add an arrow; for *too*, add the word *also*; for *two*, draw twins with the numeral 2 on their shirts. These three sight words are frequently confused.

2. Researcher Tatiana Gordon suggests a story such as the following about a friend, sibling, or pet as practice. Enlarge the print of the story so that the children can see it as it is read. Use a pointer to point to each word. When *to*, *too*, and *two* come up, pause and ask the children which it is—the direction *to*, the *too* that means also, or the *two* that means more than one.

   This is me and this is _____.

   When I go to _____ , _____ goes too.

   That makes two of us.

   When I go to the _____ , _____ goes to the _____ too.

   That makes two of us.

   When I go to sleep, _____ goes to sleep too.

   That makes two of us.

Picture Book Recommendations

Berger, Samantha. 2009. *Martha Doesn't Say Sorry!* Boston, MA: Little, Brown. **(P, K, 1st)**

In this sequel to *Martha Doesn't Share!* a personified otter with a pink dress and headband stubbornly refuses to apologize. She soon learns, however, that being nice is an important part of family life. Discuss Martha's naughty behaviors with the students and role-play an apology.

Cleminson, Katie. 2012. *Otto the Book Bear.* New York: Hyperion. **(P, K)**

Otto resides at the library in the pages of a book, and his favorite thing is to come alive as children read. He gets lost from his family but they are reunited at the public library.

Cooke, Lucy. 2013. *A Little Book of Sloth.* New York: Margaret McElderry. **(1st, 2nd, 3rd)**

Who knew that sloths could be so adorable? This book, illustrated with photographs from a Costa Rican sanctuary, encourages children to focus on print with all of the interesting facts, such as the two types of sloths—three-fingered Bradypus and the two-fingered Choloepus.

Idle, Molly. 2014. *Flora and the Flamingo.* San Francisco, CA: Chronicle. **(P, K, 1st, 2nd)**

In this Caldecott Honor book, a little girl in pink leotards and a pink flamingo learn to coordinate their best dance moves and build a friendship in the process.

Parr, Todd. 2010. *Reading Makes You Feel Good.* Boston, MA: Little, Brown. **(P, K, 1st)**

A colorful, light-hearted look at the advantages of learning to read.

Pinfold, Levi. 2012. *Black Dog.* London, UK: Templar. **(K, 1st, 2nd)**

A huge stray dog appears on the property, and everyone is afraid of it—except a tiny child. The drama and bravery draw children into the story.

Rosenthal, Amy. 2012. *Wumbers.* San Francisco, CA: Chronicle. **(1st, 2nd, 3rd)**

Children familiar with texting will enjoy deciphering these words that use numbers in place of letters; for example, *2na* is for *tuna* and *10nts* is for *tents.* Appreciating this book requires children to look very carefully at print.

| T = Toddlers (ages 1–2) |
| P = Preschool (ages 3–5) |
| K = Kindergarten (ages 5–6) |
| 1st = First grade (ages 6–7) |
| 2nd = Second grade (ages 7–8) |
| 3rd = Third grade (ages 8–9) |

Stewart, Dawn. 2000. *Harriet's Horrible Hair Day*. Atlanta, GA: Peachtree. **(K, 1st, 2nd, 3rd)**

> Determined to get her untamed hair under control, Harriet and her siblings attempt comical remedies that only make matters worse. Have children list the failed solutions on a plot diagram of the story.

Willems, Mo. 2012. *We Are in a Book!* New York: Hyperion. **(K, 1st, 2nd)**

> The zany gray-and-pink duo strikes again. This time, Elephant and Piggie realize that they are the ones being read about, so they decide to put words into the readers' mouths, a feature of the book that draws attention to print.

What Is It?

Intentional Vocabulary Instruction to Increase Comprehension

Teachers who make a deliberate effort to teach vocabulary and expand children's word knowledge exert the most powerful, positive impact on young children's vocabulary learning. Although young children learn about four hundred new words per year, more than four or five new words in one lesson can be overwhelming, particularly for English language learners. It usually takes at least eight to ten encounters with a word before students know it, and even more repetition may be necessary when the word is not in the child's first language, so repetition of the word in various contexts is essential.

Why Is It Important?

It takes multiple exposures to a word for children to store it, understand it, and make it part of their vocabulary. According to researchers Isabel Beck, Margaret McKeown, and Linda Kucan, for every one hundred unfamiliar words met in reading, between five and fifteen of them will be learned. Researchers James Byrnes and Barbara Wasik have found that, to attain the goal of a ten-thousand word vocabulary in six years, the child has to learn an average of two thousand words a year, thirty-eight words per week, and five to six words per day.

How Does It Work?

Research has identified several strategies that help to build young children's vocabularies: selecting important words to teach, providing student-friendly definitions, teaching the word in different contexts, and providing repeated encounters with the word.

Experts emphasize the importance of asking questions in the reading process.

- **Observing, gathering, and organizing data.** Encourage children to look carefully and to describe what they see. They can use observational data to support their ideas and try to organize what they have observed.
- **Comparing and classifying.** Encourage children to look for similarities and differences and to relate new information and ideas to what they already know. Remind children of previous learning that will help them solve the current problem.
- **Summarizing and interpreting.** Encourage children to recap what they know so far and to explain things from their own points of view.
- **Identifying assumptions and suggesting hypotheses.** Ask children to make educated guesses about the assumptions they have made.
- **Imagining and creating.** Encourage children to use visualization or to create mental images that will help them solve the problem.

Connections with the Common Core State Standards

Age	Category	Standard
Kindergarten	Craft and Structure	RL.K.4. Ask and answer questions about unknown words in a text.
First Grade	Key Ideas and Details Key Ideas and Details	RL.1.1. Ask and answer questions about key details in a text. RL.1.4. Identify words and phrases in stories or poems that suggest feelings or appeal to the senses.
Second Grade	Key Ideas and Details	RL.2.1. Ask and answer such questions as who, what, where, when, why, and how to demonstrate understanding of key details in a text.
Third Grade	Key Ideas and Details	RI.3.1. Ask and answer questions to demonstrate understanding of a text, referring explicitly to the text as the basis for the answers.

Leveled Adaptations

Level I: Relying on Actions and Oral Language

1. Use a small video camera or smartphone video camera to record and narrate everyday school activities. Many of these recording devices have a preview feature so that you can see the video instantly and transfer it to the computer.
2. Use these webcam stories to review activities with the children immediately after they happen.
3. After you have modeled how to narrate the film, give children an opportunity to do this.

Level II: Relying on Visual Images

1. Compose and illustrate a humorous step-by-step expository picture book with the class using a book such as Laura Numeroff's *10-Step Guide to Living with Your Monster* as an example.
2. Invent a webcam story to accompany the book.

Level III: Beginning to Use Symbols

Make an "all about" book, such as *How Big Is It? A BIG Book All About BIGness* by Ben Hillman.

Extensions

1. For older students, combine fact and fiction by producing a story that includes both, using *Lady Liberty: A Biography* by Doreen Rappaport as inspiration.
2. In conjunction with a mathematics unit on measurement, create an actual-size book, using *Actual Size* and *Prehistoric Actual Size* by Steve Jenkins as models. Or, use the Magic Schoolbus series that combines science facts with imaginary field trips taken by Mrs. Frizzle's class.

Picture Book Recommendations

Church, Caroline. 2012. *Let's Get Dressed.* New York: Scholastic. **(T, P)**

    This book can be used to teach the names of different articles of clothing and parts of the body.

Clanton, Ben. 2013. *The Table Sets Itself.* London, UK: Walker. **(P, K, 1st, 2nd)**

    This book uses words for eating utensils such as *dish, table, fork, knife,* and so on. Make a matching game with pictures and words for the utensils mentioned in the book.

Coffelt, Nancy. 2009. *Big, Bigger, Biggest!* New York: Henry Holt. **(K, 1st, 2nd)**

    An introduction to the concept of comparison. Use it in conjunction with folktales that feature comparisons, such as "The Three Bears" or "The Three Billy Goats Gruff."

Fleming, Denise. 2011. *Shout! Shout It out!* New York: Henry Holt. **(K, 1st, 2nd)**

    In this engaging interactive book, children are invited to "name that category"—colors, letters, animals, transportation, and so on.

Frasier, Debra. 2007. *Miss Alaineus: A Vocabulary Disaster.* Boston, MA: HMH Books. **(3rd)**

    In this picture book, a child attends school with a cold and misunderstands a vocabulary word, much to her embarrassment. Third-graders will be interested in this glimpse of expectations for vocabulary learning in their futures.

Martin, Bill, Jr. 2011. *Ten Little Caterpillars.* San Diego, CA: Beach Lane. **(T, P, K, 1st)**

    Beautiful illustrations from Lois Ehlert teach children the ordinal numbers (first, second, and so on).

McMullan, Kate. 2012. *I'm Fast!* New York: Balzer and Bray. **(T, P, K)**

    This book about a race between a car and a train uses bright pictures and interesting vocabulary to describe their speed.

Wilson, Karma. 2010. *The Cow Loves Cookies.* New York: Margaret K. McElderry. **(T, P, K, 1st)**

    All of the animals eat what is expected as the farmer makes his rounds. But in a surprise ending to this story told in rhyme, the farmer and the cow enjoy a cookie break together.

Wolff, Ashley. 2009. *When Lucy Goes Out Walking.* New York: Henry Holt. **(T, P, K)**

    A playful black-and-white pup takes a rhyming journey through the seasons and matures into an adult dog as the months pass.

T = Toddlers (ages 1–2)

P = Preschool (ages 3–5)

K = Kindergarten (ages 5–6)

1st = First grade (ages 6–7)

2nd = Second grade (ages 7–8)

3rd = Third grade (ages 8–9)

STRATEGY 53

Easy Readers as Supports in Learning to Read

What Is It?

An easy reader is a controlled vocabulary text; this means that it uses simple language and few words. Easy readers are like bicycles with training wheels; they offer greater control and support to the child who is just learning the task. By building on what the child already knows, using the illustrations to give hints about what the text says, and keeping the vocabulary simple, these books support children in making more accurate guesses about what the book "says." This bolsters children's confidence and competence as readers.

Why Is It Important?

Easy readers, also called controlled vocabulary texts, are intended to build children's confidence so that they are not overwhelmed when attempting to read. By limiting the amount of text, using simple language, and relying on words that are phonetic (can be "sounded out"), easy readers give children the greatest chance to experience success.

How Does It Work?

Common features of easy readers include the following:

- Predictable connections between pictures and print so that struggling readers can search illustrations for answers
- Wide spacing, large print, few words per page, and short sentences that do not discourage the beginner
- Controlled vocabularies that use commonly known high-frequency nouns, verbs, adjectives, and adverbs
- Literal language rather than symbolic language, such as limited use of idioms and metaphors
- Structures that make the text more predictable: question-and-answer, rhyme, days of the week, repetition of phrases

Connections with the Common Core State Standards

Age	Category	Standard
Kindergarten	Vocabulary Acquisition and Use Vocabulary Acquisition and Use	LK.4. Determine or clarify the meaning of unknown and multiple-meaning words and phrases based on kindergarten reading and content. LK.6. Use words and phrases acquired through conversations, reading and being read to, and responding to texts.
First Grade	Vocabulary Acquisition and Use	L.1.4. Determine or clarify the meaning of unknown and multiple-meaning words and phrases based on first-grade reading and content, choosing flexibly from an array of strategies.
Second Grade	Phonics and Word Recognition Fluency	RF.2.3. Know and apply grade-level phonics and word analysis skills in decoding words. RF.2.4. Read with sufficient accuracy and fluency to support comprehension.
Third Grade	Phonics and Word Recognition	RF.3.3. Know and apply grade-level phonics and word analysis skills in decoding words.

Leveled Adaptations

Level I: Relying on Actions and Oral Language

1. *Orange Pear Apple Bear* by Emily Gravett tells a story using just five nouns. See this book read at Toddler Story Time 1, 2, 3 on YouTube.com. (Type "Orange Pear Apple Bear baby toddler story" into the search bar.)
2. Using plastic fruit replicas of each food item and a teddy bear, have the children enact the story.

Level II: Relying on Visual Images

1. Teach the children the folk song "Take Me Riding in Your Car, Car." A version of the song, featuring babies, is available on YouTube.com. (Type "Take Me Ridin' in Your Car waykuy" in the search bar.)
2. Read the book *Woody Guthrie's Riding in My Car.* Another video that is suitable for older children and is based on the picture book and shows the lyrics is available on YouTube. com. (Type "Riding in My Car by Woody Guthrie" in the search bar.)
3. Introduce the book *Brownie and Pearl Go for a Spin* by Cynthia Rylant. Supply a toy car, a doll to represent Brownie, and a stuffed toy cat to represent Pearl. Let the children view a reading of the book on YouTube.com. (Type "Brownie and Pearl Go for a Spin reading level 1 book 6" into the search bar.)

Level III: Beginning to Use Symbols

1. *Good News, Bad News* by Jeff Mack tells the entire story about a picnic using three words. The rest of the story is communicated through the pictures, all of which appear on the inside cover. Teach the children to recognize the words *good, bad,* and *news.*

2. The good/bad pairs are *rain/umbrella*, *apples/worms*, *cake/bees*, and *cave/bear*. Have children recap the story by making picture-word cards for each good and bad thing. Let them arrange the cards in order as you revisit the story.

3. Relate this book to the classic *Fortunately* by Remy Charlip, also rereleased as *What Good Luck! What Bad Luck!* Then, have the children write their own good news/bad news stories.

Extensions

1. Give the children a list of common words, and have them use those words to invent an easy reader for other students.

2. Involve them in illustrating the book and making it into a big-book version so that it can be shared in a small group.

Picture Book Recommendations

T = Toddlers (ages 1–2)	
P = Preschool (ages 3–5)	
K = Kindergarten (ages 5–6)	
1st = First grade (ages 6–7)	
2nd = Second grade (ages 7–8)	
3rd = Third grade (ages 8–9)	

There are a number of easy-reader series available, such as those by Aladdin Paperbacks Ready-to-Read, Bantam/Bank Street Ready-to-Read, HarperCollins: My First I Can Read Series, Harper Trophy I Can Read Books, Puffin Easy-to-Read, Random House Step into Reading, Scholastic Hello Reader, School Zone Start to Read, and The Wright Group.

Beaumont, Karen. 2011. *Where's My T-R-U-C-K?* New York: Dial. **(P, K, 1st)**

In this book suitable for beginning readers, Tommy's truck goes missing, and it looks like the family dog is the culprit.

Butler, John. 2005. *Ten in the Den.* Atlanta, GA: Peachtree. **(T, P, K)**

A variant of the counting rhyme "Ten in the Bed" that invites children to sing along.

Cabrera, Jane. 2005. *Ten in the Bed.* New York: Holiday House. **(T, P, K)**

Large, bright illustrations bring the old counting rhyme to story time.

Dewdney, Anna. 2012. *Llama, Llama Hoppity-Hop.* New York: Penguin. **(T)**

In this rhyming board book that is part of a series about Llama Llama, the activities are clapping, jumping, stretching, and moving.

Gravett, Emily. 2014. *Orange Pear Apple Bear.* New York: Little, Simon. **(T, P, K)**

This very simple book manages to tell a story using just five words: *orange, pear, apple, bear,* and *there*.

Hills, Tad. 2014. *Drop it, Rocket!* New York: Random House. **(P, K, 1st, 2nd)**

The popular spotted dog character goes on a search for new words, including a leaf, a hat, and a star. When he finds a red boot, however, he doesn't want to give it up.

LaRochelle, David. 2013. *Moo!* New York: Walker. **(P, K, 1st)**

Using just the word *moo* to express his excitement, glee, fear, consternation, and embarrassment, a cow has the adventure of a lifetime when he steals the farmer's car.

Mack, Jeff. 2012. *Good News, Bad News.* New York: Scholastic. **(P, K, 1st)**

The only words in the book are *good news* and *bad news* in this story about a picnic. Some good news: umbrella, apples, cake, and cave. Some bad news: rain, worms, bees, and bear.

Parenteau, Shirley. 2007. *One Frog Sang.* Somerville, MA: Candlewick. **(P, K, 1st)**

Frogs make different sounds, counting from one to ten, until a car drives by and disturbs their symphony. After that, it is a countdown from ten to one.

Rylant, Cynthia. 2012. *Brownie and Pearl Go for a Spin*. New York: Beach Lane. **(T, P)**

A simple text follows a girl and her kitten on a big trip to the mailbox at the end of their house's sidewalk.

Spinelli, Eileen. 2003. *Bath Time*. New York: Cavendish. **(T, P, K)**

Toys take up so much space in the tub that there isn't any room for the child in this variation on the theme that there isn't always room for one more.

Wood, Audrey. 2005. *Deep Blue Sea*. New York: Blue Sky. **(T, P, K)**

A cumulative story about the colors and the sea.

Information Books Presented Interactively

What Is It?

Information books present new information; explain how to do something, such as how to plant a vegetable garden; describe real things, such as reptiles; or report on real events, such as Hurricane Katrina. When choosing information books, consider the "Five A's":

- **Authority** of the author
- **Accuracy** of the content
- **Appropriateness** of the book for children
- **Artistry** of the language
- **Artistic** appeal of the book

Why Is It Important?

Teachers of young children tend to read storybooks aloud much more often than expository (information) books. Early childhood teachers are being urged to read information books aloud to children, teaching them new vocabulary, discussing these books with children, and guiding children to understand them. The use of expository texts in the early childhood years helps children to make a more successful transition into the increased use of informational textbooks as they enter third and fourth grades.

How Does It Work?

According to researchers, it is important for teachers to present informational texts interactively, particularly for English language learners, so that children are engaged in the material. Here is a procedure recommended by Peggy Hickman, Sherolyn Pollard-Durodola, and Sharon Vaughn for interactive read-alouds of information books with English language learners:

1. Read through the entire book yourself before sharing it with the children, and segment the book into sections.
2. Introduce the text and three new vocabulary words prior to reading each section.
3. Draw the children's attention to each of the three vocabulary words by supplying a definition, pointing out something in the picture, or dramatizing and pantomiming.
4. Ask three questions: two that require recall and one that is inferential.
5. Reread the section of the text, and emphasize the vocabulary words.
6. Encourage the children to demonstrate their comprehension by recalling elements of the book, connecting with their experiences, or explaining vocabulary in their own words.

Connections with the Common Core State Standards

Age	Category	Standard
Kindergarten	Comprehension and Collaboration Comprehension and Collaboration	SL.K.2. Confirm understanding of a text read aloud or information presented orally or through other media by asking and answering questions about key details and requesting clarification if something is not understood. SL.K.3. Ask and answer questions to seek help, get information, or clarify something that is not understood.
First Grade	Comprehension and Collaboration	SL.1.3. Ask and answer questions about what a speaker says to gather additional information or clarify something that is not understood.
Second Grade	Ideas and Details Comprehension and Collaboration	RI.2.1. Ask and answer such questions as who, what, where, when, why, and how to demonstrate understanding of key details in a text. SL.2.2. Recount or describe key ideas or details from a text read aloud or information presented orally or through other media.
Third Grade	Range of Reading and Level of Text Complexity Comprehension and Collaboration	RI.3.10. By the end of the year, read and comprehend informational texts, including history/social studies, science, and technical texts, at the high end of the second- and third-grades text complexity band independently and proficiently. SL.3.2. Determine the main ideas and supporting details of a text read aloud or information presented in diverse media and formats, including visually, quantitatively, and orally.

Leveled Adaptations

Level I: Relying on Actions and Oral Language

After hearing a true account of someone's personal experience, children can invent spontaneous dialogue, replay the story with a different cast, create the original or a different setting, and evaluate their efforts. Read *Rosa Parks* by Eloise Greenfield or *The Story of Ruby Bridges* by Robert Coles so that children can enact the scenes that affect them most deeply.

Level II: Relying on Visual Images

Read a story together, and then ask questions such as these:

- What do the pictures tell me?
- Are there any special kinds of pictures, such as close-ups, diagrams, or maps, that help me to understand?
- Are there some new words that I didn't know before?
- What kind of pictures are these?
- What kind of book is this?
- How do you know?
- What do you expect to find out in this book?

When sharing information books, define key terms; make comments that show how ideas are interconnected; use words and phrases that point out relationships, such as *because* or *that's why*; recap information periodically, as in "So, the steps in the process are . . ."; and invite the children to explain and retell while using the new vocabulary they have acquired.

Level III: Beginning to Use Symbols

Show the children a pair of books—a storybook and an information book—and then ask questions such as these:

- How are these two books different? Look at size, shape, topic, purpose of text, and purpose of illustrations.
- Do you read an information book like this the same way as a storybook? Why? Why not?
- Can you think of another pair of books—one that is real and the other, pretend?

For preschoolers, compare *Clifford, the Small Red Puppy* by Norman Bridwell and *My Puppy Is Born* by Joanna Cole. For children in the primary grades, try *If Dogs Ruled the World* by Faith McNulty and *Stella Unleashed! Notes from the Doghouse* by Linda Ashman contrasted with *Sled Dogs* by Lori Haskins and *Medical Detective Dogs* by Frances Ruffin.

Extensions

1. Read books such as *Riki's Birdhouse* by Monica Wellington, *How Is a Crayon Made?* by Oz Charles, and *Food Creations: From Hot Dogs to Ice Cream Cones* by Jacqueline Ball to give the children a model of the informational writing style.

2. Let them write a book about how something is made and use digital photos or drawings to illustrate it.

3. Do an author study of a writer with many nonfiction books, such as Aliki, George Ancona, Claire Cherry, Ruth Heller, Margy Burns Knight, Ann Morris, Jim Arnosky, Arthur Dorros, Gail Gibbons, Barbara Brenner, Walter Dean Myers, Anne Rockwell, or Millicent Selsam.

4. There are loads of information-book series, including the Face to Face With series by National Geographic, I Wonder Why by Kingfisher, Touch and Feel and DK Eyewitness by DK Publishing, National Geographic Little Kids First Big Book of, Scholastic Discover More, and Discovery Links Science by Newbridge.

Picture Book Recommendations

Charbonnel-Bojman, Severine. 2012. *My Picture Book of Animals.* Towanda, NY: Firefly. **(T, P)**
   This padded board book is illustrated with photographs of animals doing what comes naturally to them.

Huber, Raymond. 2013. *Flight of the Honey Bee.* Somerville, MA: Candlewick. **(P, K, 1st, 2nd)**
   A day in the life of a honey-bee scout is full of drama, excitement, and danger as it zigzags from flower to flower, spreading pollen all around.

Jenkins, Steve, and Robin Page. 2011. *How to Clean a Hippopotamus.* Boston, MA: Houghton Mifflin. **(K, 1st, 2nd)**
   This fascinating look at the interdependence of various species introduces children to unusual animal partnerships. For teacher reference or older students, there are detailed end notes.

Jenkins, Steve, and Robin Page. 2013. *My First Day.* Boston, MA: Houghton Mifflin. **(P, K, 1st, 2nd)**
   With captivating cut-paper illustrations, this successful author-illustrator team describes in simple language the first day of life for twenty-two different creatures. Children will be surprised to learn that some animals, unlike human beings, are expected to start walking immediately and without adult help.

Kelly, Irene. 2011. *Even an Octopus Needs a Home*. New York: Holiday House. **(K, 1st, 2nd, 3rd)**

A picture book that uses illustrations to invite listeners and readers into various animals' homes and tells them the name of each one's habitat. Link to other books that show how animals live, such as *A Strange Place to Call Home: The World's Most Dangerous Habitats and the Animals That Call Them Home* by Marilyn Singer or *Who Lives in the Snow?* by Jennifer Jones.

McCarthy, Meghan. 2011. *Pop! The Invention of Bubble Gum*. New York: Simon and Schuster. **(2nd, 3rd)**

Chewing gum gets much more interesting when it offers the opportunity to blow bubbles. This book combines cartoon-style drawings with fascinating facts about that childhood favorite—bubble gum.

McElroy, Jean. 2011. *It's Harvest Time!* New York: Simon and Schuster. **(T, P, K)**

A fold-out board book illustrated with photographs that teaches the very young how five fruits and vegetables progress from plants to dinner plates.

Munro, Roxie. 2011. *Hatch!* Tarrytown, NY: Marshall Cavendish. **(K, 1st, 2nd)**

This book invites children to guess what bird produced an egg and gives some clues before the answer is revealed. Additional information about each bird and a glossary are supplied.

Newman, Mark. 2011. *Polar Bears*. New York: Macmillan. **(K, 1st, 2nd)**

This book combines captivating photographs and a clear, accurate text about these beautiful creatures. Additional facts and information about protecting the species are included as well.

Peterson, Cris. 2012. *Seed, Soil, Sun: Earth's Recipe for Food*. Honesdale, PA: Boyds Mills Press. **(K, 1st, 2nd)**

Children learn about a plant's requirements for optimal growth in this interesting book.

Sayre, April Pulley. 2013. *Eat Like a Bear*. New York: Henry Holt. **(P, K, 1st, 2nd, 3rd)**

Strong illustrations portray a hungry grizzly bear as it wakes up in the spring and begins its determined search for food.

Sill, Cathryn. 2011. *About Hummingbirds: A Guide for Children*. Atlanta, GA: Peachtree. **(2nd, 3rd)**

There are many fascinating facts about these tiny, jewel-toned birds that will surprise teachers as well as children.

Trumbore, Cindy. 2013. *Parrots over Puerto Rico*. New York: Lee and Low. **(1st, 2nd, 3rd)**

A story of the rescue and return of the Puerto Rican parrot, a species once so abundant it blotted out the sun.

T = Toddlers (ages 1–2)

P = Preschool (ages 3–5)

K = Kindergarten (ages 5–6)

1st = First grade (ages 6–7)

2nd = Second grade (ages 7–8)

3rd = Third grade (ages 8–9)

Dolch Sight Words to Increase Fluency

What Is It?

The Dolch sight-word list consists of 220 sight words that often are used on spelling lists, flashcards, and various tests of knowledge of the English language. It takes many, many repetitions of these words for them to become part of a sight-word vocabulary, particularly for children with attention deficits or language disorders and delays. Working with the Dolch list over time can support English language learners as they build a larger sight-word vocabulary in their visual memory.

Why Is It Important?

According to Donald Hayes and Margaret Ahrens, a few thousand words account for 90 percent of the spoken vocabulary anyone uses or hears on a regular basis. A highly educated adult has an active listening and speaking vocabulary of about ten thousand words but likely knows nearly ten times as many words in reading and writing, or about a hundred thousand words, according to James Byrnes and Barbara Wasik. Approximately 50–75 percent of the words used in everyday reading are called "sight words" because readers are expected to quickly identify the word and its meaning.

How Does It Work?

When children have many common words stored in their visual memory, they do not have to stop to decipher each word. This ability, referred to as Rapid Automatic Naming (RAN) is essential for reading fluency. There are many different sight-word apps available, such as Ace Writer for the iPad. Children who are advanced in language can master the Dolch sight-word list at a rapid pace as a way to increase their reading fluency.

Connections with the Common Core State Standards		
Age	**Category**	**Standard**
Kindergarten	Vocabulary Acquisition and Use	L.K.6. Use words and phrases acquired through conversations, reading and being read to, and responding to texts.
First Grade	Vocabulary Acquisition and Use	L.1.4. Determine or clarify the meaning of unknown and multiple-meaning words and phrases based on first-grade reading and content, choosing flexibly from an array of strategies.
Second Grade	Fluency	RF.2.4. Read with sufficient accuracy and fluency to support comprehension.
Third Grade	Fluency	RF.3.4. Read with sufficient accuracy and fluency to support comprehension.

Leveled Adaptations

Level I: Relying on Actions and Oral Language

1. Make some reversible signs, such as a paper plate on a stick that has *stop* on one side and *go* on the other or a face with *yes* and *no*.
2. Have the children walk around in a circle when the sign says go, then have them stop.

Level II: Relying on Visual Images

1. Print out illustrated flash cards in Spanish of common words by typing, "Ms. Blanca flash cards" in the search bar on YouTube.com.
2. Teach the children the sentence stem "This is a ____." Place the flash cards in the blank so that children can read different sentences.
3. Have them make their own books that repeat the phrase, "This is a ____."

Level III: Beginning to Use Symbols

Print out the free, illustrated flash cards of common Spanish words at Spanish Kids Stuff http://www.spanishkidstuff.com/flashcards.html to give children practice with words.

Extensions

1. Visit http://www.mrsperkins.com/dolch.htm to download Dolch lists suitable for different grade levels, in different formats, such as Word, pdf, worksheets, and computer software.
2. Make a sight-word Bingo or other games.

Picture Book Recommendations

Bebop Books (http://www.leeandlow.com/p/overview_bebop.mhtml#LeveledLibrary)
    Is a leveled library of books available for purchase that use high-frequency words.

Bob Books (http://bobbooks.com)
    Offers controlled vocabulary books for purchase that give practice with sight words.

I Can Read Series from HarperCollins (http://harpercollinschildrens.com/Kids)
    Has easy readers that are leveled with characters such as Biscuit the puppy, Pete the Cat, and Little Critter.

Keep Kids Reading (http://www.keepkidsreading.net)
    Offers free sight-word books for families.

T = Toddlers (ages 1–2)

P = Preschool (ages 3–5)

K = Kindergarten (ages 5–6)

1st = First grade (ages 6–7)

2nd = Second grade (ages 7–8)

3rd = Third grade (ages 8–9)

STRATEGY 56

Participation Books to Address Low Book Interest

What Is It?

Books with flaps to lift, parts that move, cutouts to peer through, and textures to touch are referred to as participation books, interactive books, or novelty books.

Why Is It Important?

Parents and families sometimes report that their young children are disinterested in picture books and do not want to sit and listen as a book is read aloud. One way of bridging the gap between playing with toys and reading books is to choose picture books that are more interactive. Researchers Joan Kaderavek and Laura Justice found that such books generated longer sentences and more questions from children during in-home readings of storybooks.

How Does It Work?

Books with moving parts can be more appealing to some children than books that are static in nature. The opportunity to manipulate books offers English language learners a chance to label not only the pictures but also their actions while operating the book. In addition, interactive books typically have simple texts and are predictable—with repeated phrases, rhymes, verses, or questions—and this supports children's attempts to make sense out of print.

Connections with the Common Core State Standards

Age	Category	Standard
Kindergarten	Integration of Knowledge and ideas	RI.K.7. With prompting and support, describe the relationship between illustrations and the text in which they appear, such as what person, place, thing, or idea in the text an illustration depicts.
	Integration of Knowledge and Ideas	RI.K.10. Actively engage in group reading activities with purpose and understanding.
First Grade	Integration of Knowledge and Ideas	RI.1.7. Use the illustrations and details in a text to describe its key ideas.
Second Grade	Key Ideas and Details	RL.2.1. Ask and answer such questions as who, what, where, when, why, and how to demonstrate understanding of key details in a text.
	Key Ideas and Details	RL.2.1. Ask and answer such questions as who, what, where, when, why, and how to demonstrate understanding of key details in a text.
	Integration of Knowledge and Ideas	RL.2.7. Use information gained from the illustrations and words in a print or digital text to demonstrate understanding of its characters, setting, or plot.
Third Grade	Key Ideas and Details	RI.3.1. Ask and answer questions to demonstrate understanding of a text, referring explicitly to the text as the basis for the answers.

Leveled Adaptations

Level I: Relying on Actions and Oral Language

1. Use a participation book such as *Tuck Me In!* by Dean Hacohen that invites children to chime in with the story. This book follows the pattern, "Who needs to be tucked in? I do! Good night, baby ____. Who else needs to be tucked in?" The subsequent page is cut to look like a blanket so that turning the page "tucks in" each story character (baby pig, baby zebra, baby elephant).

2. Have the children dramatize the story using toy animals and pieces of fabric. Invite them to add new animals to extend the story.

Level II: Relying on Visual Images

1. In the book *Dear Zoo* by Rod Campbell, a child writes to the zoo to request a pet but sends each animal back for not being suitable. The text follows the pattern "So they sent me a ____. And did you keep him? He was too ____. I sent him back." Read the book with the children.

2. List the animals and the reasons for return: elephant, too big; giraffe, too tall; lion, too fierce; camel, too grumpy; snake, too scary; monkey, too naughty; frog, too jumpy. Finally, the zoo sends a puppy, and he is perfect.

3. Watch the book converted into a song using the tune of "Down by the Bay" on YouTube. com. (Type "Pop-Up Dear Zoo by Catherine Huang" in the search bar.)

Level III: Beginning to Use Symbols

1. Have children practice deciphering print with an electronic book. Hear Frank Leto's echo song "Ladybug, Ladybug" from Montessori Home, and see the lyrics appear as they are sung on YouTube.com. (Type "Frank Leto Ladybug Ladybug song" into the search bar.) This song teaches some different parts of the body in English.

2. After learning the song, have the children make a small ladybug finger puppet to point out each part of their body as it is mentioned.

Extensions

1. Have older children work in small groups to engineer a book with tactile elements. The series of board and cloth participation books by Jellycat, including *If I Were an Owl . . .* by Anne Wilkinson, offer many examples. Another source of inspiration is *Jungly Tails* posted on YouTube.com. (Type "Little Jellycat Jungly Tails soft baby book" into the search bar.)

2. Let the children read their creation with younger students.

Picture Book Recommendations

T = Toddlers (ages 1–2)
P = Preschool (ages 3–5)
K = Kindergarten (ages 5–6)
1st = First grade (ages 6–7)
2nd = Second grade (ages 7–8)
3rd = Third grade (ages 8–9)

Campbell, Rod. 2007. *Dear Zoo: A Lift-the-Flap Book.* New York: Little Simon. **(T, P, K, 1st)**

A child in search of the perfect pet writes to the zoo, and many animals are shipped out and returned to the zoo. Each picture of the shipping crate for the pet can be opened by lifting the flaps. Finally, when a puppy arrives, the search for a pet is successful.

Hacohen, Dean. 2010. *Tuck Me In!* Somerville, MA: Candlewick. **(T, P)**

A series of animals responds to the question, "Who needs to be tucked in at night?" with "I do!" Half pages serve as "blankets" for each baby animal in the story.

Hines, Anna Grossnickle. 2002. *Which Hat Is That?* Boston, MA: Harcourt. **(T, P, K)**

A lift-the-flap book and guessing game that focuses on different types of headwear.

Isadora, Rachel. 2008. *Peekaboo Bedtime.* New York: Putnam. **(T, P)**

A companion book to *Peekaboo Morning,* this book follows the toddler as he plays peekaboo before bed.

Isadora, Rachel. 2002. *Peekaboo Morning.* New York: Putnam. **(T, P)**

An African American toddler plays the traditional game and sees many familiar faces in this book for babies. Introduce the book by covering the page with a cloth and then pulling the cloth off, saying, "Peekaboo!"

Krauss, Ruth. 2005. *Bears.* New York: HarperCollins. **(P, K, 1st)**

First published in 1948, this book depicts bears and all their interesting behaviors. The new edition includes illustrations by Maurice Sendak, and he adds the Max character from *Where the Wild Things Are,* who is searching for his teddy bear.

Merberg, Julie. 2013. *My Favorite Shoes: A Touch-and-Feel Shoe-Stravaganza.* New York: Downtown Bookworks. **(T, P, K)**

This book sparkles (literally) with different types of footwear to touch and admire, from leopard print flats to furry boots.

Sirett, Dawn. 2008. *Animals.* New York: Dorling Kindersley. **(T, P)**

This book offers textured pictures that a baby will want to touch and explore.

Sirett, Dawn. 2013. *Sophie la Girafe: Sophie's Busy Day.* New York: Dorling Kindersley. **(T)**

A touch-and-feel baby book in French and English about a teething toy for a baby.

Van Fleet, Matthew. 2010. *Heads.* New York: Simon and Schuster. **(T, P)**

This pull-the-tab companion to *Tails* includes a bevy of animals, all doing something interesting or comical.

Van Fleet, Matthew. 2003. *Tails.* New York: Simon and Schuster. **(T, P)**

Pull tabs, flaps, and other tactile features let children interact with this delightful book.

Wells, Rosemary. 2009. *Shopping.* New York: Penguin. **(T, P)**

A trip to the grocery store features the popular siblings Ruby and her independent little brother, Max. Throughout this rhyming board book with flaps that lift, Max puts things in the cart that he likes to eat.

Writing Prompts to Increase the Motivation to Write

What Is It?

One effective early writing strategy is to provide children with a structure for producing writing. Some of these writing prompts can be suggested by a picture book with a particular structure, such as *Brown Bear, Brown Bear What Do You See?* by Bill Martin, Jr., and Eric Carle. At other times, teachers can suggest an organizational pattern for the child's work.

Why Is It Important?

In the past, it often was assumed that young children who had not mastered printing the letters of the alphabet and the correct spelling of words were not capable of writing. As a result, time to write often was reserved for children who were particularly advanced or did not occur when children were in the primary grades. We now know that children are capable of communicating using a variety of strategies. The emphasis in early writing instruction should be on conveying meaning through the written word.

How Does It Work?

Young writers need to understand that writing is, first and foremost, a way of communicating thoughts and feelings. Here is a recommended way to make the teaching of writing more interactive.

1. Suggest a structure for the writing such as a picture-book pattern, one of the ones recommended below or one invented by the teacher.

2. Stimulate thinking and prepare to write by asking open-ended questions about what ideas the child has.

3. Decide on a way to record the child's ideas. For example, the child who is not yet writing could work with an aide, a cross-age tutor, or community volunteer to write down her ideas. Technology could be used to record the child's ideas, oral or written. Make sure to put the child's name on the page.

4. Reread for meaning. After the child's entry is written, it needs to be read aloud so that any changes the child wants to make can be incorporated.

5. Share the writing with others. All of the children's work can be compiled into a book for which each child contributed one page. Send the writing to another class at school, put it on the class webpage, post it on the wall in the hallway, make it into an interactive presentation using free software, such as VoiceThread, and invite comments from families, and so forth.

Connections with the Common Core State Standards

Age	Category	Standard
Kindergarten	Production and Distribution of Writing	W.K.5. With guidance and support from adults, respond to questions and suggestions from peers and add details to strengthen writing as needed.
First Grade	Production and Distribution of Writing	W.1.5. With guidance and support from adults, focus on a topic, respond to questions and suggestions from peers, and add details to strengthen writing as needed.
Second Grade	Production and Distribution of Writing	W.2.5. With guidance and support from adults and peers, focus on a topic and strengthen writing as needed by revising and editing.
Third Grade	Production and Distribution of Writing Production and Distribution of Writing	W.3.5. With guidance and support from peers and adults, develop and strengthen writing as needed by planning, revising, and editing. W.3.6. With guidance and support from adults, use technology to produce and publish writing (using keyboarding skills) as well as to interact and collaborate with others.

Leveled Adaptations

Level I: Relying on Actions and Oral Language

1. Use a picture book about pets, or print images of many common pets from online. Books about unusual pets, such as a penguin in *One Cool Friend* by Toni Buzzeo and a sloth in *Sparky!* by Jenny Offill, will stimulate children's thinking.
2. List the animals on the whiteboard or a piece of chart paper. Include a category of "Other" for unusual pets.
3. Conduct a quick survey with the class. If a child has a particular pet, put his initials next to each type of pet he actually owns.
4. Tally the results to see which pet is most popular in the class.
5. Talk about "wished for" pets. Have each child draw, dictate, or write their ideas in response to the following writing prompt:

   My dream pet is _____. My dream pet likes _____. My dream pet needs _____. My dream pet would _____.

Level II: Relying on Visual Images

1. When cold and flu season hits, read the book or watch the video of *Bear Feels Sick* by Karma Wilson. (On YouTube.com, type "Bear Feels Sick mp4" into the search bar.)
2. Make a list of Bear's symptoms. How can he tell that he is getting sick? Then, make a list of all the things Bear's friends do to take care of him when he's sick.
3. Relate this book to the humorous book *How Do Dinosaurs Get Well Soon?* by Jane Yolen, and have the children draw examples of things to do (and not to do) to feel better.

Level III: Beginning to Use Symbols

In her book *Teaching Young Children a Second Language*, Tatiana Gordon suggests the following structure for student writing:

If I were _____ , I would live in _____.

If I were _____ , I would eat _____.

If I were _____ , I would sleep in _____.

If I were _____ , my pet would be _____.

If I were _____ , I would travel to _____.

Extensions

1. Use the structure from Margaret Wise Brown's classic *The Important Book* to generate original writing. One example follows:

   The most important thing about grass is that it is green.

   It grows and is tender with a sweet, grassy smell.

   But the important thing about grass is that it is green.

2. Children can follow the pattern:

   The important thing about _____ is that _____.

   It _____ and is _____.

   With _____

   And _____

   But the important thing about _____ is that _____.

Picture Book Recommendations

T = Toddlers (ages 1–2)
P = Preschool (ages 3–5)
K = Kindergarten (ages 5–6)
1st = First grade (ages 6–7)
2nd = Second grade (ages 7–8)
3rd = Third grade (ages 8–9)

Auch, Mary Jane. 2008. *The Plot Chickens*. New York: Holiday House. **(K, 1st, 2nd, 3rd)**

A group of fowl model the writing process in this humorous book. Have children make a sequence chart that corresponds to the steps the chickens follow.

Llanas, Sheila. 2011. *Picture Yourself Writing Fiction: Using Photos to Inspire Writing*. Bloomington, MN: Capstone. **(3rd)**

Photographs can be a powerful tool for inspiring children's original writing. This book encourages children to use photos as the basis for their written compositions.

Menchin, Scott. 2007. *Taking a Bath with the Dog and Other Things that Make Me Happy*. Somerville, MA: Candlewick. **(T, P, K)**

Sweet Pea starts out grumpy, but her mood begins to brighten as she catalogues twenty things that make her happy. Readers can use the illustrations to help them recall the text on each page and then write or draw their own books about what makes them happy.

Portis, Antoinette. 2010. *Kindergarten Diary*. New York: HarperCollins. **(P, K, 1st)**

A child who enjoyed preschool and was reluctant to go to kindergarten is now settled in and describes what happens over the course of a month. A good introduction to keeping a journal in kindergarten and thinking about what comes next—first grade!

Ray, Deborah. 2008. *Wanda Gág: The Girl Who Lived to Draw*. New York: Viking. **(1st, 2nd, 3rd)**

This is the true story of the author of the first true picture book, *Millions of Cats*, and how she used her talents to support her five siblings. Link this book with other picture-book author or illustrator biographies, such as *A Caldecott Celebration: Seven Artists and Their Paths to the Caldecott Medal* by Leonard Marcus and *Ashley Bryan: Words to My Life's Song* by Ashley Bryan.

Watt, Melanie. 2010. *Chester's Masterpiece.* Toronto, Canada: Kids Can Press. **(P, K, 1st, 2nd)**

In this book from the series about a calico cat named Chester, he challenges his owner's role as an illustrator and author by hiding all of her tools in his litter box. The owner tries to communicate with Chester via post-it notes about genre, setting, plot, heroes, and ending, but he is determined to do things his own way.

Wilson, Karma. 2007. *Bear Feels Sick.* NY: Margaret K. McElderry. **(P, K, 1st)**

Bear's sneezing and sniffling will be something that children have experienced. Invite the children to chime in on the refrain of "Bear feels sick." Afterward, children can create a "word splash" of vocabulary that describes how they feel when they are sick.

Yolen, Jane. 2010. *How Do Dinosaurs Get Well Soon?* New York: Scholastic. **(P, K, 1st)**

When dinosaurs get sick, everything that could go wrong is super-sized. Fortunately, they learn to go along with the program and are restored to health.

STRATEGY 58

Using Children's Interests to Increase Motivation to Read

What Is It?

Interests are enduring attractions to topics, experiences, and activities. Researcher Brian Cambourne has found that learners are apt to become fully engaged in a task when they are free from anxiety and are being taught by a person whom they respect, admire, trust, and would like to emulate; believe they are capable of learning or doing whatever is being demonstrated; and see the value of and purposes for the learning.

Why Is It Important?

Research indicates that the acquisition of reading skills and motivation to read are interrelated. However, when children feel they are not "good at" reading, they may find ways to avoid reading or simply refuse to read. One powerful way to invite them into reading is to match literacy materials to their interests. Particularly for young English language learners, a book that they can identify with enables them to see themselves in literacy activities and become more fully engaged.

How Does It Work?

When learners are interested in something, they will focus better and will persist at a challenging task for a longer period of time. It is also possible to build situational interest. This occurs when a child does not have a preexisting interest in something, but the task that the teacher designs is so engaging that the child becomes interested.

Connections with the Common Core State Standards

Age	Category	Standard
Kindergarten	Range of Reading and Level of Text Complexity Research to Build and Present Knowledge	RL.K.10. Actively engage in group reading activities with purpose and understanding. W.K.8. With guidance and support from adults, recall information from experiences or gather information from provided sources to answer a question.
First Grade	Comprehension and Collaboration	SL.1.1. Participate in collaborative conversations with diverse partners about first-grade topics and texts with peers and adults in small and larger groups.
Second Grade	Presentation of Knowledge and Ideas	SL.2.4. Tell a story or recount an experience with appropriate facts and relevant, descriptive details, speaking audibly in coherent sentences.
Third Grade	Comprehension and Collaboration	SL.3.1. Engage effectively in a range of collaborative discussions (one-on-one, in groups, and teacher-led) with diverse partners on third-grade topics and texts, building on others' ideas and expressing their own clearly.

Leveled Adaptations

Level I: Relying on Actions and Oral Language

1. Most children are attracted to animals, particularly baby ones. Show the children pictures of baby animals, and have each child select a favorite.
2. Gather the children and have them take turns saying what they like about their favorite animals. Show the photo of each animal as the child describes it.

Level II: Relying on Visual Images

1. Watch the video "Pattern Practice: What Do You Like to Do?" by ELF Kids Videos, published in January 2014 on YouTube.com. (Type "Pattern Practice What Do You Like to Do" into the search bar.) Have the children practice reading the answers.
2. Have the children watch the more advanced "Pattern Practice: What Do You Like to Do?" ELF Kids video published February 2014 on YouTube.com.
3. Let the children create their own slide show of things that they like to do.

Level III: Beginning to Use Symbols

1. Teach the children the song "¡Colores, Colores!" in Spanish about favorite colors. The song illustrates all of the lyrics and gives a reason for liking a particular color. Find it on YouTube.com by typing "colors colors colores colores" into the search bar.
2. Have the children conduct a simple survey with the other students about their interests. A simple survey could include favorite color, toy, TV show, song, food, play or game, place to visit, and so forth. Ask an aide, parent volunteer or cross-age tutor to compile the results.

Extensions

1. Share a book that chronicles history on a topic of interest to children, such as *Chavela and the Magic Bubble* by Monica Brown that tells the story of chewing gum or *chicle* or *From Rags to Riches: A History of Girls' Clothing in America* by Leslie Sills.

2. Have the children choose a topic, locate interesting facts about it, and make it into an original book.

Picture Book Recommendations

T = Toddlers (ages 1–2)

P = Preschool (ages 3–5)

K = Kindergarten (ages 5–6)

1st = First grade (ages 6–7)

2nd = Second grade (ages 7–8)

3rd = Third grade (ages 8–9)

Beaumont, Karen. 2011. *Shoe-La-La!* New York: Scholastic. **(P, K, 1st)**

On a quest for the perfect party shoes, four girls shop until the salesman drops, but they don't buy anything. Instead, they go home and decorate their own shoes, inspired by all of the ones that they tried on.

Brown, Monica. 2010. *Chavela and the Magic Bubble.* New York: Clarion. **(1st, 2nd, 3rd)**

A young girl, whose father worked to harvest *chicle* in Mexico before coming to the United States, loves chewing gum. One day she gets magic *chicle*, blows a bubble, and takes off on a journey into the rain forest where her family once lived.

Buzzeo, Toni. 2012. *One Cool Friend.* New York: Dial. **(P, K, 1st, 2nd)**

The appeal of having a very unusual pet is brought to life here when Elliot brings a penguin home after a visit to the aquarium. Introduce the book by asking children to name their favorite animals and the ones they have—or dream of having—as pets.

DaCosta, Barbara. 2012. *Nighttime Ninja.* Boston, MA: Little, Brown. **(P, K, 1st)**

A young boy stalks through the house at night, pretending to be a ninja as he attempts to raid the refrigerator.

Dempsey, Kristy. 2011. *Mini Racer.* London, UK: Bloomsbury. **(P, K, 1st)**

The competitors in this book each have a distinctive vehicle, such as the rabbit's carrot-car. As they race along to the finish line, racers use their special skills to get ahead. Children who love things that go will enjoy this fast-paced fun.

Eversole, Robyn. 2012. *East Dragon, West Dragon.* New York: Atheneum. **(P, K, 1st, 2nd)**

Two dragons live in different parts of the world where they are regarded very differently. In the East, the dragon is admired and lives in splendor. In the West, the dragon is feared and lives in a cave. Nevertheless, the two become friends, help one another, and celebrate their success.

Isadora, Rachel. 2012. *Bea at Ballet.* New York: Penguin. **(T, P, K)**

Many young children enroll in dance classes; this book shows toddlers learning the basics of ballet.

Light, Steve. 2012. *Trains Go.* San Francisco, CA: Chronicle. **(T, P, K)**

Bold watercolor images on the two-page spreads of this board book introduce seven different types of trains and the sounds that each one makes. A good way to extend children's interest in Thomas the Tank Engine.

Lord, Cynthia. 2010. *Hot Rod Hamster.* New York: Scholastic. **(K, 1st)**

An ingenious hamster not only builds a race car but also takes on bigger opponents in the race in this fast-paced, rhyming text. See also the sequel, *Happy Birthday, Hamster,* in which the choice of birthday cake is the main event.

Ransom, Candice. 2011. *Big Rigs on the Move*. New York: Lerner. **(T, P, K)**

A simple text and photographs give a realistic look at things that go.

Redeker, Kent. 2012. *Don't Squish the Sasquatch!* New York: Hyperion. **(P, K, 1st)**

A procession of hybrid creatures, such as Mr. Octo-Rhino, board a bus along with Señor Sasquatch, who can't bear to be cramped. Finally, Señor Sasquatch passes out, and the other passengers pitch in to revive him. Entertaining fun as children imagine other not-so-scary monsters.

Salas, Laura. 2011. *Book Speak! Poems about Books*. New York: Clarion. **(1st, 2nd, 3rd)**

This lively collection is focused on literacy topics and is well suited for the primary grades.

Schertle, Alice. 2009. *Little Blue Truck*. Boston, MA: HMH Books. **(T, P, K)**

A pickup truck gets stuck in the mud and receives help from several different farm animals. Lots of action and sounds will invite children to talk about this book.

Schoenherr, Ian. 2010. *Don't Spill the Beans!* New York: Greenwillow. **(P, K, 1st)**

Bear won't tell his secret to the listeners and readers, but he tells all his animal friends as he carries a set of cards and a wrapped box behind his back. The surprise is a big happy birthday message for the reader, so sharing the book with the class on a child's birthday is ideal.

Wheeler, Lisa. 2011. *Dino-Baseball*. Minneapolis, MN: Carolrhoda. **(P, K, 1st, 2nd)**

Two of children's enduring interests—dinosaurs and baseball—are combined in this book.

Autobiographical Memory Supported with Voki

What Is It?

Autobiographical memory (AM) refers to one's personal recollections of life. Children and adults recall events from their personal pasts and use them to construct the stories of their lives. Increasingly, AM is being studied through neuroimaging technology.

Voki is a free, web-based character-speaking program that can be accessed on the Internet at http://www.voki.com. Voki can be used to create personalized characters that can speak using the child's voice. The finished Voki can be emailed, uploaded, or embedded in a variety of web-based applications. When children compose autobiographical stories and add pictures, this material is easier for them to read because the ideas are familiar and they are the authors.

Why Is It Important?

Family stories about personally significant experiences shape a child's sense of self. Children may ask to hear these stories over and over again about the day that they were born, a time when they got lost, or a favorite family activity. Such memories become part of their life history or autobiography.

How Does It Work?

Young children develop autobiographical memory through discussing events that have meaning for them and their cultures. Research suggests that autobiographical memory is highly individual, built over time, modified with additional experience, and solidified by discussion with others—particularly family members—through telling and retelling life stories. Researcher Katherine Nelson asserts that when there is no one with whom to share family stories, autobiographical memory does not develop fully because children's recollections are not reinforced.

Connections with the Common Core State Standards		
Age	**Category**	**Standard**
Kindergarten	Presentation of Knowledge and Ideas	W.K.3. Use a combination of drawing, dictating, and writing to narrate a single event or several loosely linked events, tell about the events in the order in which they occurred, and provide a reaction to what happened.
First Grade	Presentation of Knowledge and Ideas	SL.1.4. Describe people, places, things, and events with relevant details, expressing ideas and feelings clearly.
Second Grade	Presentation of Knowledge and Ideas Presentation of Knowledge and Ideas	SL.2.4. Tell a story or recount an experience with appropriate facts and relevant, descriptive details, speaking audibly in coherent sentences. SL.2.5. Create audio recordings of stories or poems; add drawings or other visual displays to stories or recounts of experiences when appropriate to clarify ideas, thoughts, and feelings.
Third Grade	Text Types and Purposes	W.3.3. Write narratives to develop real or imagined experiences or events using effective technique, descriptive details, and clear event sequences.

Leveled Adaptations

Level I: Relying on Actions and Oral Language

Children can create an avatar—an imaginary character—with characteristics similar to their own and can record their own voices making some statements about themselves. Use a simple format such as the following: My name is _____. I am a (boy, girl). I am _____ years old. There are _____ people in my family. My favorite color is _____. My favorite food is _____. My favorite animal is _____. I like to _____. Something that is good about me is that I _____.

Level II: Relying on Visual Images

1. Begin by teaching children the song "I Love My Shirt" by Donovan. You can find it on YouTube.com. (Type "Donovan Smothers Brothers I Love My Shirt" in the search bar.) Create a song chart of the words.
2. Ask the children to talk about a favorite article of clothing. The book *I Had a Favorite Dress* by Boni Ashburn illustrates this concept.
3. Have the children tell or record a story about a favorite article of clothing using the free software Voki.

Level III: Beginning to Use Symbols

1. Share books that tell a story with great personal significance for a family, such as *A Chair for My Mother* by Vera Williams, or choose some from the Picture Book Recommendations.
2. The children can dictate or write a family story, illustrate it, and then record it using Voki. These stories can be downloaded and shared with their family members.

Students who are gifted and talented with language can create an avatar to represent a historical figure or themselves. Watch a tutorial on how to do this on YouTube.com. (Type "Official Voki tutorial how to create and publish your Voki" into the search bar.)

Picture Book Recommendations

T = Toddlers (ages 1–2)

P = Preschool (ages 3–5)

K = Kindergarten (ages 5–6)

1st = First grade (ages 6–7)

2nd = Second grade (ages 7–8)

3rd = Third grade (ages 8–9)

Ashburn, Boni. 2011. *I Had a Favorite Dress*. New York: Harry N. Abrams. **(P, K, 1st)**

As a child's favorite dress wears out, it is transformed to a shirt, tank top, scarf, and so forth with help from her mom. Finally, all that is left is the memory.

Berne, Jennifer. 2013. *On a Beam of Light: A Story of Albert Einstein*. San Francisco, CA: Chronicle. **(2nd, 3rd)**

Cartoon-style illustrations introduce children to the intellectual giant and his contributions to society. Use this book to encourage older children to investigate admirable people and learn about their lives through books.

Graham, Bob. 2012. *A Bus Called Heaven*. Somerville, MA: Candlewick. **(P, K, 1st, 2nd)**

A bus with a destination sign that reads "Heaven" is abandoned on an urban street and is transformed into a community gathering spot. When the bus is towed to the junkyard, a young girl figures out a way to get it back. Relate this book to the classic book by Vera B. Williams, *A Chair for My Mother*, a story about the community rallying to help after a house fire. Then invite children's stories about when they were helped or offered help to neighbors.

Kahn, Rukhsana. 2010. *Big Red Lollipop*. New York: Viking. **(K, 1st, 2nd)**

A Pakistani child is required to take her younger sister to a friend's birthday party in this story about different cultural traditions and sibling relationships.

McDonnell, Patrick. 2011. *Me . . . Jane*. Little, Brown. **(1st, 2nd, 3rd)**

A biography of the naturalist Jane Goodall, whose favorite toy was a stuffed chimpanzee named Jubilee. She began to dream of visiting Africa after the Tarzan stories got her interested in the continent. She dedicated her life to helping animals.

Rocco, John. 2011. *Blackout*. New York: Hyperion. **(P, K, 1st)**

Everyone is too busy to play a board game with a young girl, but after the power goes off, everything changes. Relate this book to *Tar Beach* by Faith Ringgold, a story in which an urban community goes up on the roof to escape the heat during a power outage. Have the children think about natural events that have disrupted their plans, and ask them to create stories about how they responded.

Uegaki, Chieri. 2005. *Suki's Kimono*. Toronto, Canada: Kids Can Press. **(P, K, 1st, 2nd, 3rd)**

Suki's most prized possession—a blue cotton kimono—reminds her of a visit to Japan with her *obachan* (grandmother). When she shares the kimono with her class, she begins humming the music and dancing the traditional dance, much to the enjoyment of her peers.

Yaccarino, Dan. 2011. *All the Way to America: The Story of a Big Italian Family and a Little Shovel*. New York: Knopf. **(1st, 2nd, 3rd)**

This true immigration story invites families to think about the history of their own families as well as family traditions.

What Is It?

Directed Listening-Thinking Activity to Improve Comprehension

The directed listening-thinking activity (DLTA) is a way to promote children's listening comprehension and ability to make inferences. It also can be combined with graphic organizers that small groups of children complete before, during, or after a story. In this way, children learn to use pictures and text to build comprehensions. The DLTA is a way of presenting a book that gets the children involved by asking them to make predictions at key points in the plot. The teacher needs to identify some natural breaks in the story and pause to have children guess what might happen next. They then listen to see if their predictions are confirmed or if they want to revise them. This makes reading the story more interactive.

Why Is It Important?

It is estimated that the young child's receptive vocabulary often is four times that of his expressive vocabulary, so listening is the basis for literacy. The old adage "listen and learn" is true. Children with listening-comprehension difficulties face serious learning challenges and are much more likely to fall behind their peers as they progress through school. Although listening is the language art that hearing children and adults use the most, it is the one taught the least. Teaching children to actively visualize information during listening and reading is a common strategy to develop and improve comprehension and memory.

How Does It Work?

1. Choose a suitable book to share with the class, and identify one, central question that will focus them on the gist of the story. For example, before sharing *The Little Red Hen*, you might say, "As you listen to the story, try to figure out why the animals keep saying, 'Not I!' but then change to 'I will!'"

2. Identify three to five places in the book to pause, ask a question, or recap so that children stay focused.

3. Before sharing the book, show the title, cover, and discuss the type of book. Students can then make specific predictions about what will happen. Write these down with the child's name or initials next to them.

4. While reading the story, refer to the predictions; ask which ones are coming true, and why the children think so. Children can revise their predictions or make entirely new ones.

5. After the story is finished, ask the children to answer the focus question. Review their predictions with questions such as: Which predictions were correct? How did you make that prediction? What "clues" can be used to make accurate guesses about a story?

Connections with the Common Core State Standards

Age	Category	Standard
Kindergarten	Comprehension and Collaboration Key Ideas and Details	SLK.2. Confirm understanding of a text read aloud or information presented orally or through other media by asking and answering questions about key details and requesting clarification if something is not understood. RLK.1. With prompting and support, ask and answer questions about key details in a text.
First Grade	Comprehension and Collaboration	SL.1.2. Ask and answer questions about key details in a text read aloud or information presented orally or through other media.
Second Grade	Comprehension and Collaboration Integration of Knowledge and Ideas	SL.2.2. Recount or describe key ideas or details from a text read aloud or information presented orally or through other media. RL.2.7. Use information gained from the illustrations and words in a print or digital text to demonstrate understanding of its characters, setting, or plot.
Third Grade	Key Ideas and Details	RL.3.2. Recount stories, including fables, folktales, and myths from diverse cultures; determine the central message, lesson, or moral and explain how it is conveyed through key details in the text.

Leveled Adaptations

Level I: Relying on Actions and Oral Language

1. Set a purpose for listening to the action song, "This Is the Way We Go to School," sung to the tune of "Here We Go 'Round the Mulberry Bush." Begin with the questions, "How do you get ready to come to school? What are some of the things that you need to do?" For example, we comb or brush our hair before we go to school. Ask the children if anyone has an idea about how we could show brushing or combing our hair.

2. Explain that you will listen to a song together, and while you are listening, they can think about how to show someone what we do to get ready to come to school. Ask the children to think about the actions you could do to go along with the song, while you watch the video.

3. Find the song on YouTube.com by typing "this is the way we go to school songs for children" in the search bar.

4. Talk about each thing that the children do in the song to get ready. Ask the children to show some actions they could do, such as pretending to brush their teeth or wash their hands.

5. Make a song chart so that children can refer to it as they revisit the song. Learn the words to the song, and then add the actions.

Level II: Relying on Visual Images

1. In *Two Bad Ants* by Chris Van Allsburg, a pair of ants leaves the group and goes through some terrifying "ant's-eye-view" adventures during someone's breakfast. A good focus question is "What do ants do that is 'bad'? As I read the story, think about whether the ants will want to go off on an adventure by themselves again."

2. As you go through the book, help the children to interpret the images they see from this unusual perspective.

Level III: Beginning to Use Symbols

1. To understand the story *Tops and Bottoms* by Janet Stevens, children need to understand the idea that the edible portion of some plants, such as lettuce, broccoli, and celery, is above the ground and for other plants, such as beets, carrots, and radishes, the edible portion is below the ground. For corn, however, the "middle" is the edible part—the silk and the roots are discarded.
2. The DLTA focus question is "What does Hare do to trick Bear?" As you read the book, point out how the various plants grow.

Extensions

Put a child in charge of leading the class in completing a discussion web. This will be a new challenge for the child to take on the teacher's role. Adapted from the article "Teachers' Choices Books and Comprehension Strategies as Transaction Tools" by Kathy Headley and Pamela Dunston, the procedure is as follows:

1. Prior to reading a book aloud to the children, identify the gist or underlying message of the story and write a single question, a discussion web statement, to focus the children's listening comprehension. In addition, identify three to six stopping points where students will reflect on the story and make predictions.
2. Pair the students and let them respond to the discussion web statement by working with their partners for approximately five minutes. They can argue both sides of the issue and provide reasons for their thinking.
3. When time is up, let the students form groups of four by having one pair join another. They can present each member's opinion and justification to the small group. For approximately ten minutes, small-group members discuss all views presented.
4. A spokesperson from each small group presents the group's views to the rest of the class. For yes-or-no questions, responses can be tallied to determine the general opinion of all groups in the class. Encourage the students to justify their thinking and question the thinking of classmates.
5. After discussion, let the students respond to additional questions.
6. On completion, read the story and draw comparisons between the ending of the story and the students' predictions.

Picture Book Recommendations

Boelts, Maribeth. 2007. *Those Shoes*. Somerville, MA: Candlewick. **(2nd, 3rd)**

A young boy who is teased about his footwear wants those "cool" shoes that other children have so badly that he buys them from the thrift store, even though they are not comfortable. This book lends itself to pausing for discussion about the boy's decision and what is truly important.

Brown, Peter. 2010. *Children Make Terrible Pets*. New York: Little, Brown. **(1st, 2nd, 3rd)**

Older children will understand the premise of this book, which is that, in comparison to dogs and cats, children are much more work! The story is told primarily through speech bubbles.

Cronin, Doreen. 2011. *Click, Clack, Moo: Cows That Type*. New York: Simon and Schuster. **(K, 1st, 2nd)**

Duck is back in this sequel to *Giggle, Giggle, Quack*. Last time, Duck was passing notes, but now she has a typewriter and launches a letter-writing campaign. Her goal is to get the farmer to improve the working conditions of the cows.

Danneberg, Julie. 2000. *First Day Jitters*. Watertown, MA: Charlesbridge. **(K, 1st, 2nd)**

Lots of people feel nervous about doing something for the first time, such as going to school. In a surprise ending, the teacher is a little worried too! Also available in Spanish as *¡Que nervios! El primer día de escuela*.

Davis, Katie. 2005. *Kindergarten Rocks!* Boston, MA: HMH Books. **(P, K)**

An older sister tells Dexter what to expect in kindergarten to calm his worries. Have children discuss what their first-day worries were like and how they were resolved.

Ravishankar, Anushka. 2008. *Elephants Never Forget!* Boston, MA: Houghton Mifflin. **(P, K, 1st, 2nd)**

In a different type of adoption story, an elephant is raised by water buffalo in this story set in India. Reminiscent of *Stellaluna* by Janell Cannon, the elephant's differences are accepted by a different species family. Even after the elephant meets an elephant herd, in a surprise ending, he decides to stay with those who nurtured him.

Stevens, Janet. 1995. *Tops and Bottoms*. Boston, MA: Harcourt Brace. **(1st, 2nd, 3rd)**

Hare, out of money after losing a bet with Tortoise, decides to dupe Bear (a very wealthy and lazy landowner) to support his family.

Thomas, Jan. 2008. *The Doghouse*. New York: Harcourt. **(P, K, 1st)**

Why do animals keep going into the doghouse? As you share this mystery with young children, pause at important breaks in the story for predictions until the answer is finally revealed.

What Is It?

Drawing as Prewriting and Narrative Prop

Both drawing and writing are composing processes. After children draw a picture, it can become the basis for a one-word label, a caption, a dictated story, or the child's original writing that uses invented or conventional spelling.

Why Is It Important?

Drawing shares many characteristics with handwriting and composition, such as requiring forethought and planning, using writing implements, communicating ideas, and fostering self-expression. Researchers have found that some children as young as two years of age are able to distinguish between scribbles that are attempts to write and those that are drawing. They may separate them on the page and point to which is the picture and which is the story. Most children can draw before they write words, so drawing is an earlier form of communication.

How Does It Work?

Scribbling is a form of prewriting and predrawing. As children enter the preschool years, most of them are beginning to attach meaning to their scribbles. For example, they may name their scribbles with a word or phrase. Gradually, children's drawings become the basis for a simple story; that is why they are referred to as a narrative prop. The link between drawing and writing is evident in the use of story paper during kindergarten, first, and second grade. This type of writing paper has a large blank portion at the top (where the child draws the picture) followed by ruled lines underneath (where the child writes the text).

Connections with the Common Core State Standards

Age	Category	Standard
Kindergarten	Text Types and Purposes Comprehension and Collaboration Presentation of Knowledge and Ideas	W.K.3. Use a combination of drawing, dictating, and writing to narrate a single event or several loosely linked events, tell about the events in the order in which they occurred, and provide a reaction to what happened. SL.K.5. Add drawings or other visual displays to descriptions as desired to provide additional detail.
First Grade	Presentation of Knowledge and Ideas	SL.1.5. Add drawings or other visual displays to descriptions when appropriate to clarify ideas, thoughts, and feelings.
Second Grade	Integration of Knowledge and Ideas Presentation of Knowledge and Ideas	RL.2.7. Use information gained from the illustrations and words in a print or digital text to demonstrate understanding of its characters, setting, or plot. SL.2.5. Create audio recordings of stories or poems; add drawings or other visual displays to stories or recounts of experiences when appropriate to clarify ideas, thoughts, and feelings.
Third Grade	Text Types and Purposes	W.3.3. Write narratives to develop real or imagined experiences or events using effective technique, descriptive details, and clear event sequences.

Leveled Adaptations

Level I: Relying on Actions and Oral Language

The classic children's book *Bark, George* by Jules Feiffer features a dog that forgets how to bark. Make a simple sketch of a the face of a dog, cat, duck, pig, and cow—all the animal sounds that George makes in the story—and arrange them in that sequence. As George makes each animal sound, have the children participate in saying it too. This demonstrates to children how pictures can become a prop for storytelling.

Level II: Relying on Visual Images

1. Using *Bark, George* by Jules Feiffer, introduce the concept of a speech bubble that represents what the animal is saying. Many examples can be found in your word processing program by clicking on Insert, then Shapes, and then choosing Callouts at the bottom of the list.

2. Print out a clip-art image of a dog, cat, duck, pig, and cow, and number them in the story sequence.

3. Type the word for the sound that each animal makes into the callout, then print it out. Make several of these so that children can work in a small group and use them to retell the story. This will show children how a series of pictures can be used to recall and share the story.

Level III: Beginning to Use Symbols

1. Use *Beautiful Oops!* by Barney Saltzberg to get children thinking about how their art—even their "mistakes"—can inspire stories. Watch the video and hear the song on YouTube.com. (Type "beautiful oops by Barney Saltzberg" into the search bar.)

2. Combine it with Ed Emberley's *Drawing Book of Weirdos* to stimulate children's imaginations in drawing things they've never seen before—and writing about them.

3. Link this book with other picture-book author and illustrator biographies such as *A Caldecott Celebration: Seven Artists and Their Paths to the Caldecott Medal* by Leonard Marcus and *Ashley Bryan: Words to My Life's Song* by Ashley Bryan.

Extensions

Have the children experiment with software that allows them to draw and write an original book, such as The Draw Write Read app for the Nook (others are listed in the Technology Supports for Strategy 61, available online). Children can make a book cover using the library of images or do something completely original. A dedication page is provided and the other pages are blank. They can be illustrated with photographs, clip art, or original artwork, and they can enter the text into text boxes. The child's book is stored on a bookshelf, and the app keeps a record of how many times it was read or added as a favorite. Children can return to the book to edit it, share it with other children, or view other children's books.

Picture Book Recommendations

Bryan, Ashley. 2009. *Ashley Bryan: Words to My Life's Song*. New York: Atheneum. **(2nd, 3rd)**
Watch the African American poet and children's book illustrator Ashley Bryan talk about his life. You can view several different videos about his work on TeacherTube by typing in "Ashley Bryan and Reading Rockets." He credits his family's support during childhood as the origin of his love of art.

Emberley, Ed. 2005. *Ed Emberley's Drawing Book of Weirdos*. New York: LB Kids. **(1st, 2nd, 3rd)**
This picture book of "weirdos" gets children thinking imaginatively about their drawings.

Kohl, MaryAnn. 2003. *Storybook Art: Hands-On Art for Children in the Styles of 100 Great Picture Book Illustrators*. Bellingham, WA: Bright Ring. **(1st, 2nd, 3rd)**
This book uses inspirational artwork that encourages children to create their own masterpieces. It can be paired with *Discovering Great Artists* by the same author to motivate young artists.

Marcus, Leonard. 2008. *A Caldecott Celebration: Seven Artists and Their Paths to the Caldecott Medal*. New York: Walker. **(1st, 2nd, 3rd)**
Biographical information about the lives of some of the most well-known and celebrated children's book illustrators are included in this book. Teachers can find interesting facts about the artists, and older children can use the book as a resource when researching a favorite illustrator.

Saltzberg, Barney. 2010. *Beautiful Oops!* New York: Workman. **(P, K, 1st)**
Not everything that artists do is preplanned; sometimes, what starts out as a mistake suggests new possibilities.

T =	**Toddlers (ages 1–2)**
P =	**Preschool (ages 3–5)**
K =	**Kindergarten (ages 5–6)**
1st =	**First grade (ages 6–7)**
2nd =	**Second grade (ages 7–8)**
3rd =	**Third grade (ages 8–9)**

Van Fleet, Mara, and Sarah Wade. 2009. *The Very Mixed-Up Princess.* Pleasantville, NY: Reader's Digest. **(T, P, K)**

> The pages of this book are split into thirds that separate the head, trunk, and legs of the characters. Young children can flip the pages to mix and match princesses, pirates, dragons, and more.

Whatley, Bruce. 2005. *Wait! No Paint!* New York: HarperCollins. **(1st, 2nd, 3rd)**

> This zany mash up of "The Three Little Pigs" and "Goldilocks" focuses on the illustrator (referred to as the Voice in the book). As he runs into problems with his paints, elements of the stories get changed completely. Use this book with older students to discuss how planning—and serendipity—affect art.

What Is It?

The programs that most teachers have on their computers at home and at school, such as Microsoft PowerPoint, Symbols 2000, and Clicker 5, can be used to develop instructional materials for young children.

Why Is It Important?

Reading is no longer limited to print on paper; today's children are accessing a wide variety of digital texts. In response to these trends, educators need to rethink what it means to read and need to consider all of the technoliteracy skills that very young children may have acquired prior to enrolling in early childhood programs and how these experiences may affect attitudes toward literacy with print.

How Does It Work?

If an activity is too easy, children get bored; if it is too difficult, children get frustrated. Identifying a task that is at the correct level of challenge is a key to student engagement in learning. Technology is an important support in this because most games and activities have different levels, and children can decide when to move on to the next level. Many programs provide corrective feedback.

Technology to Differentiate Instruction

Connections with the Common Core State Standards		
Age	**Category**	**Standard**
Kindergarten	Production and Distribution of Writing	W.K.6. With guidance and support from adults, explore a variety of digital tools to produce and publish writing, including in collaboration with peers.
First Grade	Presentation of Knowledge and Ideas	SL.1.5. Add drawings or other visual displays to descriptions when appropriate to clarify ideas, thoughts, and feelings.
Second Grade	Presentation of Knowledge and Ideas	SL.2.5. Create audio recordings of stories or poems; add drawings or other visual displays to stories or recounts of experiences when appropriate to clarify ideas, thoughts, and feelings.
Third Grade	Presentation of Knowledge and Ideas	SL.3.5. Create engaging audio recordings of stories or poems that demonstrate fluid reading at an understandable pace; add visual displays when appropriate to emphasize or enhance certain facts or details.
	Production and Distribution of Writing	W.3.6. With guidance and support from adults, use technology to produce and publish writing (using keyboarding skills) as well as to interact and collaborate with others.

Leveled Adaptations

Level I: Relying on Actions and Oral Language

Use the free software Studyblue, available on https://itunes.apple.com, to make flashcards for use with the students. For example, if children are studying animals, they can make some simple flashcards of familiar pet animals, cards for common insects, or more challenging cards that can be sorted into domesticated, forest, and jungle animals. The program has additional features, including making multiple decks of cards, sharing your cards with others, making study guides, and using the cards to create quizzes.

Level II: Relying on Visual Images

1. For children who join the class during the year, create a video tour of the classroom and an overview of class routines narrated in English, American Sign Language, and other languages spoken by children in the classroom. The video with accompanying narration can be burned onto a CD so that children can share it with their families.

2. A class digital big book illustrated with digital photos that document important events can help to orient newcomers to the class. Loan it to the child, or give the child an opportunity to view it at school if there is no video equipment in the home.

Level III: Beginning to Use Symbols

When children move away, send them off with a digital memory book that recounts their accomplishments or a class book to which every former classmate contributes a page and gives a reason that the student will be missed. This way, the children who move away can establish their credentials in the new setting by sharing their memory books with their new classmates. Try the program Eyejot (http://corp.eyejot.com) to produce a video and post it on the classroom website.

Extensions

Get children involved in making a movie using programs such as Microsoft Movie Maker, Audacity, or Apple iMovie. Movies can be burned on CDs, copied to MP3 players, or even uploaded to a secure website as a podcast so that anyone with a computer and Internet connection (and the login information) can access them.

Picture Book Recommendations

Bradley, Deborah. 2013. *Alphabet Book of Animals*, Kindle ed. VitaMamaOnline.com. **(P, K)**
   This book presents the alphabet through the animals of Africa.

Brown, Marc. 1985. *The Bionic Bunny Show*. Boston, MA: Little, Brown. **(K, 1st, 2nd, 3rd)**
   Children get a look behind the scenes at a television studio as the special effects that make a wimpy character appear to be a superhero are revealed.

Rocco, John. 2011. *Blackout*. New York: Hyperion. **(K, 1st, 2nd, 3rd)**
   After the power goes out in an urban neighborhood, the residents decide to make the most of the situation. Surprisingly, no longer being wired in leads to new forms of connection—parents who aren't too busy to play a board game, neighbors who have time to talk and share food before it melts, and a veritable rooftop party. A thought-provoking book that suggests we aren't always the ones controlling the media; it sometimes controls us.

Smith, Lane. 2010. *It's a Book*. New York: Roaring Brook. **(1st, 2nd, 3rd)**
   A character with a technology mindset and extensive video-gaming experience fires questions about the traditional printed page: "How do you scroll down? Can you blog with it? Can you make the characters fight?"

Zink, Rui. 2004. *The Boy Who Did Not Like Television*. Monterey, CA: MacAdam/Cage. **(P, K)**
   A child has parents who watch television constantly, so he keeps turning off the set. The adults assume that something is wrong with him, so they take him to a doctor, a teacher, and a magician to try to find a solution. Finally, the adults leave the TV off and sit with him—problem solved!

T = Toddlers (ages 1–2)

P = Preschool (ages 3–5)

K = Kindergarten (ages 5–6)

1st = First grade (ages 6–7)

2nd = Second grade (ages 7–8)

3rd = Third grade (ages 8–9)

Electronic Talking Books (E-Books) to Support Reading Comprehension

What Is It?

E-books are digitized versions of books, often with interactive features. Many e-books offer numerous enhancements, such as musical backgrounds and animations, the ability to adjust the size of the print or the rate at which it is read, click-accessible definitions, background information, questions for the children to answer, and activities to extend the experience.

Why Is It Important?

The e-book for children makes recorded books more interactive. It gives them on-demand practice with a text, accompanied by animated images so that the words make sense. It also gives ELLs opportunities to listen to different native speakers in English. In addition, many e-books are available in second-language versions, which is a tremendous help for English language learners. While these books cannot replace reading aloud with parents and families, electronic talking books can provide enrichment and practice.

How Does It Work?

E-books can be downloaded on readers, such as Kindle or Nook, on computers, tablet computers, and some smartphones. Most have a read-while-listening tool that supports children's graphophonemic awareness, word recognition, fluency, and pronunciation. Some e-books allow the user to choose a voice for the narration, and many have a "read by myself" option. Some offer a tracking system that can provide feedback to the teacher on the words that were problematic for each child.

Connections with the Common Core State Standards		
Age	**Category**	**Standard**
Kindergarten	Vocabulary Acquisition and Use	L.K.6. Use words and phrases acquired through conversations, reading and being read to, and responding to texts
First Grade	Craft and Structure	RI.1.5. Know and use various text features, such as headings, tables of contents, glossaries, electronic menus, icons, to locate key facts or information in a text.
Second Grade	Integration of Knowledge and Ideas	RL.2.7. Use information gained from the illustrations and words in a print or digital text to demonstrate understanding of its characters, setting, or plot.
Third Grade	Integration of Knowledge and Ideas	RL.3.7. Explain how specific aspects of a text's illustrations contribute to what is conveyed by the words in a story.

Leveled Adaptations

Level I: Relying on Actions and Oral Language

1. Use an e-book of an action rhyme, such as "Teddy Bear, Teddy Bear," and ask the children to perform the gestures or actions as they listen.

2. Find a toy dragon or use a clip-art picture. Demonstrate all of the motions using the toy or picture with this chant:

    Dragon, Dragon, turn around.

    Dragon, Dragon, touch the ground.

    Dragon, Dragon, flap your wings.

    Dragon, Dragon, whisper things.

    Dragon, Dragon, jump up high.

    Dragon, Dragon, soar and fly.

    Dragon, Dragon, breathe out flame.

    Dragon, Dragon, roar your name—DRAGON!

Level II: Relying on Visual Images

Use the free sample app of the classic Dr. Seuss book *The Cat in the Hat,* available on https://itunes.apple.com. Let the children experiment with the interactivity of the e-book. The child can touch any image in the story, and the printed word zooms onto the screen for children to read.

Level III: Beginning to Use Symbols

1. Children can experience the familiar fairy tale "Cinderella" in a new way with the award-winning app from Nosy Crow, available on https://itunes.apple.com for $4.00. The e-book has charming illustrations, the sound of turning pages, an orchestral background, and a script read by professional actors. With a touch, children can replay bits of dialogue, watch as Cinderella cares for animals, and choose "read and play," "read to me," or "read by myself" modes.

2. Have the children compare and contrast this version with other versions of the fairy tale, such as *The Salmon Princess: An Alaska Cinderella Story* by Mindy Dwyer.

3. Let them experiment with changing the setting to make their own versions of the story.

Extensions

Some sources for reviews of electronic talking books include Lunchbox Reviews, Digital Storytime, iPadCurriculum, and Teachers with Apps. After children have read many reviews of e-books, give them an opportunity to review a new e-book using the same system, such as five-star ratings. Project Listen is an advanced computerized reading "tutor" that "listens" as the child reads and "talks" when the child makes a mistake, gets stuck, or clicks for help. To view a video explaining how it works, go to http://www.cs.cmu.edu/%7Elisten.

Picture Book Recommendations

T = Toddlers (ages 1–2)

P = Preschool (ages 3–5)

K = Kindergarten (ages 5–6)

1st = First grade (ages 6–7)

2nd = Second grade (ages 7–8)

3rd = Third grade (ages 8–9)

Christelow, Eileen. 2012. *Five Little Monkeys Go Shopping.* Boston, MA: HMH. **(T, P, K, 1st)**
Eileen Christelow's popular series is based on the chant "Five Little Monkeys Jumping on the Bed." Have children watch the video version at http://www.youtube.com/watch?v=tVMzrd5D7xM

Doyle, Bill. 2011. *My Dad Drives a Roller Coaster Car.* New York: Crab Hill Press. **(K, 1st)**
Offered as an e-book on https://itunes.apple.com for $0.99, this sweet book lets children enjoy unlimited access to all of the amusement park rides, from merry-go-round to spinning teacup.

Potter, Beatrix. *The Tale of Benjamin Bunny.* http://www.gutenberg.org/e-books/14407 **(T, P, K, 1st)**
Now in the public domain, the original text and illustrations of the Beatrix Potter story are available. The story can be played with a touch of a button, or an adult can read the book aloud to the child.

Sierra, Judy. 2004. *Wild about Books.* New York: Knopf. **(1st, 2nd, 3rd)**
A librarian drives a bookmobile into a zoo with hilarious results.

What Is It?

If children do not engage in literacy with print activities over the summer, they frequently arrive at school at a lower level of reading proficiency than what they had acquired at the end of the previous school year. The term *summer slump* refers to this decline in reading skills. Students who attend summer programs have better outcomes than their peers who do not attend these programs. According to the Smart Television Alliance, during the summer months, children's television viewing increases by 150 percent.

Why Is It Important?

Children's out-of-school literacy practices often require them to quickly process fleeting visual images. Formal school, however, usually requires children to concentrate on stationary print. Researcher James Kim found that, irrespective of race, socioeconomic status, or previous achievement, children performed better on fall reading-achievement measures when families documented that they had read books and had written something about them.

How Does It Work?

Summer literacy activities engage children and families in different types of literacy events. Literacy events are activities that children find engaging and that focus on working with print as a listener, a reader, or a writer. Often, these activities are linked with summer fun, such as a rebus recipe for making s'mores, a booklet of the lyrics to songs that are sung in the car, or a story about learning to swim. By linking literacy learning with these interesting pursuits, children avoid losing ground as listeners, speakers, readers, and writers.

Connections with the Common Core State Standards

Age	Category	Standard
Kindergarten	Integration of Knowledge and Ideas Range of Reading and Level of Text Complexity	RL.K.9. With prompting and support, compare and contrast the adventures and experiences of characters in familiar stories. RL.K.10. Actively engage in group reading activities with purpose and understanding.
First Grade	Key Ideas and Details Comprehension and Collaboration	RL.1.3. Describe characters, settings, and major events in a story, using key details. SL.1.1. Participate in collaborative conversations with diverse partners about first-grade topics and texts with peers and adults in small and larger groups.
Second Grade	Vocabulary Acquisition and Use	L.2.4. Determine or clarify the meaning of unknown and multiple-meaning words and phrases based on second-grade reading and content, choosing flexibly from an array of strategies.
Third Grade	Phonics and Word Recognition	RF.3.3. Know and apply grade-level phonics and word analysis skills in decoding words.

Leveled Adaptations

Level I: Relying on Actions and Oral Language

1. Send home the words and gestures to accompany "We're Going on a Bear Hunt" so that children can sing it and read the text, based on their familiarity with the chant. Find it on YouTube.com by typing "Michael Rosen's We're Going on a Bear Hunt" into the search bar.
2. Relate the chant to the book *Where Are We Going?* by Elliott Kreloff.
3. Teach other chants, such as "Who Stole the Cookies from the Cookie Jar?" in the same way.

Level II: Relying on Visual Images

1. Watch a Toddler 123 video of the counting book *One Mole Digging a Hole* by Julia Donaldson, which has a gardening theme. Find the video by typing "toddler 123 One Mole Digging a Hole" into the search bar.
2. Have the children identify clip art pairs of rhyming words, such as *mole/hole, snakes/rakes, bears/pears, foxes/boxes, storks/forks, parrots/carrots, frogs/logs, crows/hose, doves/gloves, bees/trees,* and *everyone/sun.*
3. Provide families with information about television and movie tie-ins to books.

Level III: Beginning to Use Symbols

1. Send home a list of recommended summer reading (see Picture Book Recommendations).
2. Work with students to plan a list of literacy activities with a summer theme. For example, suggest that they cut out a jar shape on paper and write a story or poem about catching lightning bugs or an imaginary dialogue between the child and the firefly. There are many suggestions in the Technology Supports for Strategy 64, available online.

Extensions

Summer often is a time when families get together, so encourage families to have their children interview family members, survey them about something, such as their favorite foods at a picnic, or create a family scrapbook or digital photo album.

Picture Book Recommendations

Arnold, Tedd. 2005. *Hi! Fly Guy.* New York: Cartwheel. **(K, 1st, 2nd)**

Flies are an inescapable part of summer, but in this story, a personified fly named Buzz becomes a pet.

Broach, Elise. 2010. *Seashore Baby.* New York: Little, Brown. **(T)**

In this lift-the-flap book, a baby participates in the special activities associated with a day at the beach.

Florian, Douglas. 2002. *Summersaults.* New York: Greenwillow. **(K, 1st, 2nd, 3rd)**

A collection of short poems about the childhood pursuits during the summer months.

Hoberman, Mary Ann. 2012. *Forget-Me-Nots: Poems to Learn by Heart.* New York: Little, Brown. **(3rd)**

A collection of poetry, illustrated by Ed Emberley, that brings together memorable poems for young children.

Kreloff, Elliott. 2008. *Where Are We Going?* New York: Sterling. **(P, K)**

This story, based on the chant "We're Going on a Bear Hunt," includes many different sound effects.

Loewen, Nancy. 2009. *Words, Wit, and Wonder: Writing Your Own Poem.* Mankato, MN: Capstone. **(2nd, 3rd)**

This book features easy-to-understand explanations of the basic elements and forms of poetry. Young readers and aspiring poets can put their rhyming skills to use using the techniques displayed in this book.

McDonald, James. 2012. *Rainy Day Poems: The Adventures of Sami and Thomas.* Salem, OR: House of Lore. **(P, K, 1st, 2nd, 3rd)**

The illustrations and rhymes in this book depict the adventures of Sami and Thomas. Young readers can learn to anticipate the ending word in each phrase given what they understand of about rhyming words.

McNamera, Margaret. 2012. *Summer Treasure.* New York: Simon Spotlight. **(P, K, 1st, 2nd)**

When Hannah goes to the beach on her summer vacation, she is surprised to see her teacher there. She finds that she can have fun with her teacher, even when it's not time for school, and they search for beach treasures together.

Oswalt, Kay. 2012. *Fred Threads, Book One: The Interview.* Bloomington, IN: Inspiring Voices. **(1st, 2nd, 3rd)**

A boy's school assignment involves him in conducting an interview with his mom. Young children can use these strategies as a model to conduct their own interviews during the summer months.

Proimos, James. 2012. *The Best Bike Ride Ever.* New York: Dial. **(P, K)**

This story about wanting a bike and learning how to ride one will allow encourage young readers to think about exciting bike rides, both real and imaginary.

| T = Toddlers (ages 1–2) |
| P = Preschool (ages 3–5) |
| K = Kindergarten (ages 5–6) |
| 1st = First grade (ages 6–7) |
| 2nd = Second grade (ages 7–8) |
| 3rd = Third grade (ages 8–9) |

Raczka, Bob. 2011. *Lemonade: And Other Poems Squeezed from a Single Word*. New York: Roaring Brook. **(2nd, 3rd)**

Each selection in this book is a puzzle as well as a poem, giving it the same child appeal as secret codes. The inventiveness of the concrete poetry (such as pepperoni turning into pizza topping) will encourage children to try some poetry puzzles of their own.

Rosen, Michael. 2012. *Bananas in My Ears: A Collection of Nonsense Stories, Poems, Riddles, and Rhymes*. Somerville, MA: Candlewick. **(1st, 2nd, 3rd)**

Pure fun is the focus of this collection illustrated by Quentin Blake that children are sure to appreciate.

Ruddell, Deborah. 2008. *A Whiff of Pine, a Hint of Skunk: A Forest of Poems*. New York: Margaret McElderry. **(1st, 2nd, 3rd)**

A lovely collection of poems about the beauty of the forest.

Salas, Laura. 2011. *Book Speak! Poems about Books*. New York: Clarion. **(P, K, 1st, 2nd, 3rd)**

This lively collection is focused on literacy topics and is well suited for the primary grades.

Swados, Elizabeth. 2002. *Hey You! C'mere! A Poetry Slam*. New York: Arthur A. Levine. **(K, 1st, 2nd, 3rd)**

A group of friends travels around a city block turning their experiences into poetic stories. Their use of slang suggests that poetry can happen even within a casual conversation with friends.

Wardlaw, Lee. 2011. *Won Ton: A Cat Tale Told in Haiku*. New York: Henry Holt. **(2nd, 3rd)**

Introduce children to the surprisingly succinct form of poetry, Japanese haiku, through this tale of a shelter cat adopted by a school-age boy. Combine with *One Big Rain: Poems for Rainy Days* by Rita Gray for additional examples of poems that do not rhyme.

Wood, Audrey. 2007. *A Dog Needs a Bone*. New York: Blue Sky. **(K, 1st)**

A very funny book that rhymes, with a persistent canine who wants a treat.

Yolen, Jane, and Andrew Peters. 2007. *Here's A Little Poem: A Very First Book of Poetry*. Somerville, MA: Candlewick. **(P, K, 1st, 2nd)**

This variety of poems and authors has something that will appeal to every reader. The multiple talented poets each bring a unique piece to the book, ensuring an enjoyable reading experience.

What Is It?

Voice Amplification to Build Listening Comprehension

Researchers Peggy Nelson, Kathryn Kohnert, Sabina Sabur, and Daniel Shaw have found that, when attempting to evaluate listening environments, three things are particularly important:

- the listener's auditory development,
- the quality and intensity of the message relative to other competing sounds, and
- the listener's prior experience with the content and format of the message.

Voice amplification makes the message that children need to hear louder than the background noise; this is referred to as the "signal-to-noise ratio." It can be accomplished through simple and inexpensive devices, such as a paper cone megaphone or a plastic gallon milk jug with the bottom cut off; with moderately sophisticated tools, such as a toy karaoke microphone; or with expensive and sophisticated technology, such as a headset microphone and amplification system.

Why Is It Important?

Researchers have identified factors that make it difficult for children to listen at school, including colds, allergies, and recurrent ear infections; specific language impairments, learning disabilities, or attention deficits; the rapid rate of speech of some teachers; background noise, distractions, and interruptions in the classroom; difficulty in adapting to the classroom's academic language; language or dialect differences between the child and teacher or peers; and lack of appropriate models for listening and learning. The fact that young children are less adept than adults at "filling in the blanks" when messages are incomplete, garbled, or ambiguous also contributes to listening difficulties. Young children in general and second language learners in particular may fail to understand when just a few words or syllables are missed. Therefore, the teacher's or a peer's message has to stand out clearly from various background noises.

How Does It Work?

Create a positive listening environment for ELLs:

- Make an effort to speak distinctly, slow your rate of speech, and use more visual aids.
- Make instructions clear, concise, and sequential.
- Strive to minimize background noise and disruptions.
- Reinforce messages with pantomime, demonstration, and print material.
- Rephrase (rather than just repeat) when children ask a question or appear to be confused.
- Enlist the support of peers to provide explanations.

Connections with the Common Core State Standards

Age	Category	Standard
Kindergarten	Integration of Knowledge and Ideas	RI.K.10. Actively engage in group reading activities with purpose and understanding.
First Grade	Vocabulary Acquisition and Use	L.1.4. Determine or clarify the meaning of unknown and multiple-meaning words and phrases based on first-grade reading and content, choosing flexibly from an array of strategies.
Second Grade	Knowledge of Language	L.2.3. Use knowledge of language and its conventions when writing, speaking, reading, or listening.
Third Grade	Knowledge of Language	L.3.3. Use knowledge of language and its conventions when writing, speaking, reading, or listening.

Leveled Adaptations

Level I: Relying on Actions and Oral Language

1. Begin with a low-tech form of voice amplification, such as a plastic gallon milk jug with the bottom cut off to use as a megaphone or a plastic toy megaphone or microphone from the dollar store. You also might try a plastic kazoo to change the quality of the child's voice. A set of them can sometimes be found as party favors at the dollar store or online. Have the children experiment with these items to see how they can change the way their voices sound or amplify them.

2. Make these tools available to children when they are dramatizing stories so that they can practice speaking with expression.

3. Teach children a game created by Tatiana Gordon called Edible/Inedible that is similar to Simon Says. Seat a small group of children in a circle. Explain that the children must listen carefully to words you say when you roll a ball. If you say a word that is something you can eat, the child should catch the ball. But, if you say a word that is not something edible, then the child should not catch the ball. Roll a foam ball to a child, and name an object such as "banana." If the child catches the ball, respond with, "Good! You ate a banana." If you name something inedible, such as "chair," the child should deliberately not catch the ball. If the child catches the ball, say, "Oops! You ate a chair!"

Level II: Relying on Visual Images

1. Even very young children are aware of what is involved in being an effective listener. Use the book *Listen Buddy* by Helen Lester to initiate discussions of good listening habits. Begin by announcing the book in a whisper, and then project your voice. Ask children how the volume affects their ability to listen.

2. Set a purpose for listening: "Today we are going to hear the story of a rabbit with big, beautiful ears. As you listen, think about why Buddy changed and decided that it is important to be a good listener."

3. When you share the video, adjust the volume so that everyone can hear it. Find it on YouTube.com by typing "Listen Buddy Helen Lester" into the search bar.

Level III: Beginning to Use Symbols

Help children to construct phonics phones that amplify their voices and the sounds that letters and words make. Instructions are posted at http://blog.maketaketeach.com/how-to-make-a-phonics-phone. Have the children use their phonics phones to read aloud, sing, recite a poem, or have a conversation with a partner.

Extensions

Best Prompter by Smartphone Ware, offered for $0.99 on https://itunes.apple.com, converts an iPad or iPhone into a teleprompter. It shows the text that the person wants to speak on the screen. SpeechPrompter by GWHQ Productions, offered for $7.99 on https://itunes.apple.com, acts like a teleprompter supplying text from a given area to scroll on the screen. Children can practice saying important information from text aloud.

Picture Book Recommendations

Balouch, Kristen. 2011. *The Little Girl with the Big Big Voice.* New York: Little, Simon. **(T, P, K)**

A very loud girl searches the jungle to find a friend, but her big voice frightens away the elephant, snake, and crocodile. Finally, she finds a friend whose voice (a roar) is even louder than hers.

Gershator, Phillis. 2008. *Listen, Listen.* Cambridge, MA: Barefoot. **(T, P, K)**

This book focuses on the sounds that are unique to seasons of the year.

Henkes, Kevin. 2006. *Lilly's Purple Plastic Purse.* New York: Greenwillow. **(P, K, 1st)**

Lilly gets so excited about sharing her new, shiny purse that the teacher temporarily takes it away from her.

Janisch, Heinz. 2009. *"I Have a Little Problem," Said the Bear.* New York: NorthSouth. **(P, K, 1st, 2nd)**

Bear tries to discuss his fear of the dark, but all of the animals are quick to offer a solution before he even gets a chance to confide in them. Finally, a fly who is a good listener offers to move into his cave, and Bear is no longer afraid.

Lester, Helen. 1997. *Listen Buddy.* Boston, MA: HMH Books. **(P, K, 1st)**

Just because a rabbit has big ears doesn't mean he is a good listener.

Stein, David Ezra. 2010. *Interrupting Chicken.* Somerville, MA: Candlewick. **(P, K, 1st)**

Even though the little red chicken is advised not to interrupt during the bedtime stories, she can't help warning characters from "Hansel and Gretel," "Chicken Little," and "Little Red Riding Hood" about what is destined to go wrong. See the book and hear it read on YouTube.com. (Type "Interrupting Chicken" into the search bar.)

T = Toddlers (ages 1–2)
P = Preschool (ages 3–5)
K = Kindergarten (ages 5–6)
1st = First grade (ages 6–7)
2nd = Second grade (ages 7–8)
3rd = Third grade (ages 8–9)

Literacy for All Young Learners

Appendices

Recommended Resources for Teaching ELLs

Common Core State Standards and ELLs

Colorín Colorado http://www.colorincolorado.org/homepage.php

> A bilingual site for Spanish-speaking families and educators of English language learners that contains ELL resources by grade, classroom videos and podcasts, community outreach ideas, recommended resources, and professional development tools.

"Common Core Curriculum Rubric: Meeting the Needs of ELLs." Colorín Colorado. http://blog.colorincolorado.org/2014/02/27/common-core-curriculum-rubric-meeting-the-needs-of-ells

> This rubric is designed to help review how well curricular units aligned to the Common Core meet the needs of ELLs.

Defining Diversity

Literacy-Connections Bilingual Spanish, ESL, and Literacy Resources: http://www.literacyconnections.com/SecondLanguage.php

> This annotated list highlights sites that support second language learning. If your school has funds available to purchase bilingual books, this site has the prices and all of the ordering information at your fingertips.

Women's and Children's Health Network Kids' Health http://www.cyh.com/HealthTopics/HealthTopicDetailsKids.aspx?p=335andnp=286andid=2345

> "What Is Diversity?" Teachers can use the child-friendly material on this site to better understand diversity issues and explore them with children.

Head Start and ELLs

Everything ESL http://www.everythingesl.net

> This website includes lesson plans, teaching tips, and professional-development resources with a focus on students whose first language is not English.

"Learning in English, Learning in Spanish: A Head Start Program Changes Its Approach." *Young Children.* DC: NAEYC. http://www.naeyc.org/files/yc/file/200907/Youngquist709.pdf.

> This article describes program changes to better meet the needs of ELLs.

Lee y Serás (Read and You Will Be) http://leeyseras.net/site/main.html

> A beautiful, click-and-turn-the-page picture book at this Scholastic site describes this program to support English language learners. Free downloadable videos, literacy tips for families, games for children, and resources for teachers are embedded in the text.

Pre-K Pages http://www.pre-kpages.com

> This site has printables, lesson plans, activities, recommended books, and teaching advice.

Teaching Tips for Working with ELLs http://www.ncela.us

> This website of the National Clearinghouse for English Language Acquisition offers many practical ideas on teaching young English language learners that are supported by research.

Teachnology http://www.teach-nology.com/tutorials/teaching/differentiate/planning

> An online tutorial gives ideas that coach teachers in ways to write lesson plans to meet the needs of diverse groups of learners.

Teachnology Lesson Plans http://www.teach-nology.com/teachers/lesson_plans

> Free, downloadable plans are available at this site. A special section for English as a second language is included as well as ESL news, practice, research, and online discussion.

Sources for Lesson Plans, Printables, and Inexpensive Teaching Materials

Lesson Plans and Printables

A to Z Teacher Stuff http://www.atozteacherstuff.com

Created by teachers, this site features lesson plans, themes, teaching tips, and other resources, many organized by the month of the year.

ABC Teach http://www.abcteach.com

Loads of resources and particularly professional-looking clip art and images. Much of it is free, but there is an annual membership to access everything.

Activity Village http://www.activityvillage.co.uk

This British site offers loads of printables, puzzles, games, and crafts and includes information about the celebrations of other countries.

Adobe Education Exchange http://edex.adobe.com

Thousands of resources for teachers, this site offers classroom-tested teaching tools and materials. Free to join.

Discovery Education's Lesson Plan Library http://school.discoveryeducation.com/lessonplans

Search a huge lesson plan library by age and grade level to get teaching ideas at this site.

DLTK http://www.dltk-teach.com

A wide variety of lesson plan resources.

Education Helper http://www.edhelper.com

Search by grade level at this site that provides thousands of lessons, leveled books, and a newsletter, *Teacher Ideas Monthly.*

Education Place http://www.eduplace.com

This site by Houghton Mifflin Harcourt has tabs for children and for parents and a bilingual resource section with lesson plans.

Education World http://www.education-world.com/a_lesson

Click on the lesson plan tab to locate lesson plans. Also has a teacher professional development section.

Edutopia http://www.edutopia.org

Sponsored by the filmmaker George Lucas, this site offers innovative lesson plans, project-based learning support, standards-based teaching ideas, and more.

Microsoft Lesson Connection http://www.microsoft.com/education/LessonPlans.aspx

Guides teachers in planning lessons keyed to the Common Core State Standards.

Mr Printables http://www.mrprintables.com

For teachers who wish they were artistic, this site has high-quality visual aids to support teaching, such as emotion cards, crafts, and a cross-stitch-pattern animal for children to make.

ProTeacher http://www.proteacher.com/020001.shtml

At this site, you type in what you are searching for and other teachers answer you on a blog.

Read-Write-Think http://www.readwritethink.org/lessons/index.asp

Includes high-quality lesson plans for all aspects of literacy.

Scholastic http://teacher.scholastic.com/lessonplans

Lesson and unit plans, discussion guides, and extension activities abound at this huge repository of teacher resources.

Sites for Teachers http://www.sitesforteachers.com

A megasite that rates sites for teachers by popularity.

Teacher Planet http://www.teacherplanet.com

    Thematic lesson plans, templates, and a special section on English as a second language are featured on this site, searchable by grade level.

Teacher Tube www.teachertube.com

    This is the educational version of YouTube that enables teachers to locate film clips on a wide variety of topics that are suitable for children.

The Teacher's Corner http://www.theteacherscorner.net

    Printables, lesson plans, bulletin board ideas, thematic units, and teacher resources.

Teacher's Net http://teachers.net/lessons

    Lesson plans, searchable by grade level and subject area, can be downloaded at this site. Many of the plans include the actual teaching materials, such as videos or clip art.

TeachersFirst http://www.teachersfirst.com

    This site links to other sites to locate teaching resources from many different sources.

TeachingBooks http://www.teachingbooks.net

    The ultimate "begin with a picture book" site. Each entry contains a reading of the book, material about the author, lesson plans, and lists of related books. The lists of related books are very helpful when creating a book pack.

Thinkfinity http://www.thinkfinity.com

    This Verizon Foundation site has great lesson-planning resources that can be searched by subject area, a portal for parents, and homework help, reading lists, and more.

Inexpensive Materials

Visit dollar stores and office supply stores.

    Find key chains, beanbag toys, plastic toys or figurines, teacher supplies, stickers, and home items such as sets of self-stick house numbers and letters. Find small whiteboards, magic slates, and chalkboards for writing practice. After Halloween, look for masks, hats, and costumes for story characters. Look in the clearance section at office supply stores.

Sponsor a toy box clean out.

    Collect from among the teachers and their families and friends, and send home a request to families. Request washable items only, and collect lots of small plastic toys to use for story retelling.

Visit the websites for Oriental Trading, CafePress, and Etsy.

    If you need multiples of an item, they may be available here—for example, Oriental Trading offers small rubber ducks. Can be good sources for inexpensive hats to represent different characters.

Visit Stuffed Safari (http://www.stuffedsafari.com).

    Carries realistic-looking stuffed animals from various manufacturers.

Collect clean dog toys.

    You often can get small, medium, and large of the same toy. Some of the newer toys have animals that hide inside a larger shape, such as bees in a hive, that are good as visual aids for counting rhymes. Check in the clearance bin at pet supply stores.

Visit craft supply vendors.

    Cake decorations—such as small plastic items or stickers—and scrapbooking supplies often have a particular theme.

Sources that Review Children's Books, Apps, and Sites

American Library Association (ALA) http://www.ala.org and http://gws.ala.org

Association for Library Service to Children (ALA) Notable Books for Children http://www.ala.org/alsc/awardsgrants/notalists

Award-Winning Picture Books and Recommended Authors and Illustrators http://childrensbooks.about.com/od/ages6101earningtoread/u/new_readers.htm#s3

Bank Street College of Education http://www.bnkst.edu/bookcom

Best Children's Books by Age http://www.parents.com/fun/book-gallery

Blackwell's Best http://www.vickiblackwell.com/childrenlit.html

Capitol Choices: Noteworthy Books for Children and Teens http://www.capitolchoices.org

Carol Hurst's Children's Literature Site http://www.carolhurst.com

Center for Media Literacy http://www.medialit.org

The Children's Book Review http://www.thechildrensbookreview.com

Children's Technology Review http://childrenstech.com

Common Sense Media https://www.commonsensemedia.org

Digital Storytime http://digital-storytime.com/review.php?id=613

The Fred Rogers Center Early Learning Environment http://www.yourele.org

Fun Educational Apps http://www.funeducationalapps.com

Goodreads http://www.goodreads.com

Grades K–2 Children's Literature http://www.literacy.uconn.edu/k2chilit.htm

International Reading Association "Children's Choices" and "Teacher's Choices" http://www.reading.org/Resources/Booklists/ChildrensChoices.aspx

KidsReads http://www.kidsreads.com

The New York Times Book Review, Children's Books Reviews http://topics.nytimes.com/topics/reference/timestopics/subjects/c/childrens_books/index.html

Notable Books for a Global Society http://www.csulb.edu/org/childrens-lit/proj/nbgs/intro-nbgs.html

Oprah's List http://www.oprah.com/search.html?q=children%27s+books

School Library Journal http://www.slj.com

Smart Apps for Kids http://www.smartappsforkids.com

Teachers with Apps http://www.teacherswithapps.com

Through the Looking Glass Book Review http://lookingglassreview.com/books

We Are Teachers http://www.weareteachers.com

Online Literacy Resources for Families

ABC Mouse http://www.ABCmouse.com

Family members can record stories that children can listen to over and over again at this fee-based, top-rated site.

About Parenting http://childparenting.about.com

This site features free number and word games such as Sudoku, crossword puzzles, or vocabulary builders for children ages three to ten years, as well as advice, articles and resources for parents.

Booklists for Families http://www.familyreading.org/i-recommended.htm

Tips on reading aloud, family activities, games, and recommended books and sites.

Family Education Network http://www.familyeducation.com

A wealth of information for families is available here, but it does contain advertising. Many helpful articles on a wide variety of issues that families face. Includes an infant-toddler section.

Great Web Sites for Kids http://www.ala.org/greatsites

Search by subject area, topic, and grade level at this American Library Association site.

Hubbard's Cupboard http://www.hubbardscupboard.org

Ideal for home schooling and faith-affiliated schools, this site offers many resources for teaching, crafts, and activities.

Let's Read as a Family http://www.rif.org/kids/leer/en/leerhome_english.htm

This site from Reading Is Fundamental (RIF) has many resources to support reading at home.

NAEYC for Families http://families.naeyc.org

Advice and tips from the leading early childhood experts.

On-the-Go Resources http://www.walearning.com/resources/on-the-go

This site from Washington Learning Systems, funded by a federal grant, offers free downloadable resources in English and in Spanish for families with young children.

PBS Kids http://pbskids.org

There are many free, engaging games related to children's favorite public television programs, such as *Caillou* for toddlers and young preschoolers and *Between the Lions* for older preschool and primary students.

Reading Rockets http://www.readingrockets.com

Loads of resources for families are available at this site. Just click on the "For Parents" section.

Super Kids http://www.superkids.com

This site offers many interactive word games for families to play together, such as Mumbo Jumbo, a sort of e-version of Scrabble.

Susan Stephenson http://susanstephenson.com.au

Download some very helpful brochures, prepared by a professional author, suitable for sharing with families.

Talk to Your Baby Campaign http://www.literacytrust.org.uk/talk_to_your_baby

Emphasizes the importance of early verbal interaction for children's language development.

Picture Books about Human Emotions and Needs

Many picture books for young children include the message that human emotions and basic needs are universal.

Ajmera, Maya, and Alex Fisher. 2002. *A Kid's Best Friend*. Watertown, MA: Charlesbridge.

Ajmera, Maya, and John Ivanko. 2000. *To Be a Kid*. Watertown, MA: Charlesbridge.

Ajmera, Maya, and John Ivanko. 2002. *Animal Friends: A Global Celebration of Children and Animals*. Watertown, MA: Charlesbridge.

Ajmera, Maya, and John Ivanko. 2005. *To Be an Artist*. Watertown, MA: Charlesbridge.

Ajmera, Maya, and John Ivanko. 2006. *Be My Neighbor*. Watertown, MA: Charlesbridge.

Ajmera, Maya, Sheila Kinkade, and Cynthia Pon. 2010. *Our Grandparents: A Global Album*. Watertown, MA: Charlesbridge.

Ajmera, Maya, Olateju Omolodun, and Sarah Strunk. 2000. *Extraordinary Girls*. Watertown, MA: Charlesbridge.

Ajmera, Maya, and Michael Regan. 2000. *Let the Games Begin!* Watertown, MA: Charlesbridge.

Ajmera, Maya, and Anna Versola. 2001. *Children from Australia to Zimbabwe: A Photographic Journey around the World*. Rev. ed. Watertown, MA: Charlesbridge.

Ancona, George. 1977. *I Feel: A Picture Book of Emotions*. New York: Dutton.

Ancona, George. 1990. *Helping Out*. Torrance, CA: Sandpiper.

Ancona, George. 2011. *Come and Eat!* Watertown, MA: Charlesbridge.

Baer, Edith. 1970. *The Wonder of Hands*. New York: Parents Magazine Press.

Baer, Edith. 1980. *Words Are Like Faces*. New York: Star Bright.

Baer, Edith. 1994. *Así vamos a la escuela: Un libro acerca de niños en diferentes países del mundo*. New York: Scholastic.

Baer, Edith. 1994. *This Is the Way We Go to School: A Book about Children Around the World*. New York: Scholastic.

Baer, Edith. 1995. *This Is the Way We Eat Our Lunch: A Book about Children Around the World*. New York: Scholastic.

Brenner, Barbara, and George Ancona. 1970. *Faces*. New York: Dutton.

Brown-Johnson, Latrecia. 2010. *Diversity Soup*. Bloomington, IN: Xlibris.

Cooper, Ilene. 2007. *The Golden Rule*. New York: Abrams.

Dooley, Norah. 1992. *Everybody Cooks Rice*. Minneapolis, MN: Carolrhoda.

Dooley, Norah. 1995. *Everybody Bakes Bread*. Minneapolis, MN: Carolrhoda.

Dooley, Norah. 2004. *Everybody Serves Soup*. Minneapolis, MN: Carolrhoda.

Dooley, Norah. 2005. *Everybody Brings Noodles*. Minneapolis, MN: Carolrhoda.

Fox, Mem. 2006. *Whoever You Are*. San Diego, CA: Voyager.

Fox, Mem. 2008. *Ten Little Fingers and Ten Little Toes*. Boston, MA: HMH.

Global Fund for Children. 2007. *Global Babies*. Watertown, MA: Charlesbridge.

Grossman, R. D. 2009. *Families*. Cambridge, MA: Star Bright.

Hull, Bunny. 2002. *Peace in Our Land*. Beverly Hills, CA: Kids Creative Classics. (Audiobook)

Isadora, Rachel. 2010. *Say Hello!* New York: Putnam.

Jackson, Jill, and Sy Miller. 2009. *Let There Be Peace on Earth and Let It Begin with Me*. New York: Tricycle.

Katz, Karen. 2006. *Can You Say Peace?* New York: Henry Holt.

Kerley, Barbara. 2009. *One World, One Day.* Washington, DC: National Geographic Children's Books.

Kinkade, Sheila. 2006. *My Family.* Watertown, MA: Charlesbridge.

Mora, Pat. 2008. *Join Hands! The Ways We Celebrate Life.* Watertown, MA: Charlesbridge.

Morris, Ann. 1993. *Bread, Bread, Bread.* New York: HarperCollins.

Morris, Ann. 1993. *Hats, Hats, Hats.* New York: HarperCollins.

Morris, Ann. 1994. *Loving.* New York: HarperCollins.

Morris, Ann. 1995. *Houses and Homes.* New York: HarperCollins.

Morris, Ann. 1995. *Weddings.* New York: HarperCollins.

Morris, Ann. 1997. *Light the Candle! Bang the Drum!* New York: Dutton.

Morris, Ann. 1998. *Play.* New York: HarperCollins.

Morris, Ann. 1998. *Shoes, Shoes, Shoes.* New York: HarperCollins.

Morris, Ann. 1998. *Work.* New York: HarperCollins.

Morris, Ann. 1999. *Teamwork.* Boston, MA: Lothrop Lee and Shepard.

Morris, Ann. 2000. *Families.* New York: HarperCollins.

Numeroff, Laura. 2009. *What Sisters Do Best/What Brothers Do Best.* San Francisco, CA: Chronicle.

Sierra, Judy. 2012. *Wild about You!* New York: Knopf.

Tyler, Michael. 2005. *The Skin You Live In.* Chicago, IL: Chicago Children's Museum.

Free Children's Books Online

Candlelight Stories http://candlelightstories.com

Click on the Stories tab for free picture books.

Children's Books Online: The Rosetta Project http://www.childrensbooksonline.org

Antique children's books with vintage illustrations, searchable by grade level, and translated into different languages are the focus of this site.

Curious George http://www.curiousgeorge.com

Listen to stories about the popular character in English and Spanish. The text is highlighted as each word is spoken. Also includes games and ideas for extension activities.

DLTK Teach http://www.dltk-teach.com/minibooks

Children (and adults) can make their own mini-books at this site and print them out.

Enchanted Learning http://www.enchantedlearning.com

Children can make their own books following the instructions here; some are free, but for access to everything, the cost is $20.00 a year.

International Children's Digital Library http://en.childrenslibrary.org

Families can find stories from virtually every country and culture at this high-quality site.

Kids English Books http://www.kidsenglishbooks.com

Find simple concept books, folktales, and fairy tales (with matching audio) that can be printed out at this site.

Magic Keys http://www.magickeys.com

Click on the Children's Storybooks Online hotspot for free picture books.

MagicBlox Your Kid's Library http://magicblox.com

Read a new, free book every day or subscribe to all seven hundred picture books that can be read on computer or mobile devices.

MeeGenius http://www.meegenius.com/store/books/free

Free, familiar tales are posted here to read on computers, tablets, or smartphones. Stories are read aloud as the pages turn, or a child can choose "read by myself." Many of them are free, but to access all of them, a $5.00 monthly subscription is required.

A Story Before Bed http://www.astorybeforebed.com/storytime

Locating a bedtime story just got easier with these recorded picture books, read aloud, that parents and families can watch on a computer together. Pages turn just like a real book, the author does the reading, and there is a pause button to stop and discuss. A "Record Your Own" feature allows parents or children to record themselves reading the book.

Storyline Online http://www.storylineonline.net

Readers (many of them celebrities) read aloud various top-quality picture books—searchable by title, author, and reader—in the videos posted on this site. Click on "View a List of All Books" to see what is available; picture book favorites such as *Harry the Dirty Dog* and *The Rainbow Fish* are included.

Appendix G: Search Engines for Children

All the Information in the Known Universe http://www.kyvl.org/kids

This tutorial and interactive website from the Kentucky Virtual Library teaches children how to find information on the Internet.

Ask Kids http://www.askkids.com

The best search engine for answering simple questions such as: "How fast do bees fly?" or "Why is the sky blue?"

Fact Monster http://www.factmonster.com

The award-winning site has child-friendly facts and articles, such as myths about sharks, and interactive tools that encourage kids to improve their math, spelling, and vocabulary.

How Stuff Works http://www.howstuffworks.com

This award-winning site, searchable by grade, clearly and concisely explains to children and adults how various things work.

Kids Click! http://www.kidsclick.org

This site was created by a group of U.S. librarians so children could find age-appropriate, noncommercial, and nonviolent links to information on just about any topic. A great resource for finding high-quality images, such as photos of animals, maps, videos, and audio.

Quintura Kids http://quinturakids.com

Most online searches require writing, spelling, and keyboarding skills. This one is a visual search engine that allows children to click on a picture, word, or phrase to conduct a search.

Yahoo! Kids http://kids.yahoo.com

A child-friendly search engine allows children to investigate their interests and questions.

References and Resources

Allington, Richard, and Anne McGill-Franzen, eds. 2013. *Summer Reading: Closing the Rich/Poor Reading Achievement Gap.* New York: Teachers College Press.

Asher, James. 1969. "The Total Physical Response Approach to Second Language Learning." *The Modern Language Journal* 53(1): 3–17.

August, Diane, and Timothy Shanahan, eds. 2008. *Developing Reading and Writing in Second-Language Learners: Lessons from the Report of the National Panel on Language-Minority Children and Youth.* New York: Routledge.

Barnyak, Natalie, and Tracy McNelly. 2014. "Supporting Young Children's Visual Literacy through the Use of E-Books." In *Young Children and Families in the Information Age: Applications of Technology in Early Childhood.* New York: Springer.

Bear, Donald, Marcia Invernizzi, Shane Templeton, and Francine Johnston. 2007. *Words Their Way: Word Study for Phonics, Vocabulary, and Spelling Instruction.* 4th ed. Upper Saddle River, NJ: Prentice Hall.

Beck, Isabel, Margaret McKeown, and Linda Kucan. 2008. *Creating Robust Vocabulary: Frequently Asked Questions and Extended Examples.* New York: Guilford Press.

Bloodgood, Janet. 1999. "What's in a Name? Children's Name Writing and Literacy Acquisition." *Reading Research Quarterly* 34(3): 342–367.

Brabham, Edna, and Susan Villaume. 2001. "Building Walls of Words." *Reading Teacher* 54(7): 700–702.

Brock, Avril. 2013. "Let's Get Talking: Communication, Language, and Literacy in the Early Years." *World Class Initiatives and Practices in Early Education: Moving Forward in a Global Age.* New York: Springer.

Bruner, Jerome. 2004. *The Process of Education.* Rev. ed. Cambridge, MA: Harvard University Press.

Byrnes, James, and Barbara Wasik. 2009. *Language and Literacy Development: What Educators Need to Know.* New York: Guilford.

Cabell, Sonia, Laura Justice, Tricia Zucker, and Anita McGinty. 2009. "Emergent Name-Writing Abilities of Preschool-Age Children with Hearing Impairment." *Language, Speech, and Hearing Services in Schools* 40: 53–66.

Cambourne, Brian. 2001. "Conditions for Literacy Learning: Why Do Some Students Fail to Learn to Read? Ockham's Razor and the Conditions of Learning." *The Reading Teacher* 54(8): 784–786.

Carr, Eileen, and Donna Ogle. 1987. "K-W-L Plus: A Strategy for Comprehension and Summarization." *Journal of Reading* 30(7): 626–631.

Conyers, Jeff. 2012. "My Very Own Imagination Library." *Childhood Education* 88(4): 221–225.

Cook-Cottone, Catherine. 2004. "Constructivism in Family Literacy Practices: Parents as Mentors." *Reading Improvement* 41(4): 208–216.

DeBruin-Parecki, Andrea, and Mary Hohmann. 2003. *Letter Links: Alphabet Learning with Children's Names.* Ypsilanti, MI: HighScope Press.

Denton, Carolyn, Richard Parker, and Jan Jasbrouck. 2003. "How to Tutor Very Young Students with Reading Problems." *Preventing School Failure* 48(1): 42–44.

Dixon, L. Quentin, Shuang Wu, and Ahlam Daraghmeh. 2011. "Profiles in Bilingualism: Factors Influencing Kindergartners' Language Proficiency." *Early Childhood Education Journal* 40(1): 25–34.

Emery, Donna. 1996. "Helping Readers Comprehend Stories from the Characters' Perspectives." *The Reading Teacher* 49(7): 534–541.

Enz, Billie, Jennifer Prior, Maureen Gerard, and Myae Han. 2008. "Exploring Intentional Instructional Uses of Environmental Print in Preschool and Primary Grades." In *Effective Early Literacy Practice: Here's How, Here's Why*. Baltimore, MD: Paul H. Brookes.

Ernst-Slavit, Gisela, and Margaret Mulhern. 2003. "Bilingual Books: Promoting Literacy and Biliteracy in the Second-Language and the Mainstream Classroom." *Reading Online*. www.readingonline.org/articles/ernst-slavit.

Evans, M. D. R., Jonathan Kelley, and Joanna Sikora. 2014. "Scholarly Culture and Academic Performance in 42 Nations." *Social Forces* 92(4): 1573–1605.

Fello, Susan, Kelli Paquette, and Mary Jalongo. 2006. "Talking Drawings: Improving Intermediate Students' Comprehension of Expository Science Text." *Childhood Education* 83(2): 80–86.

Fisher, Bobbi, and Emily Medvic. 2000. *Perspectives on Shared Reading: Planning and Practice*. Portsmouth, NH: Heinemann.

Franklin-Guy, Sherri, and Rosalind Scudder. 2011. "Environmental Print and Spelling Ability: An Investigation of Kindergartners' Emergent Orthographic Skills." *International Journal of Learning* 18(5): 361–374.

Frith, Uta. 2006. "Resolving the Paradoxes of Dyslexia." In *Dyslexia and Literacy: Theory and Practice*. New York: John Wiley and Sons.

Garcia, Eugene, and Ellen Frede. 2010. *Young English Language Learners: Current Research and Emerging Directions for Policy*. New York: Teachers College.

Giles, Rebecca, and Karen Tunks. 2010. "Children Write Their World: Environmental Print as a Teaching Tool." *Dimensions of Early Childhood* 38(3): 23–30.

Gillanders, Cristina, and Dina Castro. 2011. "Storybook Reading for Young Dual Language Learners." *Young Children* 66(1): 91–96.

Goldschmied, Elinor, and Sonia Jackson. 2004. *People under Three: Young Children in Day Care*. 2nd ed. London: Routledge.

Goodman, Kenneth. 1967. "Reading as a Psycholinguistic Guessing Game." *Journal of the Reading Specialist* 6: 126–135.

Gordon, Tatiana. 2006. *Teaching Young Children a Second Language*. New York: Praeger.

Goswami, Usha. 2001. "Early Phonological Development and the Acquisition of Literacy." In *Handbook of Early Literacy Research*. New York: Guilford.

Grande, Marya, and Joyce Downing. 2004. "Increasing Parent Participation and Knowledge Using Home Literacy Bags." *Intervention in School and Clinic* 40(2): 120–126.

Gunning, Thomas. 1995. "Word Building: A Strategic Approach to the Teaching of Phonics." *The Reading Teacher* 48(6): 484–488.

Harvey, Stephanie, and Anne Goudvis. 2013. "Comprehension at the Core." *The Reading Teacher* 66(6): 432–439.

Haupt, Sharon. 2013. "Kindergarten B.E.A.R. Bags." *Teacher Librarian* 40(3): 18–19. *The Reading Teacher* 54(3): 260–268.

Hayes, Donald, and Margaret Ahrens. 1988. "Vocabulary Simplification for Children." *Journal of Child Language* 15(2): 457–472.

Helman, Lori, et al. 2012. *Words Their Way with English Learners: Word Study for Phonics, Vocabulary, and Spelling*. 2nd ed. Upper Saddle River, NJ: Pearson.

Hendrick, Joanne, and Patricia Weissman. 2009. *The Whole Child: Developmental Education for the Early Years*. 9th ed. Upper Saddle River, NJ: Pearson.

Hickman, Peggy, Sherolyn Pollard-Durodola, and Sharon Vaughn. 2004. "Storybook Reading: Improving Vocabulary and Comprehension for English-Language Learners." *The Reading Teacher* 57(8): 720–730.

Hogan, Tiffany, Mindy Bridges, Laura Justice, and Kate Cain. 2011. "Increasing Higher Level Language Skills to Improve Reading Comprehension." *Focus on Exceptional Children* 44(3): 1–20.

Horn, Martha, and Mary Ellen Giacobbe. 2007. *Talking, Drawing, Writing: Lessons for Our Youngest Writers.* Portland, ME: Stenhouse.

Isbell, Rebecca. 2008. *The Complete Learning Center Book.* Rev. ed. Beltsville, MD: Gryphon House.

Jasmine, Joanne, and Pamela Schiesl. 2009. "The Effects of Word Walls and Word Wall Activities on the Reading Fluency of First Grade Students." *Reading Horizons* 49(4): 301–314.

Jones, Jill, and Jill East. 2010. "Empowering Primary Writers through Daily Journal Writing." *Journal of Research in Childhood Education* 24(2): 112–122.

Jones, Steven, Lynne Murphy, Carita Paradis, and Caroline Willners. 2012. *Antonyms in English: Construals, Constructions, and Canonicity.* Cambridge, UK: Cambridge University Press.

Kaderavek, Joan, and Laura Justice. 2005. "The Effect of Book Genre in the Repeated Readings of Mothers and Their Children with Language Impairment: A Pilot Investigation." *Child Language Teaching and Therapy* 21(1): 75–92.

Kalmar, Kathy. 2008. "Let's Give Children Something to Talk About: Oral Language and Preschool Literacy." *Young Children* 63(1): 88–92.

Kim, James. 2004. "Summer Reading and the Ethnic Achievement Gap." *Journal of Education for Students Placed at Risk* 9(2): 169–199.

Koskinen, Patricia, Robert Wilson, Linda Gambrell, and Susan Neuman. 1993. "Captioned Video and Vocabulary Learning: An Innovative Practice in Literacy Instruction." *The Reading Teacher* 47(1): 36–43.

Krashen, Stephen. 2008. "Free Voluntary Reading: Still a Great Idea." *CEDER Yearbook V: Education for a Changing World.* College Station, TX: Texas A&M University.

Kucan, Linda. 2012. "What Is Most Important to Know about Vocabulary?" *The Reading Teacher* 65(6): 360–366.

Lefebvre, Pascal, Natacha Trudeau, and Ann Sutton. 2011. "Enhancing Vocabulary, Print Awareness, and Phonological Awareness through Shared Storybook Reading with Low-Income Preschoolers." *Journal of Early Childhood Literacy* 11(4): 453–479.

Manning, Maryann. 2005. "Reading Aloud." *Teaching PreK–8* 35(5): 80–82.

Mantzicopoulos, Panayota, and Helen Patrick. 2011. "Reading Picture Books and Learning Science: Engaging Young Children with Informational Text." *Theory into Practice* 50(4): 269–276.

Marinak, Barbara, Martha Strickland, and Jane Keat. 2010. "Using Photo-Narration to Support All Learners." *Young Children* 65(5): 35–38.

McGee, Lea, and Lesley Morrow. 2005. *Teaching Literacy in Kindergarten.* New York: Guilford.

McNair, Jonda. 2007. "Say My Name, Say My Name! Using Children's Names to Enhance Early Literacy Development." *Young Children* 62(5): 84–89.

Merkley, Donna, and Debra Jefferies. 2000. "Guidelines for Implementing a Graphic Organizer." *The Reading Teacher* 54(4): 350–357.

Miller, Pat. 2001. *Reaching Every Reader: Promotional Strategies for the Elementary School Library Media Specialist.* Worthington, OH: Linworth.

Moss, Barbara, and Virginia Loh. 2010. *35 Strategies for Guiding Readers through Informational Texts.* New York: Guilford.

National Center for Education Statistics. 2003. *Learner Outcomes: Early Childhood (Indicator 2).* Available at http://nces.ed.gov/pubs2003/2003067_2.pdf.

National Clearinghouse for English Language Acquisition. 2011. Data and Demographics. http://www.ncela.us/data-demographics.

National Early Literacy Panel. 2011. *Developing Early Literacy: Report of the National Early Literacy Panel.* http://www.earlychildhoodwebinars.org/wp-content/uploads/2010/12/Timothy_Shanahan_Early_Childhood_InvesitGations_Webinar_NELP_upload1.pdf.

National Education Association. n.d. NEA Read Across America. Available: http://nea.org/readacross.

Nelson, Katherine. 2007. *Young Minds in Social Worlds: Experience, Meaning, and Memory.* Cambridge, MA: Harvard University Press.

Nelson, Peggy, Kathryn Kohnert, Sabina Sabur, and Daniel Shaw. 2005. "Classroom Noise and Children Learning through a Second Language: Double Jeopardy?" *Language, Speech, and Hearing Services in Schools* 36(3): 219–229.

Neu, Renee. 2013. "An Exploration of Oral Language Development in Spanish-Speaking Preschool Students." *Early Childhood Education Journal* 41(3): 211–218.

Neuman, Susan, Ellen Newman, and Julie Dwyer. 2011. "Educational Effects of a Vocabulary Intervention on Preschoolers' Word Knowledge and Conceptual Development: A Cluster-Randomized Trial." *Reading Research Quarterly* 46(3): 249-272.

Neumann, Michelle. 2007. *Up Downs: A Fun and Practical Way to Introduce Reading and Writing to Children Aged 2–5.* Sydney, Australia: Finch.

Nutbrown, Cathy. 2011. *Threads of Thinking: Schemas and Young Children's Learning.* London, UK: Sage.

Ogle, Donna. 1986. "K-W-L: A Teaching Model that Develops Active Reading of Expository Text." *The Reading Teacher* 39(6): 564–570.

Ogle, Donna, and Amy Correa-Kovtun. 2010. "Supporting English-Language Learners and Struggling Readers in Content Literacy with the 'Partner Reading and Content, Too' Routine." *The Reading Teacher* 63(7): 532–542.

Pacific Resources of Education and Learning. 2004. *Exploring Comprehension through Retelling: A Teacher's Story.* Honolulu, HI: Pacific Resources for Education and Learning. http://files.eric.ed.gov/fulltext/ED490189.pdf.

Paciga, Kathleen, Jessica Hoffman, and William Teale. 2011. "The National Early Literacy Panel and Preschool Literacy Instruction: Green Lights, Caution Lights, and Red Lights." *Young Children* 66(6): 50–57.

Paquette, Kelli, Susan Fello, and Mary Jalongo. 2007. "The Talking Drawings Strategy: Using Primary Children's Illustrations and Oral Language to Improve Comprehension of Expository Text." *Early Childhood Education Journal* 35(1): 65–73.

Pennsylvania State Education Association. 2008. "Smart Television Alliance Launches 'OutSmart the Summer Spike!' Campaign." Available at https://www.psea.org/general.aspx?id=608.

Peterson, Debra, and Barbara Taylor. 2012. "Using Higher Order Questioning to Accelerate Students' Growth in Reading." *The Reading Teacher* 65(5): 295–304.

Pew Hispanic Center. 2012. *Statistical Portrait of Hispanics in the United States, 2012.* Washington, DC: Pew Research Center.

Richardson, Maurine, Margaret Miller, James Richardson, and Mary Kathleen Sacks. 2008. "Literacy Bags to Encourage Family Involvement." *Reading Improvement* 45(1): 3–9.

Richgels, Donald. 2008. "Practice to Theory: Invented Spelling." In *Effective Early Literacy Practice: Here's How, Here's Why.* Baltimore, MD: Paul H. Brookes.

Ritter, Gary, Joshua Barnett, George Denny, and Ginger Albin. 2009. "The Effectiveness of Volunteer Tutoring Programs for Elementary and Middle School Students: A Meta-Analysis." *Review of Educational Research* 79(1): 3–38.

Rodriguez, Diane, Angela Carrasquillo, and Kyung Soon Lee. 2014. *The Bilingual Advantage: Promoting Academic Development, Biliteracy, and Native Language in the Classroom.* New York: Teachers College.

Roginski, Dawn. 2014. *A Year in the Story Room: Ready-to-Use Programs for Children.* Chicago, IL: American Library Association.

Rowe, Meredith, and Susan Goldin-Meadow. 2009. "Differences in Early Gesture Explain SES Disparities in Child Vocabulary Size at School Entry." *Science* 323(5916): 951–953.

Rule, Audrey. 2001. "Alphabetizing with Environmental Print." *The Reading Teacher* 54(6): 558–562.

Rule, Audrey. 2007. "Mystery Boxes: Helping Children Improve Their Reasoning." *Early Childhood Education Journal* 35(1): 13–18.

Salomo, Dorothe, Elena Lieven, and Michael Tomasello. 2013. "Children's Ability to Answer Different Types of Questions." *Journal of Child Language* 40(2): 469–491.

Saracho, Olivia. 2007. "Fathers and Young Children's Literacy Experiences in a Family Environment." *Early Child Development and Care* 177(4): 403–415.

Sibold, Claire. 2011. "Building English Language Learners' Academic Vocabulary: Strategies and Tips." *Multicultural Education* 18(2): 24–28.

Snow, Catherine. 2008. Foreword. In *One Child, Two Languages: A Guide for Early Childhood Educators of Children Learning English as a Second Language.* 2nd ed. Baltimore, MD: Paul H. Brookes.

Society of Illustrators. 1993. *The Very Best of Children's Book Illustration.* Cincinnati, OH: North Light.

Souto-Manning, Mariana. 2007. "Immigrant Families and Children (Re)develop Identities in a New Context." *Early Childhood Education Journal* 34(6): 399–405.

Spodek, Bernard, and Olivia Saracho. 1993. *Yearbook in Early Childhood Education, Volume 4: Language and Literacy In Early Childhood Education.* New York: Teachers College Press.

Tabors, Patton. 2008. *One Child, Two Languages: A Guide for Early Childhood Educators of Children Learning English as a Second Language.* 2nd ed. Baltimore, MD: Paul H. Brookes.

Typadi, Evi, and Karen Hayon. 2010. "Story Telling and Story Acting: Putting the Action into Interaction." In *Supporting Children's Creativity through Music, Dance, Drama, and Art.* London, UK: Routledge.

Van Kleeck, Anne, Ronald Gillam, Lori Hamilton, and Cassandra McGrath. 1997. "The Relationship between Middle-Class Parents' Book-Sharing Discussion and Their Preschoolers' Abstract Language Development." *Journal of Speech, Language, and Hearing Research* 40(6): 1261–1271.

Van Kleeck, Anne, Judith Vander Woude, and Lisa Hammett. 2006. "Fostering Literal and Inferential Language Skills in Head Start Preschoolers with Language Impairment Using Scripted Book-Sharing Discussions." *American Journal of Speech-Language Pathology* 15(1): 85–95.

Van Oers, Bert, and Debbie Duijkers. 2013. "Teaching in a Play-Based Curriculum: Theory, Practice, and Evidence of Developmental Education for Young Children." *Journal of Curriculum Studies* 45(4): 511–534.

Viard, Armelle, Béatrice Desgranges, Francis Eustache, and Pascale Piolino. 2012. "Factors Affecting Medial Temporal Lobe Engagement for Past and Future Episodic Events: An ALE Meta-Analysis of Neuroimaging Studies." *Brain and Cognition* 80(1): 111–125.

Whitebread, David, and Helen Jameson. 2005. "Play Beyond the Foundation Stage: Storytelling, Creative Writing, and Self-Regulation in Able 6–7-Year-Olds." In *The Excellence of Play.* 2nd ed. Maidenhead, Berkshire, UK: Open University Press.

Whitehead, David. 2002. "'The Story Means More to Me Now': Teaching Thinking through Guided Reading." *Reading* 36(1): 33–37.

Xu, Shelley, and Amanda Rutledge. 2003. "*Chicken* Starts with *Ch*! Kindergartners Learn through Environmental Print." *Young Children* 58(2): 44–51.

Zucker, Tricia, Amelia Moody, and Michael McKenna. 2009. "The Effects of Electronic Books on Pre-Kindergarten-to-Grade 5 Students' Literacy and Language Outcomes: A Research Synthesis." *Journal of Educational Computing Research* 40(1): 47–87.

Zucker, Tricia, Laura Justice, Shayne Piasta, and Joan Kaderavek. 2010. "Preschool Teachers' Literal and Inferential Questions and Children's Responses during Whole-Class Shared Reading." *Early Childhood Research Quarterly* 25(1): 65–83.

Zygouris-Coe, Vicky, Matthew Wiggins, and Lourdes Smith. 2004. "Engaging Students with Text: The 3-2-1 Strategy." *The Reading Teacher* 58(4): 381–384.

Index